GUIDE TO CHANGE AND PROJECT MANAGEMENT

ABOUT THE AUTHOR

Paul Roberts has been managing projects since 1988 and is a founding director of Fifthday (*www.fifthday.com*), a provider of project management expertise, education and resource. He has worked with some of the world's largest, most influential organisations, and many of the smallest, both public and private, helping them to embed the principles, techniques and culture of effective change and project management.

GUIDE TO CHANGE AND PROJECT MANAGEMENT

Getting it right and achieving lasting benefit

Third edition

Paul Roberts

Published under exclusive licence from The Economist by
Profile Books Ltd
29 Cloth Fair
London EC1A 7JQ
www.profilebooks.com

Copyright © The Economist Newspaper Ltd, 2007, 2013, 2020
Text copyright © Paul Roberts, 2007, 2013, 2020

A CIP catalogue record for this book is available from the British Library

ISBN 978 1 78816 603 4
eISBN 978 1 78283 747 3

Typeset in Milo by MacGuru Ltd
Printed and bound in Great Britain by Clays Ltd, Elcograf S.p.A.

FSC
www.fsc.org
MIX
Paper from
responsible sources
FSC® C018072

Contents

Acknowledgements

I WOULD LIKE TO THANK Ed Lake at Profile Books for offering sound advice, and Kate Parker for managing the process towards publication. I would also like to convey my gratitude to the clients of my company, Fifthday – many at *The Economist* – who have shown their enthusiasm for this book and offered me their insights into the practical challenges that must be overcome in order to deliver successful change through projects.

Preface to third edition

DURING THE MONTHS when I was completing the third edition of this book, calamity struck. News arose of a virus that was travelling at speed around the world, affecting the lives and livelihoods of anyone in its path. As a catalyst for transformational change, not much else can compare. The consequences have been felt in every aspect of life, and will be with us for years to come. What it also shows is that leadership and management are needed in equal measure to address such challenges. Indeed, the importance of both is proven not just by the value they can provide when exercised well, but also by how their absence can invite further disaster.

Together, good leadership and management can mitigate panic, provide direction and offer a method for transition, if not to a new normal, then at least to the next stage. Having change imposed on us only increases the importance of navigating our way effectively through its emerging consequences. Now, more than ever, leadership and management of change is essential.

Much else has changed since this book was first published in 2007. In that year, Apple released its first-ever iPhone, ushering in an era of mobile computing that has transformed the way we engage with each other, our shopping habits, our business transactions, our access to knowledge and our very behaviour. It may be true to say that, at that time, few of us imagined that we might need anything more sophisticated than a mobile phone that could perhaps also take photographs and play music. However, someone had a bigger vision. A project followed and the iPhone was born, with the potential to transform our lives. But that potential may never have been realised had mobile computing not been so enthusiastically promoted to – and embraced by – a community of users, eager for something new. In other words, change happened because there was a vision, an engaged and eager audience, and a sense of motivation among them to adopt something different.

I mention this as a way of introducing the significant changes that have been made in this book's third edition. Where, a decade or two ago, it was necessary to persuade many institutions that effective project management was required, it is now very widely accepted as an essential discipline. Why? Because as the pace of change has increased, there has been a growing realisation among senior managers that only effective project management has the potential to deliver the transformation they seek. However, a greater awareness of the benefits that change can bring does not necessarily go hand in hand with successful project delivery. What I have noticed is how many projects, no matter how well managed, have failed to deliver the outcomes that their sponsors anticipated. Too many have produced apps, buildings, processes, products and services that remain on the shelf, unadopted, and a costly reminder that projects are vehicles that can just as easily deliver failure as success. So the revisions in this edition – including its title – are significant. Agile development has understandably gained significant traction; an entirely new chapter is now devoted to this most important of topics. And other new chapters and sections place emphasis on the methods and effort needed to envisage what change looks like, engage people to join the journey towards it, educate them sufficiently so that they can use what the project delivers, and adopt the anticipated values, actions and behaviours with enthusiasm.

Paul Roberts
July 2020

Introduction

MOST ORGANISATIONS USE PROJECTS to deliver change. Projects are management vehicles that transport people to a "new normal". Whether or not that new way of doing things is fully adopted depends very much on the extent to which arrangements have been made for its arrival. Therefore, a project must not only prepare a solution to an institution's problem or opportunity, but it must also prepare the institution for the solution. All too often, the latter is forgotten until it is too late. Without the adoption of change, its benefits can never be fully realised. Any project that delivers an output that is not sufficiently utilised or adopted may be considered a failure. So it follows that, if we are to understand and practise effective project management, it is necessary to understand and apply the principles and practices of change management. This book brings together these two interconnected subject areas.

Project and change management have the power to affect the prosperity of entire institutions. It is important to remember that while many organisations have benefited from change, many have suffered for having failed to manage its delivery. In some cases, the mismanagement has resulted in a complete business or institutional failure. This is because managing change cannot be separated from managing business-as-usual; each affects the other. If an organisation is serious about improving the way it manages change, it will have an opportunity to improve its business.

If projects are to deliver successful change, then it is crucial to ensure that the entire institution is configured to do so. No-one is immune from its draw or impact. However, people play vastly different roles in directing, delivering or adopting change, depending

FIGURE 0.1 **Executive layers involved in change**

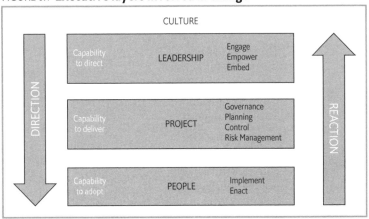

on their role in an organisation. Figure 0.1 identifies three executive layers.

Each layer is marked by its respective authority: those at the top of an organisation are commonly held to have more executive power than those at the bottom. However, those who are expected to implement changes to fit into their way of life also wield power by virtue of their level of readiness to adopt it. In between, a delivery layer exerts its own authority in the shaping and governance of the change.

The layers also reflect different responsibilities. These range from the obligation to engage and empower the workforce and to embed new behaviours, to the governance of the programme of change, to its eventual implementation and enactment.

It follows that each layer must also have the capability – that particular combination of skills, knowledge, experience and character – to discharge their respective responsibilities. Each participant makes a contribution, whether directing change, delivering it, or adopting it.

The provision of direction from the top is matched in importance by the reaction from affected stakeholders. This results in a dynamic flow which acknowledges the co-dependence between the layers. Within this relationship lies the potential for co-operation and collaboration, and also for confusion and conflict.

The leadership has the most significant responsibility to manage change in the direction of a positive and calculated outcome. It can be shaped according to the needs of an organisation to grow or contract, respond to competition or threat, or simply to keep pace with the world around it. Typically, leaders are expected to have the capability to identify opportunities for change, to direct it, and to engage and educate communities of people to embed it.

A layer of management is necessary to govern and deliver change. Usually, this happens through the use of projects. If projects are to deliver successful change, then it is crucial to ensure that each individual project can be well governed.

Yet project management is too often considered a discipline that applies only to a select few. It is often delegated to people who struggle against sometimes impossible odds to deliver a successful outcome. So effective project management means much more than having an effective project manager.

Critically, if the rewards of change are to be enjoyed, targeted groups of people must adopt it as an improvement to the status quo. For example, the introduction and embedding of new project and change management practices may represent just such an institutional transformation. To achieve this, it will be necessary to deliver not only a myriad of new processes, practices and deliverables, but also adjustments in mindset, behaviour and values. It may involve abandoning norms and some sacred cows, educating people to work differently, and persuading customers to buy something new.

All of this is enacted within an environment defined, in part, by its culture. This will have a material impact on the way in which change is understood and handled. So, when success depends on changing the way people think, speak and act, it may be understood that organisation-wide collaboration is needed, including among those who commission and finance the change, those who build the end product, and those who will use and adopt it.

Although it may appear that change follows a project, it is more the case that change begins to happen from the moment the idea has been conceived. The enactment of a project is merely further evidence that change is taking place. In other words, change precedes, accompanies and follows project activity; change and projects occur in parallel, not in sequence. However, for the structural integrity of this book, and to aid the reader's understanding of its complex and interrelated content, the leadership's direction of change will be explored in Chapter 2, people's adoption of it in Chapter 13, and project management as a delivery capability will be widely covered throughout. A further significant addition to this third edition is an entirely new chapter (Chapter 11) devoted to the management of projects that have chosen to employ an agile development approach.

The components of effective change management

FOR ANY NEW FORM OF MANAGEMENT to be accepted, it must be sold to those who do not yet believe in it. Until an organisation has had time to get used to the new way of working, apathy and cynicism towards its introduction are likely. It is common for the promoters of change to be subject to some friendly fire because not everyone will think as positively about project management as they do.

Project management has much to do with identifying and managing the risks a project may face. It can be unsettling for those who are used to solving problems once they have arisen rather than working in advance to prevent the problem arising. This is the essential difference between risk management and "issue" management, and is central to the introduction of a project-based culture. Many people may be impressed by the hero who charges in to solve problems, but arguably those who studiously identify things that could go wrong and do a great job of avoiding the need to call in support deserve greater praise and assistance. These two extremes of character can be seen not only in individuals, but also in organisations. There are issue-managing and risk-managing organisations. The former encourage and reward heroics in managing current problems and challenges. The latter praise those who seek in advance to mitigate the likelihood or impact of those problems and challenges. Project management is more effective in an environment that supports the management of risks because this gives the organisation greater control over its fortunes.

This is not the only challenge that promoters of change face. Effective project management, like any form of governance, brings with it a necessary element of administration needed to control the project. This too will be challenged by those who object to the introduction of a new way of working, procedures, routines and regulations. Care should be taken that the administrative measures are not stifling and are light enough to ensure that the right decisions are made by the right people at the right time, and that the value of them is generally understood.

Sooner or later (probably sooner), the cost of introducing a new form of management will be questioned and a budget will be needed. Senior managers have a great many priorities on which to spend scarce resources, so the money being spent on embedding change and project management must be promoted as an investment with a planned, measurable return. In other words, embedding the principles of change and project management within an organisation should be managed as a project in itself. This will help mitigate some of the challenges identified above.

Any attempt to alter opinions or working practices will face difficulties. If the approach being described here is considered along the lines of changing a culture, the following risks identified by leadership expert John Kotter in his book *Leading Change* will need to be mitigated:

- there is no sense of urgency;
- a powerful, guiding coalition is not adequately created;
- the programme lacks clear vision;
- the vision is poorly communicated;
- essential change is prevented by a will to protect the status quo;
- short-term wins are not systematically planned or delivered;
- victory is declared too soon;
- changes are not anchored in the organisation's culture.

Later chapters consider how these risks may be mitigated through the introduction of effective change and project management.

Selling the benefits

Change and project management must address issues that matter and that people want to solve. It is essential to ask questions before presenting solutions. What are the problems that the individual or organisation faces? Where do their priorities lie? Where could the greatest gains be achieved for the least investment?

For example, if there is a concern that too much project work is duplicated, it could be suggested that effective project management encourages everyone to work to a plan. But what is the benefit of a plan? It helps to explain that once people are clear about their own and each other's responsibilities, there is likely to be a reduction in rework and duplication. In seeking a form of words persuasive enough to overcome the objections of others, it is often illuminating to ask "So what?" in order to expose the heart of the benefit and to make it clear how the changes the project will bring will make their lives better.

Not every benefit will carry the same weight with every stakeholder. Some, such as the project's end users, will be encouraged to hear that effective project management provides for the definition, design, implementation and control of quality, thereby reducing the risk of a poor outcome. Others, such as those with commercial responsibilities, will be more interested in knowing that it requires the justification for the initiative to be regularly reappraised, thereby managing the risk of making a poor investment. Arguments should be tailored to meet the interests of different stakeholders.

It can help to have a list of the benefits to refer to when facing objections to the introduction of change and project management, or simply to articulate how it will make everyone's lives more ordered. Effective change and project management allow an organisation to:

- involve the right people at the right time for the right reasons to ensure that the best quality decisions are made;
- encourage customers and suppliers to participate so that the result is mutually beneficial;
- focus on the milestones of the endeavour to encourage a greater and common understanding of what will be delivered;
- reappraise the justification for the change regularly, thereby reducing the risk of making a poor investment;
- demonstrate how resources can be used as effectively as possible, thereby allowing their efficient use across the organisation;

- emphasise the risks the project faces so that the likelihood of their occurring and their impact can be managed;
- agree on the definition, design, implementation and control of quality, so reducing the risk of a poor outcome;
- minimise the dangers of unmanaged "change";
- be clear about who does what, thus reducing duplication of effort and removing the potential for "responsibility without authority";
- manage unforeseen problems sensibly and practically;
- increase the likelihood of adoption such that the benefits are more likely to be realised.

Addressing risk

An organisation that does not put sufficient resources into the management of its change management activity is running several risks:

- An organisation's normal business can be compromised. As managers focus more on failing or inefficiently managed change, they pay less attention to the business the organisation is seeking to maintain and develop (and which is funding change).
- Projects will be conducted as a second priority. Unless projects are discretely and efficiently scoped, planned and resourced, the workforce will remain focused on the normal operation of the business. Projects will be funded by "goodwill" rather than the ring-fenced budget they deserve.
- An organisation's reputation with its customers will suffer. This is especially the case if products and services are delivered by means of projects. When customers depend on delivery on time, on budget and to their specification, any failure of that project to meet their standards can affect the commercial relationship between supplier and client.
- Costs will escalate. Projects are undertaken because they are necessary or essential for the continuation or growth of the business. Their abandonment is not seen as an option. If projects are not adequately managed, they will consume increasing

resources. If they have to be abandoned, the financial and other costs can be enormous. For the business, there may be a direct impact on profitability with implications for shareholder value and investor relations.

■ Competitors will use their project management capabilities to their advantage. Their innovations will be delivered more quickly or economically. The market will welcome other organisations that can deliver products and services more efficiently.

■ An organisation's management competence will not grow. Competent managers will either burn out from the pressures of working in an environment that is not suited to the effective delivery of change through projects, or seek positions in organisations where they have an opportunity to work in a culture that is supportive and conducive to success.

If change management remains unrecognised as a specialist discipline in its own right, the organisation will probably fail to deliver the changes it needs to stay, or become more, competitive.

What are a project's characteristics?

A project has several characteristics that set it apart from an organisation's "business-as-usual". Business-as-usual can be characterised as:

■ requiring activities to be carried out repeatedly and/or regularly;
■ employing resources of similar skill-sets;
■ being constrained by annual, cycle-driven deadlines or budgets.

An organisation's typical business-as-usual activities may include:

■ delivering its products and/or services to its customers;
■ maintaining its financial affairs;
■ managing its people;
■ keeping its systems and processes running from day to day.

Business-as-usual is what departments do to maintain the performance of the organisation. If it can be established that a project differs from this, it can be shown why projects need and deserve a tailored form of management. There are several things that differentiate a project from business-as-usual:

- **A project produces a "defined deliverable".** A project is a vehicle for delivering change. It provides the governance by which an organisation can move from one steady-state to another, from A to B. One result of a project is a "defined deliverable", something which, by its use, enables the new steady-state to operate effectively. So this deliverable must be of sufficient quality to serve the purpose demanded of it.

- **A project has a defined end date.** There are many examples of projects whose deadlines are revised time and time again. For example, the European Fighter Jet had several delivery dates set and missed. This may be because the defined deliverable was not defined as well as it should have been. A project should have a target end date otherwise it will lose focus, probably go over budget and delay the business from benefiting from its investment. Furthermore, since a project is temporary, any delay in its completion means that those working on it cannot be released for other tasks.

- **A project has a defined budget.** This will extend for the life of the project, in contrast to a departmental budget, which will cover the financial year.

- **A project uses a wide range of resources.** A project will need to benefit from the capabilities, knowledge, skills and experience of people from a wide range of backgrounds from within and, possibly, outside the organisation. However, a business-as-usual department is, almost by definition, characterised by a narrower range of knowledge and skills.

- **People will be involved in peaks and troughs during the project.** Whereas a department is likely to have roughly the same number of people working in it throughout the financial year, a project will use a variety of people at different times in its life. For instance, the people specifying what the project must achieve will probably be most heavily involved at the beginning and at the end, whereas those developing the end product may be most involved during the middle phase.

- **A project has a life cycle.** Philip Larkin, a 20th-century English poet, once described the structure of a novel as having "a beginning, a muddle and an end", and many projects feel as though they are in a constant muddle. A project needs attention every day to reduce the risk of disorder and confusion, but it also needs direction from senior managers to ensure that it starts and stops according to plan. So the beginning is intended to create governance suitable for the project's management, and the end is to make sure that the project has an outcome that meets expectations.

Business-as-usual may share some of the hallmarks of a project. For instance, every month management reports will be produced to assist the company's decision-making. These reports are defined deliverables, but their creation is a repeatable, low-risk activity that does no more than maintain the steady-state of business. Similarly, business-as-usual requires a defined budget. However, it is usually calculated in order to maintain or improve performance during the coming year.

A project is intended to deliver a step change. Such changes may transform processes, performance or culture. In seeking to improve something, a project is moving firmly into a territory where expectations are less easy to predict or manage. It must produce something that, perhaps, has not been produced before, at least not in the same circumstances. There will be expectations about when the project will be completed, how much it will cost and what it will deliver. Articulating a clear and commonly held understanding of these variables is what makes each project both unique and risky.

Risk is a feature of projects. That so many fail is often because the risk of failure has been managed inadequately. Common reasons for failure include:

- inadequacy of the plan;
- absence of a plan;
- poor monitoring or control;
- unmanaged change;

- inadequate communication;
- constrained budgetary provision;
- poor management of expectations.

If uncorrected, such failures will lead to any one or a combination of the following:

- missed deadlines;
- exceeded budgets;
- substandard quality.

Time, cost and quality are the three criteria by which failure is most commonly measured. But what about success? Can a project be judged a success if it delivers:

- on time;
- to budget;
- to specification?

These may be measures of successful project management, but they are not adequate measures of a successful project. A project may result in a fit-for-purpose output, on time and on budget, and may have excited those who were involved, but did it make a positive difference? If it failed in this respect, what was the point of the investment? A successful project is best characterised by the change it delivers.

How can projects deliver change?

The outcome of any project is for an issue or opportunity to have been addressed. This means that, for the project to be considered a success, something must have been changed intentionally and by design. Although planned change is often considered to be positive, it may also be costly, risky and upsetting. For this reason, many organisations prefer to implement incremental change as part of their business-as-usual activity, to match the pace of the world around them and minimise potential resistance from within the organisation. However, it is often not possible to do this. Sometimes, an organisation is required to react to something unforeseen, or to address a problem arising from change

FIGURE 1.1 **A plan to develop operating procedures**

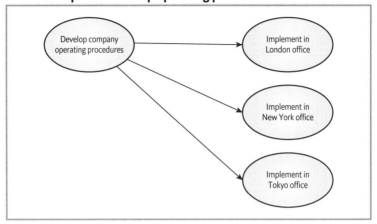

having been delayed for too long. At such times, a more significant transformation is needed. Given the heightened risk, a project is the safest and most secure means by which to respond.

Projects are undertaken to produce benefits and add value. The output should result in benefits that outweigh the investment. Later chapters will consider how to describe and quantify benefits, but first it is important to understand how the comparison of benefits and costs can help to define the scope of the project.

Figure 1.1 illustrates a company's plan to develop operating procedures that its international offices will be required to implement to gain savings from consistent and improved working practices. There are clear dependencies. For example, none of the implementations can happen until the operating procedures have been developed.

How many projects are needed to deliver this outcome? It could be four, one for each area of work. Or it could be two, one to develop the procedures and one to implement them in the offices. Or perhaps there could be economies from treating the whole endeavour as one project.

The decision is made easier when taking into account the value that must result. None of the implementations can take place if the operating procedures are not developed. But would the initiative be viable if it was not implemented in the Tokyo office? This is not clear. The critical question is whether the exclusion of Tokyo would so

FIGURE 1.2 **Cost versus income generation**

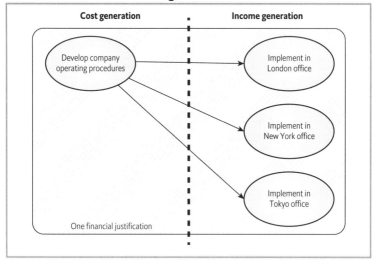

significantly reduce the benefits of the initiative that the investment could no longer be justified.

In any project there will be a point at which the investment being made is outweighed by the expected return on that investment. In this way, a project and a commercial business are no different. The question about how many projects there are can be addressed by taking a commercial perspective, as illustrated in Figure 1.2.

The development work on the left-hand side of Figure 1.2 will contribute to the costs of the project, while the implementation activities, although requiring some investment, will principally contribute to the generation of value. Whether the investment can be justified depends on knowing what value each implementation will generate. One may be insufficient, two may be enough and perhaps the third would be needed to make the case indisputable. Therefore, all four areas of work should fall under the same governance to ensure that the intended positive difference between costs and benefits is protected. This balance, with cost on one side and income (or benefit) on the other, is the foundation of any individual project. It answers the crucial question: "Why do we want to undertake this project?"

What is a project?

Every characteristic described so far has helped to describe the nature of projects, but what is a project? Many definitions exist, including the following:

- a unique set of events with a main goal and defined objectives and agreed plans for achieving that goal;
- an activity with a specified beginning and end date that is intended to meet stated objectives;
- a temporary effort undertaken to create a unique product or service;
- any organised campaign to change/improve something.

A project is better defined succinctly as a temporary management environment created to deliver a specified output according to a defined business justification:

- **A temporary management environment.** A project can be thought of as a commercial company intended to last for a defined period. It will share many of the characteristics of a business, being composed of people, objectives, plans and controls. It is the governance that knits them together and provides the order and structure that maximises the probability of success. The management environment needs to stay in place no longer than it takes to implement the specified output.
- **Created to deliver a specified output.** This is the goal, objective, product, service or situation referred to in some of the other definitions. The desired result must be defined in terms of timescale, cost and quality.
- **According to a defined business justification.** This is why the temporary management environment has been created. It is not simply to produce a deliverable; that deliverable must benefit the organisation. Change is the consequence.

What is project management?

Project management is doing what it takes to make sure that all those with an interest in the project always have the same clear answers to the following questions:

- **Who needs to be involved in managing a project?** There may be many people who have an interest in the project for a wide variety of reasons. These are the project's stakeholders. While the project may benefit from their views and opinions, not all of them need to be involved in managing it. So it is necessary to establish clearly the roles, responsibilities and reporting arrangements of those specifically charged with directing and managing a project from start to completion.

- **What must a project deliver?** A way of describing an output is to talk of it in terms of a deliverable. So the project must deliver a defined output such as the company operating procedures described in Figure 1.1. However, there will also be deliverables needed along the way, all of which must be articulated sufficiently well in advance to increase the likelihood of achieving the intended result. Examples may include a project plan, a feasibility study report, a business case, a requirements specification, a marketing report or a piece of machinery.

- **When must it deliver?** It is clearly necessary to identify a date for the end of the project, but there will be additional milestones that must be achieved throughout its life, such as those identified above. Each must have its own completion date.

- **How much must be invested?** How much will the project cost? The many projects that exceed their budgets are salutary evidence that costs must remain in focus throughout a project's life.

- **Why is this project necessary?** It is essential that the reason for the project is clearly and commonly understood. If the need or desire for the change cannot be articulated authoritatively and persuasively, it is doubtful that the project is justifiable.

Each of these five questions must be answered, and the answers must be genuinely understood and agreed by a project's authorities not merely at the beginning but also throughout a project's life. Furthermore, they must be clearly documented as part of the governance of the project.

But what about the environment outside the project? John Donne, an English poet and preacher who died in 1631, wrote, "No man is an island, entire of itself." The same is true of projects; they exist in a world in which they must compete with the demands of business-as-usual and the benefits other projects are proposing. Therefore, the wider organisation must support the concept of project management, not just a single project.

The components of effective change and project management

For a project to thrive, it must exist within surroundings that are supportive of its commissioning, management, funding, specification, building, testing and delivery. Projects launched in the wrong environment rarely succeed. The characteristics of a change-focused environment are illustrated in Figure 1.3.

The extent to which any of the components in Figure 1.3 already exist is a measure of an organisation's maturity in change and project management. It follows that there will be not only different levels of competence in different organisations, but also a path from one level of maturity to the next which will depend very much on the culture and needs of the organisation.

A case for every change

For change to be planned and delivered, it is first necessary to be able to articulate its purpose and objective. As noted earlier, this should take the form of a commercial justification for a project. Without governance and a culture that requires every change to be justified in this way, projects may be undertaken on a whim, driven by the enthusiasm of a sponsor and the strength of their argument. In their wake, other equally worthy or more worthy projects may be dismissed or overlooked. Therefore, all projects should be subject to the same discipline; the case for change should always be made in a way which

FIGURE 1.3 **Characteristics of a project-focused environment**

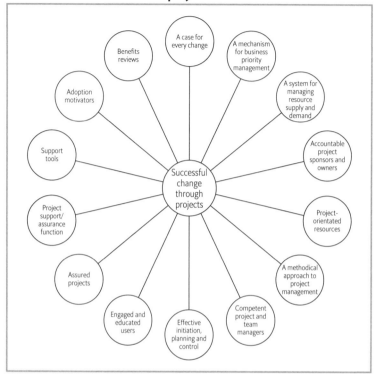

both articulates the change itself and allows it to be compared and contrasted with other proposals.

A mechanism for business priority management

An organisation may receive many proposals to change in some respect. As a result, it is common to have a portfolio of projects that have to be identified, selected, prioritised, commissioned and initiated. This usually results in a number of projects competing for attention for a variety of reasons, including:

■ mandatory or legal imperatives;

■ commercial opportunities;

■ cost-reduction opportunities;

- learning and developmental opportunities.

However, just as many organisations devote too little time and attention to change management, others try to achieve too much. In their enthusiasm to deliver everything, some organisations pursue numerous projects simultaneously. This can create other challenges:

- shortage of funds;
- conflict between projects;
- demanding or unrealistic timescales;
- increases in risk to the portfolio;
- damage to business-as-usual.

To combat these problems it is best to prioritise projects using several criteria to rank initiatives and then to back only those that are most deserving and rewarding.

A system for managing resource supply and demand

The demand for resources to deliver change will almost always outstrip the available supply. This is especially the case, given the need to continue business-as-usual activity. So while the business may be able to determine its priorities, it still has to fund them. Therefore, any organisation that wishes to deliver change through projects must have a means of identifying the resources available to deliver it, and of managing the tension of competing demands for that finite resource pot. The mechanism to do this may be a spreadsheet or computer system that compares and contrasts the available resources with the demand, identifying mismatches. More commonly, any such system will be supported by people who actively manage the portfolio's pipeline of work. Either they will ensure that the necessary resource is there when it is needed, or that preparations have been made for a forecast shortfall.

Accountable project sponsors and owners

If projects are to thrive, they need people who will promote them actively. A project's business case is its sales pitch. The document itself will not sell the merits of the project, nor make decisions about when and whether the project should start or stop. This is the role of its sponsors, and those charged with delivering a beneficial result. However, the discipline of project management also requires sponsorship. Given that not everyone will be instantly persuaded of the merits of this way of working, enough senior and authoritative individuals in the organisation must be prepared to endorse the approach and uphold its influence and value.

Project-orientated resources

Any organisation may have within it a project manager or two. Whether the wider organisation is literate in the language of project management is another matter, yet the whole organisation's structure has a part to play in making project management effective. If the organisational structure is unsupportive, projects are more likely to fail. If a culture of effective project management is to be encouraged, the language used in managing projects must be clearly understood and commonly applied by all those involved. The practical consequence of this is that the organisation must manage its resources to carry out both business-as-usual and change activity.

A methodical approach to project management

This is a defined and clearly articulated approach to project management. Sometimes it is called a methodology and is often a document that describes the processes, responsibilities and deliverables involved in the approach. Methods can be wildly misunderstood. They can be considered too expensive, too bureaucratic or too restrictive. It is important that the value of a particular approach is properly considered before it is either backed or dispensed with.

A methodology is a support for management, not a substitute for it. It is only useful when applied. No value will come from an operating manual nobody uses.

A methodical approach usually includes:

■ an overview to articulate the methodology sufficiently well to describe its scope and demonstrate how the parts fit together;

- a list of project roles and responsibilities to outline the expectations placed on the key stakeholders;
- procedures describing the steps people must take to make the project a success;
- a list of results describing what the procedures must produce;
- templates to outline the look and feel of the most common deliverables;
- examples that provide guidance on what a completed template might look like;
- hints and tips to serve as a body of reference for answers to questions that are likely to come up.

Most companies would use a book like this or an industry-standard project management methodology as the starting point for creating their own tailored approach. There are plenty of methodologies that focus on information technology (IT) projects. Surprisingly, there are few off-the-shelf pure project management methodologies available. A leading example of a pure project management approach is PRINCE.*

PRINCE (an acronym derived from PRojects IN Controlled Environments) recognises projects as endeavours that may take place in a variety of environments, both technical and non-technical. It was originally developed in the 1980s by the UK's Central Computer and Telecommunications Agency (CCTA) as a standard for IT project management. However, it was quickly recognised as an approach that could be tailored to the needs of almost any project. Its wide use identified improvements and changes that were incorporated in PRINCE2†, which was released in 1996 and is used in more than 50 countries. In keeping with trends in software development to adopt a more agile approach, there is a version of PRINCE2 – PRINCE2 Agile – that has been adapted for use in such projects.

---

* PRINCE® is a registered trademark of AXELOS Limited, and is registered in the US Patent and Trademark Office.
† PRINCE2™ and PRINCE2 Agile™ are registered trademarks of AXELOS Limited.

Whichever method an organisation chooses, it must satisfy important criteria. It should be:

■ successfully used elsewhere;

■ robust, internally consistent and free of evident fault;

■ clear enough to be sold and communicated to others, readily and easily understandable;

■ viable – it must be able to promise real value in return for the investment made in it;

■ scaleable – as it must serve a range of projects that vary in size, complexity and risk;

■ relevant – because it should cover the wide discipline of project management. There are many methodologies that focus on a limited technical approach to project management that may be relevant only to those technical projects.

Competent project and team managers

For a project to be successfully delivered it requires competent project managers and team leaders. They must understand project management and have appropriate project experience. It is not good enough that they are competent specialists with knowledge of IT, or pharmaceuticals, or engineering. Their position in the project may be enhanced if they are literate in the nature of the initiative, and also that they are employed within a project to manage the time, cost and quality expectations of the project's stakeholders. Project managers are like the hub of a wheel, holding the spokes together so that motion can be achieved. But they are not the only, or indeed most important, people involved in the project. There will be others such as the project's sponsors and owners who will have considerable influence too.

Training may help to bring about the desired culture change, but, like each of the other components listed here, it will be of little value on its own. At best, training will provide people with the skills and knowledge to do things better or differently. Training may motivate people, but the investment in it will be worth little if the principles and techniques it promotes are not applied in the workplace.

Training is not the only development tool in the box. There are other methods that may be used to develop the capabilities of individuals and the organisation itself. The turnaround of an organisation so often depends on the gradual embedding of preferred practice in real projects. The investment made in training, education and recruitment will be worthwhile only when people work and learn together.

This can be achieved in many ways, including the following:

- **Post-training coaching events.** A cost-effective way of ensuring that the lessons of a course become embedded in a person's way of working soon after receiving the training.

- **Working-lunch refreshers.** It is helpful to refresh knowledge and skills with support in specific topics of interest.

- **Skills forums.** An ideal way to share experience, improve the approach and raise everyone's standards. However, without proper ownership and control, forums can quickly become worthless.

- **Newsletters.** A helpful way of describing the ever-changing context within which the projects sit to an audience that would otherwise look mostly inwards.

- **Roadshows.** Like newsletters, these aim to maintain an interest in the relevance of project management. They invite participation but require investment. However, in mature project management cultures it is not unusual for two or more roadshows to be scheduled throughout the year.

- **Intranet sites** (web-based sites available to a restricted, usually internal, audience). Common today, intranets provide a means of storing and making accessible the organisation's approach so that it is not just available to anyone deemed to need it, but also represents the most current, single version of the truth (SVOT).

- **Buddying.** This works best when it is requested rather than enforced. Individuals are assigned a buddy with whom they can learn more about themselves and project management. This has huge advantages in that it is an organic, self-regulating approach, becoming only as large a mechanism as it needs to be; if people find little value in it, they will cease to participate. It allows participants to share experience, ask for advice in an unthreatening, informal environment and grow as managers and leaders.

Effective initiation, planning and control

Projects need the best start in life if they are to thrive. Initiation is a specific project management phase within which a project's management environment is created. During this phase, the merits of the project are further scrutinised to confirm its viability so that, if worthy, it may be planned within agreed expectations of time, cost and quality. With effective plans and controls in place, the project management team, including the project manager, may then guide it through its various stages.

Engaged and educated users

For change to stick, new ways of thinking, speaking, acting and behaving must be adopted. Commonly, those who are to use the project's output are those who are required to change most. Such users may include employees, customers and suppliers, but may extend to include diverse groups within the wider population. Success depends on how they react. Well before they are able to transform in the ways anticipated by the sponsors of change, they must first be engaged sufficiently to accept that change is coming, and that there will be consequences that may impact them personally. Assuming that they may be persuaded of the merits of the change, they must be educated in new ways of working. This may involve being shown how to use a new product or service, a new computer system or working practice. Unless such people have the confidence to use what the project has delivered, they are unlikely to change their behaviour and may well remain wedded to the status quo. It follows that both individual projects and the institutions that sponsor them must have the capability to engage and educate all such stakeholders.

Assured projects

It is helpful to have a mechanism by which projects may be checked against a series of criteria to ascertain both the effectiveness of their management and their continued potential to deliver the intended benefit. Assurance does not automatically mean audit. Indeed, the use of the word "audit" can make people fearful, which in turn may make it difficult to identify problems and their causes. A range of assurance measures can be used to give an organisation greater confidence in managing projects. The purpose in all cases is to review the project (not the project manager) with the aim of increasing the likelihood of a successful result. The following are forms of project assurance:

■ **Project management health check.** The project is reviewed (perhaps by invitation) by project management experts from elsewhere in the organisation, often drawing on the use of buddies. The outcome will be a report identifying areas of strength that could be promoted to other people and actions that need to be taken. There may or may not be a need for an external party to check progress following the report.

■ **Project management internal audit.** The project is reviewed formally, perhaps as a result of an alert or some evidence of a failing. It is likely that the audit will be conducted by someone who is impartial and competent to identify opportunities for improvement and propose solutions for the project management team to implement. Progress is tracked by the reviewer.

■ **Project management external audit.** This is similar to an internal audit but is conducted by an external party to specific terms of reference. As with any formal audit, there will be a requirement to attend to any areas of concern within a defined timetable, after which some sanctions may be applied.

Although an audit can sometimes be an uncomfortable experience, project assurance should be seen as a natural and supportive part of the discipline of project management because it seeks to improve processes, people and projects.

Project support/assurance function

A support/assurance function (SAF) is often called a project or programme office. Most mature, project-focused organisations have some form of project support and/or assurance function. The function's scope, objectives and way of working will be as unique as the project(s) it seeks to support. Many will offer a combination of support and assurance to an audience potentially composed of the most junior and senior extremes of management. The services the function offers may be equally diverse, ranging from administrative support to the development and maintenance of an organisation's approach to project management. Where the function is placed in the organisation will depend on its brief; it may support one project, a portfolio of projects, or a company-wide programme (which will be described later).

Support tools

There is a multitude of project support software on the market. Solutions are available on most computing platforms with an array of specialist applications to suit all users, whether office-bound or mobile. This particularly supports projects that feature remote working and varied time zones. Cloud computing and software-as-a-service (SAAS) have addressed many of the complexities formerly experienced by institutions wishing to implement and operate new systems and processes across their organisations. Additionally, the increasing sophistication of data analytics tools has provided opportunities for truly supportive management information to be available to all management levels involved in change.

The features of such systems vary greatly. Tools that may not be thought of as central to project management nevertheless provide functionality that may be invaluable to workers. For example, the widespread use of video and voice conferencing, and the automated configuration and version management of shared documents and files, are part and parcel of modern working practice for many people, especially those working in projects. At the opposite end of the scale are enterprise resource planning (ERP) systems which, as the name suggests, encompass the integrated management of key business processes, including those that are changing. In between are those more tailored applications that assist in the specific management of projects and change. These help managers to identify projects, qualify, quantify and prioritise them, plan them, and control their resources.

Despite these advances, project tools remain limited by the data they contain, the way in which they are set up and operated, and the organisation's willingness to adopt the relevant behaviours that lead to the realisation of their potential benefits. For example, if project workers believe that data they have entered into a time recording system will be used to unfairly challenge their performance, they may be unlikely to complete timesheets, or to do so accurately.

Therefore, expectations of the value such systems can deliver must always be compared to the risk of a workforce failing to adopt the associated working practices.

Adoption motivators

As noted previously, the benefits promised by a project may only be realised when new behaviours or ways of operating are manifested among key communities. This will not happen by chance. Nor will engagement and education alone result in people abandoning old habits and taking up new ones. Therefore, the solution or outcome that the project promises to deliver must be promoted sufficiently well so that people are motivated to adopt it. Many of the methods are described more fully in Chapter 13.

Benefits reviews

As the purpose of a project is to deliver a transformation that injects value to the organisation, it is surprising how few organisations conduct post-project reviews to assess the success of their projects.

At best, a completed project will have succeeded in producing a deliverable of acceptable quality, on time and to budget. But these are not measures of true project success; all they determine is that the project finished. The organisation deserves evidence that the promised return on investment has been achieved and that change has taken place.

In this respect, the mark of a mature project management culture is that it contains a benefits realisation phase in its project management life cycle, and conducts a benefits review during or at the end of this phase. Yet even when the benefits realisation phase is part of the methodical approach, the benefits review does not always take place automatically. Although many organisations recognise that benefits need time to accrue after a project is complete, a much smaller proportion actually measure them to confirm that they outweighed the investment made. This is strange, given that the point of a project is to deliver measurable value. However, it is understandable. Benefits are notoriously difficult to quantify. For instance, how can a commercial value be placed on increased customer satisfaction or improved morale? If a benefit cannot be valued, it is almost impossible to determine how much should be spent on delivering it. Benefits must be quantified at the outset and measured at the end of the benefits realisation phase if an organisation is to judge whether or not it made a worthwhile investment in the project.

2

Change leadership

PSYCHOLOGISTS AND MANAGEMENT THINKERS have, for many years, remarked on the human tendency for self-improvement. Change may bring new momentum, periods of creativity and invention, new ways of working and behaving, and commercial rewards. But when it is uncontrolled or poorly managed, it can cause chaos. This may result in the destruction of the status quo, or a reversal of fortune. Change may also be avoided. On the positive side, this may result in longer periods of stability, but it might equally lead to stagnation, or decline.

Any of these extremes may be experienced in the workplace.

The sources of change

The sources that fuel change are numerous. They include a range of external and internal factors that often apply in combination.

External factors

■ **Economic conditions.** One of the most significant drivers of change is the opportunity presented by a growing or diminishing economy. This can motivate individuals and organisations to move into new markets or to withdraw from others. For example, many companies around the world have invested in changes to their products and services, production processes, supply chains, and sales and marketing activity, to benefit from the rapid and significant growth in the Chinese economy.

■ **Technological innovation**. Much of the collapse of traditional retailing is due to technological innovations that have facilitated shopping online. Many of those who have been unable or slow to provide mobile or web-based solutions for their customers have seen their business fall away.

The invention of new technology can bring with it the opportunity for commercial exploitation, but this is not always an automatic consequence. Famously, when it was invented in the 1960s, the laser was considered to be "a solution looking for a problem". Since then, practical and commercial applications have been identified, including fibre-optics, optical disk-drives, barcode scanners, surgical interventions and military functions.

■ **Competition.** The woes of high-street retailers have been compounded by the emergence and growth of powerful competition. Large, internet-based retail giants have presented a challenge for traditional retailers of all forms, including those that already trade online. The ways in which retailers have responded to such competitive pressures have varied. Some have sought to copy the trading model of successful competitors. Others have sought to differentiate either through service, product offerings or price. Yet more have found new opportunities operating as market traders on the proven trading platform of an established online retailer. Of course, many others have faced change by closing up shop altogether.

■ **Local legislation and government policy.** It may seem obvious that local or government policymakers can initiate change. However, their action or inaction can have both planned and unintended consequences. For example, for many years, diesel-fuelled vehicles were promoted by many governments as a more efficient choice for drivers who made long journeys, and therefore as a more environmentally friendly option. As a result, the number of diesel vehicles on our roads grew. However, since the early 2010s, emissions scandals and pollution studies have revealed new truths about the fuel, so legislation has been progressively introduced to try to curb the use and sale of diesel-fuelled vehicles. This change of strategy has contributed to a sense of confusion among many consumers, who remain unclear as to the relative merits and risks of competing forms of fuel, and whether policy decisions about the future can be depended upon.

Inaction or delay by policymakers can have an equally significant impact. For example, research* suggests that in those countries where the food industry is self-regulated, children are exposed to more unhealthy food and drink advertising on television than those children in countries with no regulation at all. Some argue that this contributor to the growth of childhood obesity may only be addressed effectively when governments enact regulation.

- **Social and cultural movements.** At the time of writing, there has been a significantly heightened global and social interest in initiatives to promote and address the impact on our planet of climate change and human activity. This corresponds with the notable rise in the movement to adopt a vegan diet or lifestyle; a third of 16- to 24-year-olds in the UK now use non-dairy milk. As a result, many restaurants are responding with an increased and more prominent display of menu options, and supermarkets are promoting vegan products and ingredients.

- **Consumer trends.** Consumers have always followed – and in some cases, created – trends. The choices we exercise in the arts, fashion and food industries are all subject to wild fluctuations and movement. The music industry is dependent on consumers following the latest artist; without the periodic introduction of novelty, sales will decline. Appreciating this, the industry invests heavily in the search for new talent, knowing full well that its own commercial future depends on finding something new or different.

- **Geopolitical pressures.** The global economic disruption that began in 2008, and the varied and extreme impact of the pandemic in 2020, demonstrated how interconnected the machinery of geographic and political institutions has become. Where once a national crisis might have remained contained within its borders,

* https://doi.org/10.1111/obr.12840

today's global economic, social, health and cultural bonds mean that change may ripple across the planet at, quite literally, the speed of light. Some argue that the prevalence of social media, news outlets and global political institutions make traditional geographic boundaries less able to contain change. More and more, a global population is demanding a global response to global issues and opportunities, whether these be political, environmental, fiscal or social. To return a final time to the transforming retail sector, a consequence of global commercial dominance by a comparatively small number of firms is that they – and the regions of the world in which they operate – may face pressure to reform their attitude to taxation.

Internal factors

- **New products and services.** All organisations depend on being able to promote a product or service. Many come to recognise that the discovery of a successful product or service can be a double-edged sword; once its popularity has been established, there develops in its wake a demand to sustain and improve it. For many years, Apple's prosperity has depended on progressive developments of its flagship product, the iPhone. Recognising that dependence on a single product was a risk, the company exercised foresight and choice by actively augmenting its investment in the delivery of services and content, considering this to be the next frontier on which the fight for consumers would be fought.

  Motor vehicle manufacturers are also anticipating – and leading – change. Faced with the prospect of arguably the greatest revolution in journey-making since mankind climbed down from a horse and into a motorised vehicle, they are actively developing a range of new ways to travel. Each is experimenting with the development of ultra-low or zero-emissions vehicles, autonomous technology, ride-sharing opportunities, subscription-based vehicle use, and the growing attraction of purchasing a journey rather than a vehicle.

- **New routes to market.** The discovery of a new way of connecting with customers or consumers presents an opportunity for considerable change. For example, motor vehicle manufacturers have, for many years, accessed and served the car-driving population through dealerships. However, many manufacturers have begun to question the cost of maintaining a network of dealers and have instigated a movement towards direct-to-consumer online sales. Such a move is of considerable significance, given the sheer volume and variety of stakeholders who may be affected by these manufacturers' actions, including – but not limited to – the manufacturers and dealers themselves, leasers, finance providers and, of course, consumers. New routes to market such as direct-to-consumer online sales have profound implications for internal business structures, with a much greater need for staff with digital skills and the flexibility to adopt new models of customer engagement.

- **New management regimes**. At the end of 2017, the average tenure for a new chief executive officer (CEO) at an S&P 500 company was five years*. This figure had already been falling steadily and, with CEO turnover rising sharply since then[†], average tenure is likely to have fallen further in 2019. Given that many of these individuals are hired to implement a transformation in the fortunes of their respective organisations, it is not surprising that a new, self-imposed change cycle tends to begin with the arrival of the next incumbent.

- **Reorganisation.** The drive to boost efficiency through instigating change means that the institution's organisational structure frequently comes under close scrutiny, either with a view to removing blocks and layers of apparently unnecessary resources, or to redesign its wider operating model. Regrettably, if not properly managed, the benefits of a reduction in operating costs or a reform of an organisation's ways of working can often be accompanied by a commensurate reduction in standards of consumer service, product quality and employee engagement.

---

* https://corpgov.law.harvard.edu/2018/02/12/ceo-tenure-rates/
† https://fortune.com/2019/12/23/ceo-exodus-adam-neumann-steph-korey-larry-page/

Therefore, although the benefits of such a self-inflicted change may promise to be considerable, so too are the risks.

■ **Loss of employees, capability and performance.** A decline in the number or quality of employees in an organisation may be a sign that either change is already having an impact, or that it is necessary. If the organisation is failing to meet its productivity targets, or employee engagement measures are declining, the cause needs to be understood and addressed. Alternatively (or additionally), the organisation may experience a loss of skills, knowledge and expertise as a consequence of an unmanaged programme of recruitment, redundancy, retirement, resignation, or contract terminations. It may be the case that a competitor is more able to offer an employment package that is more attractive, or that the market simply cannot provide the capabilities needed by the organisation. In any case, a feature of human resource management is to anticipate, prepare for, and manage such periods of change.

What this list demonstrates is that change may be imposed, sought, lobbied for, promoted and resisted. It may even be ignored. But to avoid being swept along towards an unplanned and unknown destination, organisations must understand and manage change. Change transports an organisation from one state to another – what was referred to in Chapter 1 as a movement from A to B. Project management helps to ensure that the journey is managed.

Some of the changes described above have been evolutionary; change has taken place over time as an organisation's well-being has been gradually eroded or developed. Others have been revolutionary, transforming an organisation overnight, for good or for ill. Where a choice may be exercised, which one is best: an evolutionary or revolutionary approach to change?

Revolution versus evolution

Those who promote revolutionary change consider it a misconception that organisations develop best when they develop gradually; progress is rarely steady, resistance may be significant, and the management of organisational change can be both demanding and exhausting.

Their preference is for change to be sudden and striking so that any opposition to it may be overcome swiftly. In practice, this involves what has been referred to as a process of unfreezing, changing and refreezing the organisation.

By contrast, others encourage the benefits of evolutionary change. Sometimes referred to as "continuous renewal", its supporters consider revolutionary change to be a failure of management to maintain pace with the worlds both inside and around the organisation. Revolutionary change may be seen as a knee-jerk response to tactical or operational challenges, and may lack the structure that a strategic perspective can bring. This can lead to cycles of change that result in an organisation lurching from one extreme to another, often revisiting models of operation that it has previously abandoned. The preference of those who advocate evolutionary change is to fund and maintain a change management capability that is alert to all sources of change, and remains on standby to anticipate and respond when necessary. In this way, the revolutionary approach of unfreezing, changing, and refreezing an organisation becomes more fluid.

There are merits to both mindsets. Evolutionary change is considered to be less risky, funding is provided by business-as-usual as a managed but continuous stream of income, and the disruption that inevitably accompanies change is minimised. It is evident that technology developments are encouraging an evolutionary approach. For example, the delivery of software-as-a-service has meant that many individuals and organisations no longer have to disrupt their operations whenever a manufacturer releases an update to an application or operating system. Likewise, management methods are evolving. Iterative developments – where a solution is implemented as a progressive series of small, functional releases – allows for the realisation of benefits to be frequent and regular. (This is covered in much greater detail in Chapter 11.) Therefore, those organisations that promote continuous, evolutionary change will fund research and development divisions, maintain a permanent business change management function, invest in the development of sponsors and project managers, and experiment with technologies and practices that encourage perpetual but incremental change.

However, there are occasions when revolutionary change becomes essential or even inevitable. The pandemic of 2020 required or forced almost every organisation on the planet to adapt instantaneously in response to an existential threat. There was no time for evolutionary change. For some, this resulted in catastrophe. For others, it presented an opportunity. Revolutionary change can be both rewarding and risky, and may represent the difference between surviving and thriving. Where surprise or timing is of the essence, a more revolutionary approach might result in being first to market. Alternatively, an unanticipated, competitive threat may demand an immediate and brazen response if the organisation is to survive.

In practice, since change is not always predictable, an organisation must be prepared for periods of revolutionary transformation which it may not have anticipated. It must also maintain a portfolio of projects which delivers the benefits of continuous change. Like nature, there are transformative events, in between which there are periods of steady growth and development.

Institutional reaction to change

Engagement in change

Figure 2.1 illustrates the relationship between the source of, and support for, a range of proposed changes.

The badges in each box suggest the behaviour that communities may demonstrate as change is anticipated: enthusiasm, caution, frustration and apathy. The stars represent examples of projects as perceived by just one of these communities – the workforce.

A programme of externally mandated training is rarely popular with a workforce, in spite of the benefits to management in keeping, say, a regulator at bay. With the prospect that it will be received with great apathy, leaders and managers may expect resistance. To avoid the usual penalties that accompany non-compliance, such a programme may only happen successfully if ways can be found to address the barriers; autocratic leadership, backed up with a scheme of penalties or rewards, may be necessary to ensure the compliance of the workforce.

Frustration may be expected – and understandable – if the size of a workforce has to be reduced as a cost-saving measure. Commonly

FIGURE 2.1 **The source of, and support for, change**

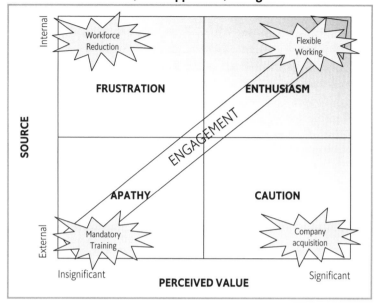

initiated following a realisation that the organisation's cost model is unsustainable, resistance can be significant, especially in industries where unions remain powerful. The nature of such a change requires a unique and tailored approach, involving the collaboration – or arbitration – of diverse and possibly antagonistic stakeholder groups.

Company acquisitions may evoke a cautious response from employees. If the acquisition means that the company avoids falling into administration, there may be a palpable sense of relief from staff. This may border on enthusiasm at first, although caution will usually follow once the details become clearer; this may mean that some jobs are sacrificed to save others. The leadership's handling of such change needs to be sensitive to the fact that a successful outcome for one group may be offset by a sense of loss for another. The change is more likely to succeed if the workforce senses that it is being managed fairly and justly.

An enthusiastic response from a workforce to a proposal for change may be welcomed by its management and leadership teams. It may suggest that the project can be conducted free from resistance. For example, the introduction of more flexible working arrangements, such as the option to work from home, is often a popular measure. Little resistance may be expected. While an eager interest may be exercised by the majority of the workforce, for some individuals, such a change may be unwelcome. An institution's apparent engagement in change can be at odds with that of an individual. The introduction of hot-desking, for instance, may upset those members of the workforce who prefer a permanent place of work.

In summary, the level of engagement determines the likely participation and commitment that may be expected, and the commensurate level and style of leadership most suited to address it.

Stakeholder identification and classification

The examples used in the model above are relevant to a workforce faced with the prospect of a change. In reality, the workforce is not the only group of stakeholders that may be affected by a change. Many people, all with differing expectations of success, will have a stake in a proposed change. It is important to identify and manage their varied expectations. When the features of the change can be articulated, it becomes possible to identify pools of individuals or groups who will have an interest in it, either because they will be affected or because they may drive the change itself. Two techniques can be helpful in first identifying who is in the pool, and then determining their respective level of influence.

The stakeholder map

Drawing up a stakeholder map is a quick and simple way of identifying everyone who may affect, or be affected by, the proposed change.

In the example illustrated in Figure 2.2, the company is being acquired. With this initiative noted at the centre, lines are extended to the stakeholder groups, subgroups and individuals. For example, the account management function is split into two divisions, each containing a number of colleagues. Each line is extended until it can be discounted, or until named individuals are identified.

Each group may be considered within the matrix in Figure 2.1 to

FIGURE 2.2 **A stakeholder map**

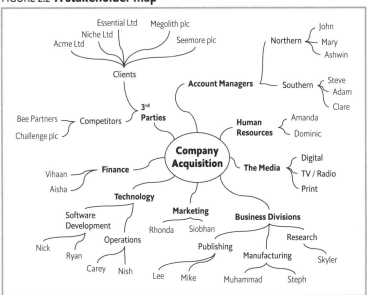

identify their possible behavioural reactions to the proposed change. This knowledge will assist the leadership team in determining the style it must exercise to gain engagement from each respective group.

The stakeholder matrix

The stakeholder matrix, shown in Figure 2.3, can help to identify the relative importance and value of these stakeholders.

This matrix allows for the placement of stakeholders in terms of their power and support. Power is not just a matter of the authority derived from a person's job but may also take account of knowledge and expertise. Support indicates the degree to which someone will back the initiative. Both may change, so although the matrix is relevant when drawn up, it may soon become out of date. This dynamic view can change as individuals fall from or rise to power. Moreover, supporters and detractors can form groups that gain power and influence as their size increases. For example, a client who expresses dissatisfaction with proposed change may exercise little individual power, but if these

FIGURE 2.3 **A stakeholder matrix**

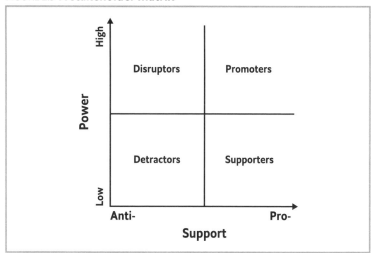

clients form a group – detractors uniting into a disruptive group – the threatened withdrawal of their custom can affect the entire commercial case for change.

As will be seen in Chapter 4, the stakeholder matrix may also be useful in identifying the candidates for the leadership and management teams.

Barriers and resistance to change

Individuals, groups and entire organisations may resist the prospect of change. The energy needed to address this must be sufficient and sustained, otherwise the forces of reaction will overpower progress. The barriers faced by those who seek to promote and deliver change may fall into three general categories: organisational resistance, cultural resistance and institutional complacency.

Organisational resistance

The organisation's operating model is composed of a unique configuration of three component parts. This fixed model is suited to serving the demands of a business-as-usual operation. However, when faced with something new, it may become apparent that any or all of these parts are unready, unable or unwilling to accommodate the proposed change:

- **People structures**. The existing reporting and control structures may not be supportive of, or appropriate for, the proposed change. For example, an organisation that has traditionally served corporate clients now proposes to market an existing product directly to retail customers. This will not be possible until retail sales and service divisions are put in place to do so. In turn, this may cause disruption to related structures, reporting lines, accountabilities and responsibilities. Furthermore, the existing structure may be well suited to the management of business-as-usual, but not to the management of change itself. The next chapter will focus on this matter.

- **Processes**. Working practices and activities can present an equally significant barrier in the face of change. For example, traditional recruitment processes may have been suited to the needs of the organisation for many years but are found to be constraining when faced with the need to develop a new division at speed.

- **Systems**. Being a set of physical tools on which many organisations depend, these can present a very real barrier to change. For example, intending to serve retail customers, the organisation is hindered not merely by the fact that its existing suite of systems is configured for corporate clients, but also that those very systems are already founded on obsolete technology. Systems may also exist in a non-computerised form. For example, an incentive scheme such as that used to reward sales people's performance, may work against the proposed change. In the case described above, unless the commission system is revised, corporate sales employees will continue to be motivated to serve corporate clients and not the retail base towards which the organisation is seeking to reorientate itself.

Therefore, no matter how well a change proposal may have been received, the very fabric of the organisation may pose a structural constraint. Before the change can happen, it may therefore be necessary

FIGURE 2.4 **Cultural resistance in an organisation**

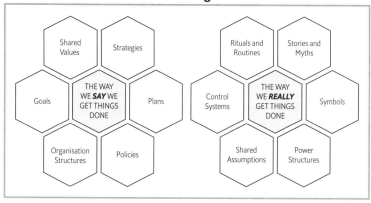

to adjust or rebuild the operating model – a change of enormous significance itself.

Cultural resistance

Considering the people described above, their configuration into an organisational structure is only one feature that can represent a barrier to change. Quite another is the obstacle represented by the culture – that combination of customs, ideas, values and behaviour that permeates the organisation. Given how ingrained this can be, the will to change is often outweighed by the desire to protect the status quo.

Consider the two scenarios illustrated in Figure 2.4.

The common machinery of management is composed of strategies, policies, plans and so forth. It is not uncommon to see an organisation's values written large on office walls and in communal areas. However, what an organisation says about the way it works is often undermined by the power of culture, which can determine how, or even if, the organisation achieves its aims.

A powerful, underlying, constraining culture is the perfect substrate on which to cultivate intransigence and complacency. Common features of a constraining culture may include:

■ **Ritual and routines**. These are practices that embed a set of beliefs or behaviours by virtue of repetition. Every organisation has its own examples. A personal favourite is of a security guard who, for 15 years, maintained a record of the number of people arriving by bicycle simply because he was one day asked to do so but was never told to stop.

- **Stories and myths.** These are tales, true or false, that have come to be treated as fact. For example, it was widely and repeatedly reported that one organisation's former CEO was removed from his position because he failed to introduce a new commission system. When the facts were examined, it was discovered that he retired because his son was gravely ill.

- **Symbols.** Cultural features can become iconic. A few examples remind us that fear of failure can have a powerful effect on how change comes to be perceived and managed in an organisation. From Coca-Cola's New Coke, which upset loyal customers to such an extent that the company had to withdraw the product, to Samsung's Galaxy Note 7, which famously had a tendency to catch fire, we are reminded of the power of symbols. More prosaically, one organisation used an extremely old computer system to capture and report on the business's portfolio of projects. The difficulty in using the system, and the poor visual quality of the material it produced, became a symbol for what project management meant to people around the organisation. It was only when the old system was replaced that people began to associate the management of change with modernity and efficiency.

- **Power structures.** As noted earlier, power is not merely a function of where in the organisation an individual or group may sit. Another personal example is of the chairman of an organisation's sports and social club, a charismatic individual who was held in such high regard by the workforce that he was regularly invited to board meetings to represent them. His position was unpaid, yet he wielded extraordinary influence. Other examples include the IT expert who was the only individual in the organisation who knew how the payroll system really worked and became so indulged by management that the size of his department grew completely out of proportion to the true value that it delivered.

■ **Shared assumptions.** This refers to commonly held beliefs that are taken to be true. For example, many of the workforce, and those in the world beyond, believed in 2008 – falsely, as it turned out – that several of the world's largest financial institutions were "too big to fail". Likewise, an entire organisation may come to assume that change can never be enacted because individuals reassure each other that "we tried that before and it didn't work".

■ **Control systems.** These are those less formal parts of the institution that can influence its fortunes. For example, after the banking crisis of 2008, many financial institutions created control systems to help them contain the sums they invested in change. Over recent years, many have discovered that these bodies are now so powerful that even essential change is challenged, constraining the organisation's growth and development .

Institutional complacency

Given that there are so many possible cultural impediments to change, organisations can quickly become complacent, confident in the comfort of the present, and blind to the challenges of the future. Institutional complacency may be apparent in a variety of behaviours:

■ **Dependence on a "burning platform".** Many believe that, to accept the need for change, a crisis is either necessary or desirable. It is true that some organisations need to be driven out of their complacency with the realisation that a threat is imminent, or upon them. The pandemic of 2020 provides an example of a motivator to change. If such an opportunity arises, it may be impossible to resist. However, if an organisation will not change until or unless it faces a crisis, it may already have passed the point of no return. As the pace of change hastens, the gap between noticing a crisis and responding to it becomes perilously small. Furthermore, as noted earlier, the capabilities needed to run a business are quite different from those needed to change it. For example, Blackberry, the producer of market-leading mobile phones and software, falsely believed that its position as the premier provider of mobile technology to businesses was unassailable. Suddenly faced with a "perfect storm" of challenges to its supremacy from outside (including, but not limited to, the arrival of Apple's iPhone and the emergence of BYOD – for "bring your own device"), as well as internal cultural barriers such as a dogged devotion to hardware development, Blackberry's eventual acceptance of a crisis came too late. New models were too slow to arrive and successive management teams were unable to govern urgent change as effectively as business-as-usual.

- **Too much fat.** Roles are duplicated or over-resourced. For example, identical IT departments existed within each division of an organisation while competitors had adopted a shared-services model. Organisations that have a tendency to revisit or continually extend failing projects also demonstrate that they are insufficiently lean to compete.

- **Poor performance or productivity.** The organisation's competitive position is falling. For example, a manufacturer excused the fact that its productivity was falling by continuing to insist that it was not only the world's only provider of its product, but that its quality was constantly improving. This exposed it to an increased risk of competition and acquisition.

- **Poor target setting and incentivisation.** Organisations sometimes measure or reward the wrong people or the wrong behaviour. For example, a service provider incentivised its sales division to deliver the highest possible standard of customer satisfaction, and its delivery division to meet profit targets. Since the sales division had no care for what they were charging for their services, they priced as low as they could and without any reference to the cost of delivery. Thereafter, the delivery division could only generate a profit by delivering at the lowest possible cost and quality. This was a model that placed two internal functions in a state of permanent tension, but worse still, reduced customer satisfaction and revenue. Unready, unwilling or unable to change a fundamental mechanism for managing its business, the firm was soon acquired by a competitor.

- **An unwillingness or inability to listen to advice.** Some leaders prefer their own interpretation to alternative perspectives, whether from inside or outside the organisation. For example, a large, traditional recruitment organisation that was enjoying its most successful year was wilfully ignorant of the risk that several digitally enabled startups posed to its own business model. This was compounded by repeated assertions by its family-run senior management team that the business model that had previously seen off much larger competitors could not be troubled by much smaller startups. No preparations or plans were put in place to mitigate the inevitable and gradual decline in business that followed.

Addressing resistance

Resistance in all its forms may be addressed with a range of tactics. However, all fall within three basic leadership strategies.

- **Directive.** This is characterised by the tendency of leaders to be autocratic. This form of leadership favours coercion and, possibly, manipulation, to drive stakeholder communities in the proposed direction. This may take the form of implicit leadership behaviour, such as placing barriers in the way of promotion for those who resist, to explicit measures designed to remove resistance entirely, such as dispensing with roles or people.

- **Consultative.** This strategy seeks to secure success through negotiation. There is an opportunity to learn from those who are pushing back against the change. Their resistance may be legitimate. Therefore, they may be engaged through negotiation with the possible outcome that they are transformed into active promoters. If this is the case, they may be offered a stake in making the change a success. If they cannot be persuaded to support the change, an attractive offer to leave may be utilised to remove them from their position of unsupportive or negative influence.

- **Democratic.** Such leaders direct, manage and deliver change by persuading others to participate in it through education and communication programmes. These promote the benefits of change such that people are encouraged to embrace it out of choice.

Whichever strategy is adopted, these institutional barriers to change must be removed. Key tactics include:

- Making the organisation's operating model compatible with the management and delivery of the change. For example, the development and launch of a new product or service may require some prior rearrangement of business processes, systems and people.

- Adopting incentive, penalty and reward measures that are consistent with the values and behaviours that the change is intended to deliver. For example, if sales teams are to successfully promote a new product or service, their existing incentive scheme must be adapted to encourage the desired behaviour.

- Engaging or confronting those who actively object to the change. For example, during a period of change designed to address unsuitable behaviour to customers, those who continue to brief against the proposal may be encouraged to leave the organisation.

- Developing a clear, commonly understood and shared expression of the vision. In this way, those who are resistant may be persuaded one by one to move towards a new set of values and behaviours. For example, a training scheme may be utilised to promote not only the benefits of the change, but also the way in which it may be achieved.

- Challenging complacency among those who are ignorant of the need for change. For example, if a competitive threat has been denied by some inside the organisation, it may be helpful to engage an external agent to present it from their impartial and objective perspective, and to use data to support the argument. Ultimately, allowing an organisation to slip into crisis may be the only way to expose reality to those who would deny it.

In summary, leaders must:

- identify and describe the "burning platform", whether it exists in the present or the future;
- challenge and disprove assumptions, rules or accepted truths where these are known to be false;
- engage a trusted advisor such as a supplier, client or consultant to present an external view of the organisation;
- knock down symbols, or replace them with new ones;
- if large scale transformation is not working, nudge values and behaviours in small steps;
- expose and acknowledge the feelings of stakeholder communities who may feel compromised or challenged by the prospect of change;
- write the future as a story, replacing any existing narratives, and share it with the organisation.

Change leadership

The ability to address resistance, encourage engagement and, ultimately change behaviour, requires leadership. Almost every definition of leadership places the ability to influence others at its heart. Notice that this is not entirely consistent with the directive approach to leadership described earlier. Almost by definition, a notable quality of leadership is that others will follow. Without followers, who is a leader leading? Therefore, to understand leadership, it is helpful to know how to influence and enable others to do willingly and enthusiastically what they might otherwise choose to avoid.

Leadership may be exercised and demonstrated in a variety of ways, dependent on the nature and personality of the individual. Leadership expert James MacGregor Burns suggested that leadership may be identified in the following forms:

Transactional leadership

This is commonly observed in discrete and contained change environments. This type of leadership adopts two practical forms of control to encourage specified actions and reactions. The first is the use of rewards or penalties in recognition of effort or performance in compliance with directives and goals. The second is commonly referred to as management by exception. Here, the status quo is maintained, whether this takes the form of a project plan or a department's existing governance; the transactional leader intervenes when specified criteria are breached.

Such leaders have a tendency to be much less attentive to the well-being of the workforce and assume that without a regime of reward or punishment, workers will not perform as required. This has much in common with Theory X, proposed by the noted management professor, Douglas McGregor, who described a form of management that assumes that the typical worker is unambitious and motivated mostly by self-interest.

Transactional leaders can deliver important and helpful outcomes that are easily measured. However, since the bare minimum of compliance may be expected from a tightly controlled workforce under such circumstances, changes may be short-lived; followers will disperse as soon as their own self-interest is no longer served by pursuing them.

As will be described later in this book, a project can be a tightly governed environment. Project managers may demonstrate this reactive, transactional form of leadership, but for change to be adopted among wider and more fluid communities, it must be supplemented with transformational leadership.

Transformational leadership

Transformational leaders take an active approach to the way in which they engage with individuals and communities. In a manner that is quite the opposite of transactional leaders, they will recognise that the organisation's governance may be a threat to, or inhibitor of, progress and that the existing culture may itself be a candidate for change. Therefore, this leader will seek to appeal to the concerns – moral and practical – of the workforce. In consequence, those who follow transformational leaders do so because they have been motivated to address the interests of the group, not of the individual.

Therefore, transformational leadership has more in common with McGregor's Theory Y, taking as a basis the assumption that workers

FIGURE 2.5 **The journey to lead and manage change**

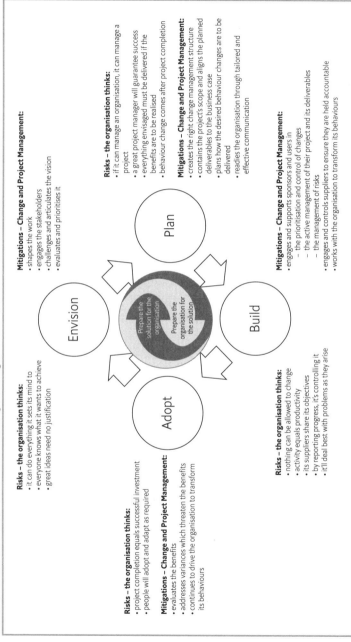

Risks – the organisation thinks:
- it can do everything it sets its mind to
- everyone knows what it wants to achieve
- great ideas need no justification

Mitigations – Change and Project Management:
- shapes the work
- engages the stakeholders
- challenges and articulates the vision
- evaluates and prioritises it

Risks – the organisation thinks:
- if it can manage an organisation, it can manage a project
- a great project manager will guarantee success
- everything envisaged must be delivered if the benefits are to be realised
- behaviour change comes after project completion

Mitigations – Change and Project Management:
- creates the right change management structure
- contains the project's scope and aligns the planned deliverables to the business case
- plans how the desired behaviour changes are to be delivered
- readies the organisation through tailored and effective communication

Risks – the organisation thinks:
- nothing can be allowed to change
- activity equals productivity
- its suppliers share its objectives
- by reporting progress, it's controlling it
- it'll deal best with problems as they arise

Mitigations – Change and Project Management:
- engages and supports sponsors and users in
  - the prioritisation and control of changes
  - the active management of their project and its deliverables
  - the management of risks
- engages and controls suppliers to ensure they are held accountable
- works with the organisation to transform its behaviours

Risks – the organisation thinks:
- project completion equals successful investment
- people will adopt and adapt as required

Mitigations – Change and Project Management:
- evaluates the benefits
- addresses variances which threaten the benefits
- continues to drive the organisation to transform its behaviours

Envision

Plan

Adopt

Build

Prepare the solution for the organisation

Prepare the organisation for the solution

are naturally self-motivated and work to better themselves in spite of whether a reward or penalty is applied.

Transformational leaders are often considered heroic as they appear able to deliver change single-handedly, whereas in fact they have tapped into the organisation's own natural resource and directed its latent energy. Such people are perfect candidates to participate in the life cycle of a change, serving first as someone who can identify the need for change and motivate others to agree, and then to sponsor the project to direct it. The important role of the project's sponsor is developed fully in Chapter 4.

Change leadership and change management

Any project needs a combination of management and leadership. Where management is concerned with logistics and is therefore of the mind, leadership has much to do with the spirit.

Management provides the ability to organise, plan, co-ordinate and control the resources to deliver change. This is something that can be learned. The people who manage are often trained, developed and appointed to positions of authority. They exist within formal structures that allow them to exercise their power within controlled limits and in so doing, are encouraged to focus on the delivery of measurable results. As noted above, when leadership is exercised by those who are more familiar with the ways and means of management, it is more transactional in its nature than transformational. Given that the risks of change are considerable, projects tend to be tightly managed environments.

Leadership provides the inspiration and motivation to change. Such qualities tend to be innate and less-easily learned; they are less common, perhaps because they remain hidden until needed. A capacity for leadership may have lain undisturbed for many years, but it has first to exist before a leader can emerge. Thereafter, the qualities of leadership may be developed further through experience. Once exposed, a leader's influence can extend well beyond the limitations of an organisational structure; indeed, this is often essential. So, although leadership is more about being than doing, in a changing environment there are essential activities that only someone with leadership qualities can carry out.

In practice, leaders and managers need each other to deliver long-lasting, beneficial change. Figure 2.5 illustrates the journey they must take together – from envisioning change, planning it, building the deliverables that will facilitate it, and encouraging the adoption of new behaviours. During that journey, they will face many risks. What follows in this book is a leader's and manager's guide to the principles and techniques that may address them.

Conceiving and prioritising projects

THE IMPULSE TO CHANGE may have been experienced by an individual or within the body corporate. If worthy, these impulses must be transformed into projects. Projects are a managed response to a variety of leadership imperatives to deliver change. Most organisations' projects are a combination of action and reaction in the face of change. Some companies prefer a selection of projects that suits their strategy; others prefer a mix that responds to their immediate operational needs; and many fall in between. In all cases, the lowest common denominator is a list of projects.

As the list lengthens, the implications for the way a company controls its projects grow. For instance, its structure may have to change in order to accommodate managing resources across several projects or it may have to become more flexible about setting priorities.

There are several ways of meeting the challenge of identifying projects.

Project identification by department

Figure 3.1 is an example of a company structure. The board oversees five directorates: operations; facilities management; technology; finance; sales and marketing. Technology is subdivided into infrastructure and applications.

How a company identifies projects usually depends on its structure. In the example, the annual business plan starts with the board and cascades through the departments. Each layer of management looks at the plan from its own perspective, identifying activity for which it will be responsible and which will help achieve the board's objectives.

FIGURE 3.1 **A company structure**

This is likely to be a combination of business-as-usual and a portfolio of several projects. The desired outcome is that by the time the plan has percolated through every layer of management, everyone knows what part they have to play in it.

Each department has a portfolio of projects to deliver, funded from a proportion of the annual budget. As the budget holder, the head of each department is often given ownership of those projects. However, their role will not be easy; as well as carrying out business-as-usual, they have a portfolio of projects which depend on resources and deliverables from other departments.

This traditional approach to identifying projects is spectacularly inefficient and demonstrates the importance of managing projects differently. Figure 3.2 shows that there are many interdependencies

FIGURE 3.2 **The traditional approach to identifying projects**

Note: BAU = business as usual.

between the projects. For example, Projects 2, 8, 17, 18 and 22 must all be delivered successfully to meet Objective 2 in the business plan. However, successfully delivering those projects may require joint activity and sharing resources with other departments.

The structure is inadequate because it was designed to deliver business-as-usual, not change. The longer projects stay within departments, the more challenging they become to co-ordinate. A specific management approach is needed if the projects are to meet Objective 2.

A classic response is to create a portfolio of management governance, which is empowered to oversee every project. This can work, but it may be costly and deliver little value beyond the tactical co-ordination of different activities and use of resources.

There is an alternative. The company could identify the projects necessary to deliver Objective 2 and assign each its own management team. This way, identifying the portfolio of projects is separated from the constraints of the organisation's structure.

Project identification by business objective

Figure 3.3 illustrates a radically different way to identify projects.

Projects are not allocated to departments but identified independently after analysis of the business plan's objectives. They are distinguished by their ability to help achieve an objective, and there are fewer of them because they are not multiplied by the number of departments involved in delivering them.

This will have a significant impact on the way the business operates. For any company that delivers much of its business or internal change through projects, the benefits will be significant, not least from avoiding inefficiencies generated by the passing of a project from one department to another. But there will be a cultural and procedural cost. It is possible to implement this approach only if an organisation is

FIGURE 3.3 **Identifying projects by business objective**

prepared to adopt the basic principles outlined in this guide. Figures 3.2 and 3.3 show the fundamental differences between an organisation that achieves change through departmental activity and one that does it through projects.

This is not to say that the departmental approach cannot be made to work. It may well be the point from which the cultural change begins. But it does not provide effective governance for projects to thrive and deliver successful outcomes. If an organisation is serious about adopting a project-focused approach, it should make sure its projects are based as directly as possible on its business objectives, not on a blinkered departmental vision. Only then is it possible to have faith that the outcome of a project will contribute directly to the strategy.

Before understanding how to derive a project from a company's business plan, it is necessary to know what is meant by a portfolio and a programme.

A portfolio

A portfolio was described earlier as a list of projects. An organisation may have one or many portfolios characterised by a common budget or a common department.

The purpose of creating a portfolio of projects is to increase the likelihood that they will succeed and to reduce the risks of failure arising from undertaking them in a complex and volatile environment. So it is better to define a portfolio as a group of projects gathered into a governable unit to facilitate their effective co-ordination and success.

Unlike a project and a programme, it is likely that the portfolio will never end. As projects are completed new ones take their place, so when judging the success of a portfolio that has no fixed outcome it is necessary to look for a steady stream of signals that:

- projects are being delivered on time;
- projects are being delivered on budget;
- projects are being delivered to specification;
- projects are enabling business benefits to be realised;
- the plan is regularly updated and approved by the business sponsors;

- the portfolio is aligned to the business plan;
- the portfolio frequently contributes to the achievement of business objectives.

These benchmarks apply to projects that fall within a common budget or department. It is possible to conceive a portfolio of projects specifically pulled together to deliver a particular business objective. In other words, a greater degree of intelligence has been applied to the creation of this kind of portfolio because it has an end target in mind. This is a programme.

A programme

A programme is a vehicle for progressing, co-ordinating and implementing an organisation's strategy, specifically by linking an often complex combination of business-as-usual activity and new projects all focused on the delivery of a defined objective. It is not business-as-usual because a programme seeks to deliver something different.

However, the term is often misused. For many people, a programme is simply a large project. A large project and a programme have similarities. They both:

- seek to deliver a beneficial outcome;
- deserve a special form of management structure.

But the shared characteristics go further than this. Some of the differences are shown in Table 3.1.

TABLE 3.1 **Differences between a project and a programme**

Project	Programme
■ has relatively few sponsors	■ has many sponsors
■ will be a contained disaster if it fails	■ may be a corporate disaster if it fails
■ is focused on a deliverable	■ is focused on a business objective
■ will deliver benefit after completion	■ will deliver benefit in phases
■ has a short- to medium-term lifespan	■ has a long-term lifespan
■ has variable risk	■ is always high risk
■ has a focused scope	■ has a wide scope
■ excludes business-as-usual activity	■ includes business-as-usual activity

For example, a project may have been identified to deliver a new sales management computer system. It conforms to the characteristics of a project:

■ There will be a limited number of sponsors, probably extending little further than the sales manager.

■ If the project fails to deliver the new system, the company can fall back on what it has used previously.

■ It must deliver an implemented sales management computer system and trained sales staff.

■ When the sales force has used the system for some time, the project costs will be recouped through extra or higher-value sales arising from slicker management of leads.

■ Implementation may be reasonably expected within a year of the project being planned.

■ The risks will be managed mainly within the sales and IT departments.

■ The scope can be contained within clear organisational, budgetary, time and geographic boundaries.

■ Business-as-usual activity should remain largely unaffected by the project (until it is completed).

Compare this project with a programme through which a manufacturer and distributor of potato snacks seeks to enter a new foreign market. The programme will have these characteristics:

■ There will be several sponsors, coming from operations, commercial management, distribution, sales, marketing and manufacturing. Virtually no part of the company will remain untouched by this endeavour.

■ Failure in the new foreign market could be corporate disaster. At the very least, the sponsoring director might be asked to resign.

■ The programme must deliver a series of co-ordinated outputs which together bring about the business objective of succeeding in the foreign market. Such outputs may themselves be delivered by projects integral to the programme. This series of co-ordinated outputs has an important implication for the economic justification of the individual projects that fall within the programme. Where a stand-alone project should be commercially justifiable, one that falls within a programme may not be on its own. Some projects within a programme may only exist to enable future projects to be undertaken. If the subsequent projects are shelved, the earlier projects may deliver little or no benefit. The business case for every project in the programme must be considered together if the programme's overall justification is to be properly understood. For instance, the programme in this example may contain a project to produce new packaging for the foreign market. On its own, it would generate no benefits. It is only justifiable as an enabler for benefit-generating projects elsewhere in the programme.

- To minimise the risk of failure, the programme may be designed to deliver benefit in phases, for instance by focusing first on one country in which demand is considered sufficient to outweigh the costs.

- The programme may have a long life, especially if it is split into phases. Conversely, if it is dropped, it may not last as long as anticipated.

- With any programme risk is inevitable. Not only is the company taking a calculated risk with a significant investment, but it is also running the risk that its existing business may be compromised during the programme's lifetime.

- Virtually every part of the business will be engaged in or affected by the programme.

- A defining characteristic of a programme, compared with a project, is that its management team must take responsibility not just for the change in activity within its scope but also for business-as-usual continuing successfully. At least until the first phase has delivered some commercial benefit, the programme will be funded by business-as-usual, whose resources will be involved in the programme. Furthermore, the company will need everyone to adapt to the demands and challenges of the new business environment the programme will deliver.

In any portfolio there may or may not be technical, strategic or commercial dependencies between the projects – it has not been constructed with them in mind. Instead, the grouping of projects is characterised by their being funded from a common budget or being overseen by a defined part of the organisation. A programme, however, is a portfolio of technically, strategically and/or commercially interlinked projects where the dependencies must be identified and managed if an objective in the business plan is to be met. Furthermore, the nature of programmes suggests that there will often be a degree of business-as-usual management required from within the programme to prepare the business for a new way of working.

Understanding these concepts is essential if projects are to be conceived and managed effectively. Project identification is not only about forming a list of projects; it is also about understanding them sufficiently well to place them in a suitable management environment, which is independent of the underlying organisational structure and which will enable them to thrive.

So although the need for a project may be raised from within one part of an organisation, it is not always the case that the eventual project must be managed, funded and resourced from the same place.

When are projects identified?

The need for a project can arise at any time, but many are identified during the annual planning cycle because the organisation is focusing on what it would like to achieve during the coming year. Yet both the organisation and the outside world will change during that year so a contingency budget should be created for initiatives approved outside the planning cycle.

When a project is identified, three things will apply:

- unless this is the first time the organisation has identified projects, it is likely that there will be a portfolio of projects that are under way, having been commissioned during the previous year, into which the new project may be slotted;

■ the project's selection, prioritisation and commissioning should be managed, not left to the whim of budget-holders;

■ some basic information must be known about each potential project if informed decisions are to be made about its future.

Most organisations have a pro forma to be used to outline a potential project. This is not only to make sure that subsequent debate is informed, but also formally to place the idea of the project in the organisation's roster of work. Thus the project does not emerge from chaos but is the product of a considered and cost-controlled process.

The pro forma is often called a project outline (see Table 3.2 for a typical example). This simple document seeks to record the answers to the most important questions at this early stage before the project is commissioned. If the senior managers think there is sufficient merit in the idea mapped out in the project outline and supported by their analysis, there is a chance of it becoming a real project.

TABLE 3.2 **A typical project outline**

Sponsor	The name of the person who has driven the initiative thus far.
Title	The name of the potential project. If the initiative is confidential, use a code name.
Objective	What is the purpose of the potential project? What problem or opportunity is it seeking to address?
Benefits	What benefits may be expected from the project, should it take place? Over what period is the return on investment expected?
Scope	Are there any specific inclusions or exclusions of note?
Key products	What will the project deliver?
Timescale	How long may the project take? Are there any important dates?
Investment	What investment will be necessary and over what period?
Investment needed for the next stage	What investment is necessary for the next stage of the project?
Planning assumptions	What assumptions had to be made when identifying key products, timescales, budgets and benefits?
Risks	What may cause the project to fail? What mitigations may there be for each risk identified?

There is a greater chance that those debating the merits of one potential project compared with another can do so when the features of each, no matter how scant, are clearly and commonly understood. Project outlines also make it possible to consider how the right projects may be selected, prioritised and commissioned for the vision to be achieved.

The way in which many organisations choose to achieve their vision is to put in place a combination of business-as-usual and change initiatives to deliver step-by-step improvements and value along the way. Once a year, those organisations develop their business plans, the result of which is usually a combination of old and new initiatives that will help achieve the business strategy.

For the most part, the once-a-year effort will focus on the initiatives the board want to deliver and will incorporate a combination of business-as-usual and change. At this level of the organisation, change is often best described in terms of programmes. Senior managers know that governance is needed to implement the delivery of something significant or new. But although programmes are designed with the innate governance to enable their control, they are still made up of interdependent projects. Add these to the other, smaller improvements that a company needs to make during the year and the organisation may have a large portfolio of initiatives that demands and deserves some form of overarching continuous governance.

Continuity is at the heart of the argument for a form of management of business change. Projects are being identified all the time, so there is a significant risk that initiatives can be identified and initiated that have little or no reference to the business plan, its sponsors or the organisation's vision for the future.

In recognising that a relationship exists between a project and the business plan, it should be possible to confirm that the list of projects being proposed or undertaken will substantially deliver the company's change agenda. So if an organisation wishes to know its true destination, it should look to the portfolio of projects it has chosen to invest in by design, by instinct or by mistake.

An organisation needs a clear line of sight between the business plan and its portfolio of projects, and assurance that the projects it undertakes will deliver the change it desires. Three steps can help to establish and maintain this line of sight. They are as easy to remember as ABC:

- **Articulating** – describing the business plan so it helps to identify projects.
- **Balancing** – making sure that the proposed portfolio of projects is constructed to deliver across a range of measures.
- **Commissioning** – sponsoring those projects that will make sure the organisation delivers the change component of the business plan.

Articulating

There are many guidelines about what should be in a business plan. Each organisation will probably have something that it uses year after year. As a result, each example will vary in its ability to describe effectively how the company's targets can be met.

Whatever the format of the business plan, a common starting point is needed. It should be possible to express the business plan as a series of statements that both summarise the content and help to identify projects. The following list, which took no more than an hour to compile, is a summary of a real organisation's wordy business plan. The company will:

- retain its most important clients;
- win new clients;
- secure recurring revenues rather than one-off fees;
- further its alliance partnerships;
- deliver increased revenue;
- deliver increased margins;
- become number one in its marketplace;
- undertake short-term, high-yield projects;
- deliver a wider range of products;
- reduce its implementation timescales;
- reduce its implementation costs;

- deliver minimum maintenance products;
- engage in fixed-price or shared-risk initiatives;
- prioritise and justify every initiative it undertakes;
- have market-leading product quality and testing processes;
- use cutting-edge product implementation processes;
- manage its projects using repeatable, proven principles and techniques;
- use new and innovative technologies;
- provide opportunities to help retain experienced staff;
- apply lessons learned from experience;
- attract and develop junior staff;
- increase the gap between itself and its competitors.

This may seem a random set of statements drawn from a document. It may be true that the business plan lacks focus or may fail across a range of success criteria. So before identifying projects that can contribute to its success, the business plan should be balanced.

Balancing

It is crucial that a portfolio of projects is balanced. This means that the selection of projects must deliver across a range of competing measures, and that an organisation must have sufficient resources to meet the project's demands.

Balancing resource supply and demand

It is probably true to say that the demand for resources to deliver projects will always outstrip their availability. Therefore, as well as identifying the right projects to undertake, it is important to ensure that there are adequate resources. A starting point can be a statement of the organisation's resource supply and demand balance (or imbalance); discussions should include such topics as where the organisation is heading and what its priorities are.

Figure 3.4 shows the resources demanded by a portfolio of projects and the supply available. When populated with an organisation's actual

FIGURE 3.4 **Resources demanded and supply available**

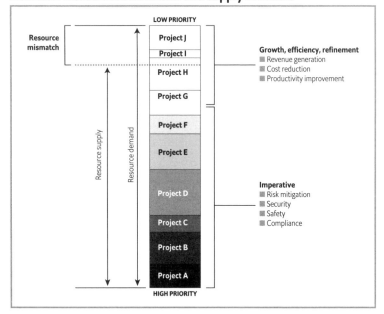

data, the dotted line shows the point up to which existing resources can be invested. In this example, the stack of projects above the line cannot be resourced unless there is additional funding or the stack is reprioritised.

The steps you should take to determine your business's position are as follows.

1 Describe what constitutes a "project"

If a business is to manage its change agenda, as distinct from business-as-usual, it must state clearly what constitutes a project. This requires more than the definition provided earlier, since that does not include the size, scale, criticality or risk of the endeavour. A set of simple criteria is needed to define which projects fall within the portfolio: for example, a piece of work requiring 15 or more days' effort, co-ordinated across more than one department.

It is crucial to specify the number of days. If it is set too high, the large number of small projects that consume much – or most – of the resources could be excluded from the controls you are seeking to implement. Since such small initiatives can compromise the successful resourcing of larger projects, they should not be allowed to fall beneath the radar.

The criterion specifying "more than one department" is justified on the basis that the wider business may lose control of its resources when individual departments make direct and unauthorised demands on one another. For example, the IT resource is finite and must be responsibly managed to ensure that business priorities are met. These institutional priorities can be compromised when departments divert IT resources to pursue non-critical or non-strategic activities.

However, the same criterion also allows for department managers to conduct discretionary projects with their own resources, providing they can fund them from their own budgets and still meet their obligations to the wider change agenda. For instance, the IT department will have a list of projects, such as software upgrades, which it will argue must be delivered for the business to continue to operate. Some will argue that these do not qualify as corporate projects, since they involve only one department. If this is the case, such work should be funded out of business-as-usual. However, if an individual software upgrade is substantial enough that it requires other departments to be involved in, say, a training programme, there is a good case for treating it in the same way as any other project. That the IT department insists it is essential does not remove its obligation to justify it along with every other initiative that the organisation is seeking to pursue.

It is worth publicising these statements to the whole organisation so that the criteria are not misunderstood. Furthermore, there is value in adding that approved projects will be:

- commissioned to satisfy the organisation's ability to conform to regulatory requirements, deliver strategic change and grow or refine itself;
- subject to formal governance to realise measurable operational or strategic benefit;
- assigned a sponsor and a cost code, without which they will not be considered legitimate.

2 Identify the projects

Compile a list of initiatives that qualify as projects according to the criteria noted above. Surprisingly, this is not as simple as it might first appear. It may soon be discovered that there are:

■ mismatched expectations – one person's understanding of a project's objective or scope is different from another's;

■ unidentified projects – those about which little is known, yet which are already under way and hungrily consuming resources;

■ unformed projects – those that have not yet been commissioned;

■ confused priorities – projects that have been incorrectly promoted or withheld;

■ pet projects – those that have the backing of an individual, but not of the business.

3 Record the projects

In seeking to resolve the problems identified above it is important to record the list of projects in a draft project register. This will be of great importance as the organisation comes to understand change; the project register will come to represent the formal portfolio of initiatives that the organisation employs to deliver its change agenda.

To begin with, a spreadsheet will be sufficient to record some basic but essential information about each project (see Figure 3.5).

The data that fill the project register describe something critical about each initiative that may not have been clear before. Much may remain unclear, but at least there is now a basis upon which to start a debate among those who have been charged with delivering the changes desired by the organisation.

At this time, the content of the project register is limited. Eventually, the data can be extended to assist in the effective management of the portfolio. For now, the most important fields are as follows:

■ Priority. Is the project imperative or not? For many projects, the answer will not be straightforward because different people will have different opinions. This is why it is important to explain what is meant by the term "imperative". It must be taken to

FIGURE 3.5 **Project register**

Priority	ID	Project name	Sponsor	Cost code	Start	End	Cost $*
Imperative	A	Project A	Sponsor A	IMP0001	01/06/2011	30/09/2011	100,000
Imperative	B	Project B	Sponsor B	IMP0002	01/07/2011	31/03/2012	135,000
Imperative	C	Project C	Sponsor C	IMP0003	01/01/2012	28/02/2012	40,000
Imperative	D	Project D	Sponsor D	IMP0004	01/08/2011	31/05/2012	250,000
Imperative	E	Project E	Sponsor E	IMP0005	01/07/2011	31/10/2011	140,000
Imperative	F	Project F	Sponsor F	IMP0006	01/05/2012	31/08/2012	120,000
Growth	G	Project G	Sponsor G	GRO0001	01/10/2011	28/02/2012	150,000
Growth	H	Project H	Sponsor H		01/11/2011	31/05/2012	315,000
Growth	I	Project I	Sponsor I		01/09/2011	31/12/2011	80,000
Growth	J	Project J	Sponsor J		01/07/2011	31/08/2011	20,000
Total							**1,350,000**

* Assumes average monthly FTE rate of $5,000

mean that the project must go ahead in order to avoid business-threatening risk. Examples would include regulatory projects, the failure or delay of which would put the business in breach of its legal obligations. If the project is not imperative according to this definition, it falls into the growth/efficiency/refinement category. This is taken to mean any other project for which a case can be made, but which is not imperative to the operation of the business. Crucially, every project must be cost justified so that its relative merits and priority may be compared.

- Project name. This will ensure that it is commonly recognised.
- Sponsor. As Chapter 4 proposes, every project should be owned by a named individual within the organisation who may be held accountable for its successful delivery. Otherwise, how will the entire portfolio be controlled?
- Cost code. No project should be authorised to commence unless it has been issued with a recognised, ring-fenced budget, indicated by the presence of a cost code.
- Start date. Has the project begun? If so, it is probably already consuming resources and needs to be brought into the control of the portfolio.

- End date. At which point can the business expect the drain of project expense to end, and the accrual of benefits to begin?
- Cost. What specific burden is the project placing on the portfolio? This may be a financial value (that is, its budget), or an expression of the person-day or full-time equivalent (FTE) resource demanded by the project. Anything will serve as long as it is applied consistently.

4 Identify the supply/demand mismatch

It is the figures in the cost column that, when added together, will equal the resource demand, one of the two crucial measures identified in Figure 3.4. The other figure that must be calculated is the resource supply available to fund the change agenda. This may be a single figure that has been set aside by the board, or a value based on the total person-days or FTEs available for the delivery of projects. Put another way, it is the resource that is not devoted to business-as-usual.

When the resource demand and resource supply figures are compared, it is possible, perhaps for the first time, to truly know the extent to which the two numbers are alike.

Figure 3.6 provides a more sophisticated illustration using some sample data. A business is faced with a resource demand of $5.15m to deliver its business-as-usual obligations and its desired portfolio of projects, yet the budget available to cover both is $4.555m. Assuming the $3.8m set aside for business-as-usual is not negotiable, the business faces a mismatch of $0.595m; $0.935m has so far been committed to projects A–G with $0.415m (projects H, I and J) remaining either uncommitted or unapproved.

This is typical of the challenges that will face the organisation. Yet to resolve the mismatch, a further, crucial piece of information is required. Effective prioritisation cannot be based only on what the organisation can afford to change. Of greater importance is taking account of what it needs to change if it is to meet its objectives. In the example, the business may decide that projects H, I and J will have to remain unachievable for now, or find new money to fund them, or reprioritise the whole register to rank them above something to which money has already been committed. The effective ranking requires

FIGURE 3.6 **The supply/demand mismatch**

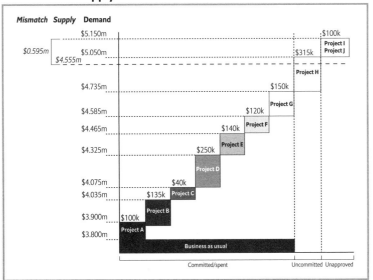

the organisation to make a judgment based not only on the balance of supply and demand, but also on what contribution each project will make to the advancement of the organisation's change agenda.

Balancing the selection of projects

The statements articulated earlier can be categorised into groups (see Table 3.3). This is a simple and early example of a business plan expressed as a balanced score card of measures, a technique developed by Robert Kaplan and David Norton, the originators of the strategic management tool the Balanced Scorecard, to describe what strategic success could look like. An organisation's targets and measures are described in four balanced quadrants: commercial, customer, process and learning. When combined, they provide a consistent and sound means of describing how to reach and measure success. This helps to identify programmes and portfolios of projects the organisation must undertake if it is to be successful.

The thinking behind the balanced score card is that commercial success can come from selling customers what they want, but the

TABLE 3.3 **Grouping business plan statements**

What will commercial success look like?	How will clients judge success?
The company will:	The company will:
■ retain its most important clients ■ bring in new clients ■ secure recurring revenues rather than one-off fees ■ further its alliance partnerships ■ deliver increased revenue ■ deliver increased margins ■ become number one in its marketplace ■ undertake short-term, high-yield projects	■ deliver a wider range of products ■ reduce its implementation timescales ■ reduce its implementation costs ■ deliver minimum maintenance products ■ engage in fixed-price or shared-risk initiatives

Which processes must be excellent?	How will we show we have learned and grown?
The company will:	The company will:
■ prioritise and justify every initiative ■ have market-leading product quality and testing processes ■ use cutting-edge product implementation processes ■ manage its projects using repeatable, proven principles and techniques	■ use new and/or innovative technologies ■ provide opportunities to help retain experienced staff ■ apply lessons learned from experience ■ attract and develop junior staff ■ increase the gap between itself and its competitors

processes needed to deliver the products and services they buy must be sleek and effective, and they get that way by using people and intellectual capital in which there is continuous investment. The investment comes from prior commercial success, so the approach looks circular.

Because the quadrants are linked by this logic, the list of statements must be checked for consistency. Engaging in fixed-price or shared-risk initiatives may not permit increased margins; developing junior staff may be a challenge while using new and innovative technologies that may create redundancies. Some objectives may be beyond the organisation's control; the most important clients may not buy the wider range of products. An organisation must ask itself: "Which would matter most: client engagement or product leadership?" If the statements are inconsistent, so may be the business plan from which they were derived and the portfolio of projects that stem from it.

TABLE 3.4 **Revised business plan statements**

What will commercial success look like?	How will clients judge success?
■ secure recurring revenues rather than one-off fees *Revised:* ■ During the coming year, the company will secure $500,000 worth of recurring revenues from clients that have always previously made one-off payments	■ reduce its implementation timescales *Revised:* ■ During the forthcoming year, the company will deliver three implementations of its standard product in seven weeks rather than nine
Which processes must be excellent?	**How will we show we have learned and grown?**
■ manage its projects using repeatable, proven principles and techniques *Revised:* ■ During the coming year, the company will implement its own project management method based on an industry-recognised standard ■ During the coming year, the company will deliver two projects using the new method	■ provide opportunities to help retain experienced staff *Revised:* ■ The company will reduce the turnover of staff with more than ten years' experience by 20%

Table 3.3 is not complete, however. There are no measures. If these statements are to be used to confirm the portfolio's contribution to the business plan, each must be quantified. Table 3.4 contains examples from each quadrant.

Despite this further analysis, it is still not possible to identify projects that will help to achieve these targets. Not every target will rely solely on a project or series of projects. Some will depend on increased or improved productivity such as reducing implementation timescales. Others may require increased vigilance but not a change of behaviour, for example securing recurring revenues rather than one-off fees. Some targets may be achieved by a combination of projects and business-as-usual; some projects already under way or under consideration might make a limited contribution to the achievement of one or more targets. However, there may be targets that can be achieved specifically as a result of a project or programme of projects. For instance, if a company wishes to implement its own project management method based on an industry-recognised standard, this may need to be commissioned as a single project.

So it is possible to derive some projects from the business plan. But an organisation moving towards a project-focused approach must be sure that other projects already under way or proposed without reference to the business plan are likely to contribute to its strategy. The organisation must assure itself that it has a portfolio of proposed and actual projects that is aligned to its vision.

This is done by challenging, not least because work on the existing portfolio has commenced. While it may seem sensible to abandon one project in favour of another, money has already been invested and it is a commercial decision to write off an investment, not an intellectual one.

However, this argument is helpful in understanding why time was taken to create a balanced set of strategic measures. The main motivation of many organisations will be to achieve the measures in the commercial quadrant, but projects and business-as-usual activity will be needed to deliver across the balanced score card if ultimate commercial success is to be achieved.

A technique that can help achieve this involves three ingredients:

- the business plan expressed as success criteria;
- the existing project portfolio;
- any newly proposed projects.

By comparing the existing portfolio and proposed projects with the list of targets, it is possible to determine the fit. If the relevant information is available, it is a relatively simple exercise. Ask whether each existing or proposed project's contribution to achieving each measure in turn is direct, indirect or absent (see Table 3.5).

Several significant conclusions can be drawn from this simple example:

- No projects are contributing to the company delivering speedier implementations. Customers will not be pleased.

TABLE 3.5 **Project contribution to strategy**

Strategic imperative	Project 1	Project 2	Project 3
Will this project contribute to the company securing $500,000 worth of recurring revenues in the coming year from clients that have always previously made one-off payments?	Direct	Indirect	Absent
Will this project contribute to the company delivering three implementations during the coming year of its standard product in seven weeks rather than nine?	Absent	Absent	Absent
Will this project contribute to the company implementing its own project management method based on an industry-recognised standard during the coming year?	Indirect	Absent	Absent
Will this project contribute to the company delivering two projects in the coming year using the new project management method?	Absent	Absent	Absent
Will this project contribute to company reducing its turnover of staff of more than 10 years' experience by 20% during the coming year?	Absent	Direct	Absent

- Even if the company develops a new project management approach (of which there is little evidence), no projects will use it.
- Project 3 is making no contribution to the company's strategic aims. Why is it being funded?

The power of this technique extrapolated across every strategic imperative and all existing and proposed projects is enormous. Here are some questions that can help in deciding which projects should be pursued:

- Are there projects contributing directly to achieving specific strategic imperatives, making them more likely to be met?
- Which strategic imperatives are unsupported by projects and so run the risk of being missed?
- Which projects are not contributing to any strategic imperative?
- Do the projects identified above give cause to reconsider whether all strategic imperatives have been identified?

- Is there a balanced portfolio of projects contributing across the four quadrants?
- Is the organisation focusing on one of the four quadrants at the expense of the others?
- Is the organisation more concerned about measurements than objectives?
- Is the organisation conducting projects because it wants to, not because it needs to?

Managers should ask themselves such questions. If direct, indirect, partial and absent are each given a value, it is possible to develop some information to aid the debate about which projects should be undertaken, which should not and where the business plan appears to be unsupported.

Figures 3.7–3.10 show examples of such data expressed in a way to encourage focused debate. In Figure 3.7, the height of each bar is less important than their relative heights in indicating a balanced portfolio. Figure 3.8 shows the portfolio's contribution to achieving a single strategic objective. Figure 3.9 shows the strategic value of an individual project. It is often valuable to add depth and substance when making a business case. Figure 3.10 shows how much each project will contribute to a specific quadrant.

However, this is not the only way of considering the relative

FIGURE 3.7 **Business balance**

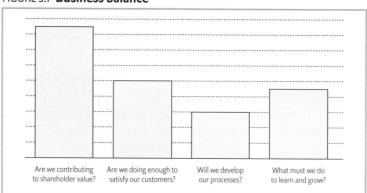

FIGURE 3.8 **Which projects will deliver recurring revenues?**

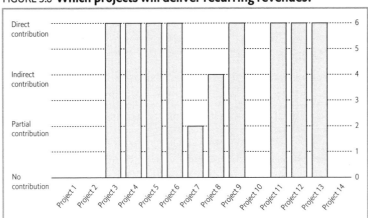

FIGURE 3.9 **The portfolio's contribution to achieving a single strategic objective**

	No contribution	Partial contribution	Indirect contribution	Direct contribution
Will this project contribute to the company securing £500,000 worth of recurring revenues during the coming year from clients that have always previously paid one-off payments?				
Will this project contribute to the company delivering three implementations during the coming year of its standard product in seven weeks rather than nine weeks?				
Will this project contribute to the company implementing its own project management method based upon an industry-recognised standard during the coming year?				
Will this project contribute to the company delivering two projects in the coming year using the new project management method?				
Will this project contribute to the company's reduction in the turnover of staff of more than 10 years' experience by 20% during the coming year?				

FIGURE 3.10 **Which projects will shareholders find most attractive?**

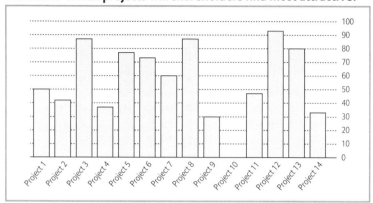

contribution of a proposed or actual project. So far the analysis has not compared each project's potential risk and reward so the proposed portfolio has not been balanced.

Every project carries a risk for every reward. For example, a new market opportunity might suggest attractive rewards but there may be operational risks in pursuing it. Almost every decision a business makes comes from weighing the potential reward against the risk. Since projects are a vehicle for delivering business change, each will bear a risk and reward profile that must be considered both independently and in the light of every other potential or actual project. The organisation will probably not be able to afford every project it wishes to undertake. The portfolio needs thinning.

Risk and reward (or benefits) management is discussed in Chapter 6; however, little detail about a project may be known in its early life. Many questions will need to be answered, but few can be pursued until fuller funding is made available. In the absence of being able to undertake a detailed analysis of the benefits and risks that any project may promise, the organisation can obtain the high-level information it needs by recording each project against a series of measures, some focused on rewards and some on risks (see Table 3.6). Each statement is answered "yes" or "no".

TABLE 3.6 **Rewards and risks of a project**

Rewards	Risks
■ This project is strategically imperative. ■ This is a regulatory or legally mandated project. ■ There is potential for long-term value creation. ■ Perceived expected financial benefits are high. ■ Expected value to customers is high. ■ Expected value to employees is high. ■ This project includes a "wow" factor.	■ The project will present significant technical challenge. ■ The project will require significant procedural change. ■ The project will require significant organisational change. ■ Implementation costs are expected to be high. ■ The project cannot be implemented quickly. ■ There is little appetite and/or capacity for this proposal. ■ There will be significant impact on business-as-usual.

Each statement with a "yes" is given a score of 1. Once each project has been measured against these statements, it is possible to assess the overall balance of risk and reward inherent in the portfolio. The matrix on which the projects will appear is shown in Figure 3.11.

■ **Empty vessels.** These can be pursued easily but will not deliver

FIGURE 3.11 **Risk and reward matrix**

much reward. They may appear attractive because of their relative ease of implementation, but if they fail to deliver much reward, they will tie up resources that could have been invested elsewhere.

■ **Money pit.** Projects that are high in risk and low in reward may appear unpalatable, but they may be necessary. Like empty vessels, they deserve debate to avoid the danger of their being discounted merely because of their risk profile.

■ **Low-hanging fruit.** These are preferable to empty vessels. Not only are they relatively low-risk projects, but they also appear to promise high rewards.

■ **Make or break.** Projects in this category will be the ones people in the organisation know about already. They will be controversial and challenging and may divide opinion. They will make or break the portfolio, the department or even the entire business. If any projects in the portfolio deserve further and full examination of their costs and benefits, these do.

Such analysis will make it much easier for senior managers to debate the merits of projects that are under consideration. The information itself may be simply expressed, but the discussion it generates will be valuable and should avoid the tacit acceptance of a portfolio of projects that may be flawed.

Commissioning

Once a potential project has been sufficiently described in outline, and its priority, risk and value have been assessed, it may be commissioned. This involves making financial provision for:

■ the first stage;
■ the whole project.

Both figures may be derived from the project outline, and although they may be based on some big assumptions, they are currently all that the organisation has on which to make projections. The first stage will require funding to explore more fully the nature of the initiative so that, among many other things, a better expression of the budget it will need can be gained. Meanwhile, the high figure in the project outline will have to serve as a guide. Under no circumstances should the budget for the whole project be given to the project management team. Funds should be provided in stages to maintain control of the emerging project.

As identified earlier, the management of the conception of a project and its subsequent governance cannot be provided adequately by the business-as-usual structure. Projects, portfolios and programmes cannot thrive in silos, so those who are to participate in project management at any level must understand and act according to a commonly agreed set of responsibilities.

Projects are a means to create value or achieve desired change and should not exist independently from the business that commissions them. Once its business plan has been developed, the company needs a management team to oversee the whole portfolio of projects. During the year it should:

■ identify further opportunities;

■ commission projects;

■ prioritise resources;

■ secure funding;

■ realise benefits.

The portfolio management team

Typically, at the beginning of a financial year, the portfolio management team will be put in charge of a range of projects, including those identified in the business plan and possibly others that have run over from the previous year. This mix of projects is known as the portfolio, which, in common with the wider business, has to flex and change throughout the year. As it does so, the portfolio management team is responsible for commissioning and delivering a value-adding mix of projects within a budget, aligned with the imperatives set out by the business.

The team will normally meet every month to:

■ identify candidate projects (from the business plan or elsewhere);

■ commission business cases;

- apportion resources across the portfolio;
- identify suitable project steering groups;
- delegate ownership of projects to project steering groups;
- prioritise projects in the portfolio;
- manage situations where benefits may be at risk.

Given the wide interest in the assorted projects, the portfolio management team may be large, increasing the risk that it will fail to operate effectively. Therefore, it is sensible to construct the team according to specific criteria:

- Do all participants carry the authority needed to make any decision required of them?
- Have participants been drawn from all areas from which decisions will be needed, including sales/marketing, operations, technology, facilities/property, legal, human resources?
- Are participants likely to remain committed to their responsibilities for the whole year?

At the end of the year, it should be possible to judge the team's success by looking at the extent to which:

- the mix of projects has helped to achieve defined business objectives as planned;
- commercial and strategic targets have been met;
- the projects within the portfolio have been delivered on time and within budget;
- the projects have produced results of acceptable quality;
- the portfolio has been administered efficiently.

If such a body is to work effectively alongside business-as-usual, it will need controlled access to the pool from which its resources will be drawn.

Resource pool management

A project is a management environment with the internal authority to make the right decisions at the right time, but as it also affects the organisation itself, it is important that an organisation examines how it provides resources to projects at the same time as carrying on its usual business.

A common complaint is that a combination of projects and business-as-usual pulls too many people in too many directions. Priorities are unclear; all the stops are pulled out for a priority project until something happens to compromise the operation of the rest of the business. At that point the project (much to the chagrin of its management team) is pushed to one side. Organisations with a strong emphasis on operational excellence often consider projects to be of secondary importance, which is understandable because business-as-usual funds projects, but this can be dangerous as it may affect their ability to change in order to prosper, or survive.

A resource pool is a group of people within a single management structure, usually with common skills. Effective resource pool management helps to balance the competing demands of the people who are responsible for business-as-usual at the same time as releasing enough of them to deliver a portfolio of value-focused projects.

Imagine installing a fish tank to be stocked with a wide variety of tropical fish. The fish come from a specialist supplier who has many pools, each containing a different species. So an assortment is chosen subject to the supplier having enough fish of each type to meet the demand and the customer having enough money to pay for them.

The same is true of projects. The management team responsible for staffing a new project requests resources from a wide variety of internal and, possibly, external sources. In this way, they obtain the mix of skills, knowledge, experience and character they believe will serve the project well. This creates a further responsibility for the people who manage the pools from which the resources have been picked. Just as the specialist supplier of fish has to manage the quantity and health of fish in each pool, so too must someone in the project-focused organisation take responsibility for managing the people who may be needed to work on projects. A project manager charged with finding a specialist team leader for a particular phase of a project may feel aggrieved if the one remaining expert has been promised to another project. This would be doubly frustrating if the only alternative on offer was one of three market analysts of which the company has a surfeit. Resource pool management is needed to ensure that both business-as-usual and projects have enough people of the quality they need at the right time.

Resource pool management can be carried out according to free market or regulated principles.

The free market

Figure 3.12 illustrates a free market. Having been given authority to deliver a successful outcome, the project management teams attempt to secure the resources they need from a variety of sources, both internal and external. External sources such as third-party resource suppliers may require a bigger investment, but the project management team has authority to deliver a commercially viable outcome. As long as

FIGURE 3.12 **A free market**

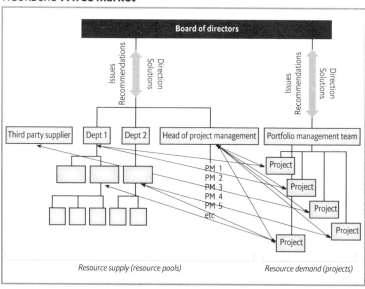

the project's benefits outweigh its costs, they can argue in favour of employing external resources.

Internal suppliers such as those in Department 1 and Department 2 can work in much the same way as an external provider, with one significant exception. Although they are resource pools, many of these internal departments must also carry out business-as-usual successfully, so most department managers are charged with managing the supply of resources to projects and business-as-usual.

Things become more complicated when a project makes a demand on the resource pools that other projects are also making demands upon. It is better for the organisation if such competition can be regulated.

The regulated market

This structure differs in two important ways from the free market model (see Figure 3.13):

- The supply and demand relationships between project and resource pool managers have been replaced with a single resource management function.
- The resolution of problems arising from shortages or oversupply of resources no longer rests with the resource pool managers but with the resource management function.

Having a resource management function does not remove the need for the resource pool managers to nurture their teams. Nor does it mean that they should not plan for future project and business-as-usual demands. It can, however, add these considerable benefits:

- forward planning of resource numbers so that cross-department recruitment campaigns can be managed;
- increased negotiating power with third-party resource providers;
- improved arbitration where resource conflicts arise;
- skills management (using skills profiles for selection rather than availability alone);

FIGURE 3.13 **A regulated market**

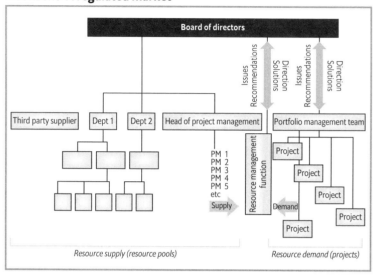

■ decreases in the incidence of potentially available resources being reserved for the personal use of their department (resource pool) managers.

To make this happen, the resource management function must:

■ plan and maintain forecasts for company-wide resource demands based on regularly gathered project resource plans;

■ plan and maintain forecasts for company-wide resource supply based on regularly gathered department resource plans;

■ match resource demand from potential and existing projects with the potential and existing supply available from internal and external resource pools;

■ identify, report and respond to resource supply and demand trends;

■ plan, co-ordinate and support recruitment campaigns across the organisation.

At the end of a year, it should be possible to judge the function's success by measuring:

- to what extent resource utilisation has been maximised;
- the availability of a current, company-wide resource plan;
- whether, at any time, all projects have a forecast of resource demand and all departments have a forecast of resource supply.

Matrix management

Both models recognise that projects are usually neither owned by, nor contained within, a single department. They are shared endeavours that draw on the skills, knowledge and experience of a variety of stakeholders whose expectations differ. Projects cut across the departmental divides, creating a matrix. Managing resources through both line and project structures is called matrix management. When used effectively, it allows organisations to deliver better business-as-usual and projects simultaneously. Without it, projects often suffer because business-as-usual takes priority.

In both the free and regulated models there is also a head of project management who plays a key role in a matrix management environment.

Head of project management

The head of project management is principally a resource pool manager responsible for managing a team of project managers to satisfy the demands of project steering groups as they seek candidates for emerging projects. This person will manage the longer-term needs of the department by recruiting, developing and retaining the best project managers required to maintain a healthy pool of personnel.

The head of project management should be an experienced person who can contribute to the continued development and application of the organisation's approach to project management. Even so, if the resource pool is small, this may not be a full-time role and could be performed by a project manager in addition to existing duties.

The head of project management should not become involved in business-as-usual or project matters other than those for which he already has specific responsibilities. Matters arising within individual projects should be managed by those involved in them.

The head of project management is, however, expected to prevent or manage anything related to the efficiency, supply or quality of project management personnel.

The person given this role may also sit on a project steering group, or possibly serve as a member of the portfolio management team.

To ensure consistency, impartiality, balance and integration of services with other stakeholders, the provision of project support and assurance to project managers (such as health checks, quality reviews, administrative support, and so on) is best provided from outside this resource pool.

The head of project management's specific responsibilities are to:

- supply project managers to project steering groups when given a demand forecast;
- manage the pool of resources effectively within the agreed headcount;
- make sure the project managers in the pool apply the company's approach to project management;
- prevent and resolve issues regarding the efficacy, supply or quality of project managers;
- recruit, retain/release, develop and reward the pool of project managers according to their performance;
- provide personal mentoring and support to project managers;
- provide training and education for the company's approach to project management.

The head of project management should be authorised to:

- recruit and release project managers to satisfy current and forecast demand effectively;
- conduct annual appraisals and to recommend rewards/penalties.

At the end of a year, the head of project management's performance should be assessed by:

- the extent to which demand for project managers has been met;

- how regularly the resource plan for project managers has been maintained;
- the extent to which project managers have achieved their targets.

This demanding role requires appropriate managerial ability and experience in project management.

Having considered the governance needed to conceive and prioritise the portfolio of projects, it is now appropriate to consider what management is needed within an individual project.

Project roles and responsibilities

WHEN CONSIDERING THE ORGANISATION of a project it is helpful to look at the structure of the company itself. A project's organisational structure should contain layers of authority that allow people at different levels to use their particular skills, knowledge and experience to take the right decisions at the right time. In the same way that the organisation's structure will (or should) have been designed to meet its particular needs, so should the organisational structure of the project be tailored to meet its objective. It must also offer a means by which the expectations of those involved or who have an interest in the project may be met.

Who should be involved in managing a project?

The people brought together to commission, manage, fund, specify, build, test, use and benefit from a project's outcome must together have the skills, knowledge, experience and personal attributes necessary to carry out the project successfully, no matter how demanding the circumstances become.

There needs to be general agreement on who:

■ defines what is required;
■ provides the budget;
■ directs the people involved in the project;
■ authorises changes;
■ manages the day-to-day work.

The project's organisational structure can be developed by identifying those in the stakeholder pool who can contribute best to its effective management and, ultimately, its success. The stakeholder map and stakeholder matrix described in Chapter 2 can be helpful in identifying and selecting who should be part of a project's organisational structure.

To begin with, the project's stakeholders are identified in the stakeholder map. When placed on the stakeholder matrix, the degree to which the project has effective and authoritative sponsorship will quickly become apparent. The top half of the matrix reveals possible candidates for the project steering group. It would be instinctive to focus on those who are promoters, but any disruptors may be best managed by being invited to participate in the project. Then their concerns can be addressed more effectively and they may be more inclined to see its benefits and move from the left side of the matrix to the right.

If there is nobody in the top half of the matrix, the project is unlikely to secure the sponsorship it needs. Those who have commissioned it must ask themselves whether their project has the necessary backing.

With little power or influence, the detractors and supporters in the lower half of the matrix are unlikely to be a source of authority for the project. However, this pool will supply some of the team members who will participate in, but not manage, the project.

In the previous chapter the portfolio management team was introduced. It has a separate role from that of the project steering groups (the various bodies to which the ownership of individual projects is delegated). In turn, the project steering groups have different responsibilities from the project manager, who plans, monitors and controls a project. However, all three must do their jobs well if an organisation's projects are to succeed. This hierarchy of management authority is shown in Figure 4.1.

Project steering group

The project steering group is accountable for the success of its project. It is responsible for making sure that the expectations set out in the business case for the project are met. If the project is seen as a small

FIGURE 4.1 **The hierarchy of management authority**

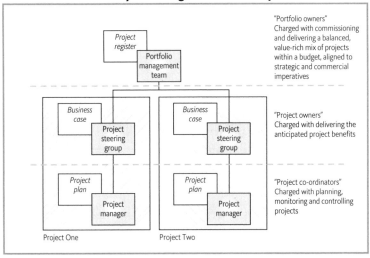

business, the steering group is its board of directors. It will commission the project plan from the project manager and, assuming it is agreed, will authorise the start of the project. It will also authorise any significant changes to the plan that are outside the project manager's authority. It secures and assigns resources. As the project manager will have only limited authority, the project steering group adjudicates on any conflicts within the project and resolves problems between the project and third parties, internal departments or other projects. It is given its authority by the portfolio management team once the financial and other resources have been allocated.

A project steering group should be made up of people who:

■ are committed to a successful project outcome;
■ are authorised to make decisions;
■ can provide or source resources;
■ are experts in their fields.

They should be chosen for a combination of experience and authority appropriate to the project.

As well as getting together at important decision-making points, most project steering groups prefer regular, scheduled meetings at which the project manager can report on the present status of the project and forecast how things are likely to proceed. Typically, this might be every month. If they need to meet more regularly, this may be an indication that their (and the project manager's) authority is not clearly defined and that the project is at risk of being managed by committee.

The project steering group should not be allowed to become a committee. It should be made up of people who are both senior enough to make decisions and expert enough in their field to add essential knowledge, skill and experience. This may suggest that it could, or should, be open to any senior individual with an interest in the project. However, the fewer people involved in the project steering group, the easier it is to make decisions. Even so, a balance has to be struck between an autocrat driving the project and a cast of thousands.

Since the project will necessarily become a shared endeavour, it will need to involve many different, sometimes antagonistic, interests. Chief among these will be the customer of the deliverable to be produced by the project, the developers who will build it and those who will fund it. The project steering group will be required to make tough choices, and it is important that its decisions are sufficiently balanced across these different perspectives. The project will suffer if one person's view always takes precedence.

These perspectives can be brought to bear on many important decisions throughout the project. It will be seen how the interests of the funders, the customers and the developers must be accommodated to ensure that effective decisions are made about changes to the project or when making judgments about the satisfactory completion of deliverables.

The interests of these three parties should be represented at an authoritative level, but these people will be part of a group and will need leadership. Consequently, the project steering group is usually chaired by a project sponsor, who is responsible for delivering the commercial benefits outlined in the business case. The project sponsor is likely to have been the driving force since the project was conceived and whose leadership capabilities have resulted in the project's configuration to address the original issue or opportunity. The project sponsor's role on the project steering group is outlined below.

The project sponsor's role and responsibilities

Role

■ promote the project's commercial imperatives;

■ assume ownership of the project on behalf of the portfolio management team;

■ seek to deliver a viable and adopted outcome.

Principal responsibilities

■ take ownership of the business case from the portfolio management team and make sure it is maintained;

■ brief the portfolio management team about project progress, alerting them if benefit escalation conditions have been met;

■ authorise the start of the project;

■ authorise the plan and agree expenditure;

■ resolve any priority or resource conflicts through arbitration with those on the project steering group who represent the customer and the developer;

■ organise and chair project steering group meetings;

■ set escalation conditions for time and costs and ensure that the project manager provides suitable notification;

■ authorise action if significant budget or timescale variances are forecast;

■ authorise the closure of the project after agreement with other members of the project steering group;

■ apply engagement, education and embracement methods to drive adoption;

■ direct and report the realisation of benefits to the portfolio management team in accordance with the agreed timetable.

The importance of balance in a project steering group and of a focused, authoritative project sponsor, became clear to those involved in the United Kingdom's FiReControl project. This initiative sought to replace 46 local fire and rescue control rooms with nine purpose-built regional centres, linked by a new computer system. When investigated by the National Audit Office (NAO) this axed project was discovered to have wasted at least £469m, having failed to deliver the IT, and with eight of the nine new centres remaining empty, but with rent accruing. The NAO's report recorded flaws in the project's governance, including a failure of the sponsoring organisation to provide the necessary leadership, mistrust and antagonism from the fire and rescue service itself, and an inadequate contractual relationship with the IT supplier. It is no coincidence that these parties represent the three interests in a project's steering group. This led to significant commercial consequences: the loss of financial control, and a failure to redress this with the delivery of any significant benefit.

This is just one example of a set of problems that can arise from a poorly constructed or absent project steering group. If there is a risk of it having too many members, separate out those who are there to provide opinions but who are not authorised to make decisions about the project. If these people represent teams or departments that will be customers of the project's deliverable, create a separate user forum through which they can express their views. Select one of them to chair the user forum and arbitrate where conflict arises. This person should sit on the project steering group to relay the forum's views and provide a single point of contact to determine the requirements the project's deliverable must satisfy and confirm they have been met at the end.

The same applies to the developers. If there are several suppliers involved, select one to lead and join the project steering group to convey their views about the design of the project's deliverable, making sure it meets any particular standards.

Sometimes the project may involve a customer from outside the organisation, for instance where a bespoke piece of machinery is being developed for an external paying client. In this case, it would be ideal for both the customer and the supplier to join the project steering group. Sometimes, however, issues such as commercial confidentiality will prevent customers and suppliers working as closely together as would be desirable. In these cases, the customer and the supplier should have their own project steering groups, in essence creating two interdependent projects where one would have been ideal.

Overall, the project steering group's performance can be judged against the extent to which:

■ the business case is maintained, is always accessible and illustrates the difference between the company's total effort or investment in the project compared with the income or benefit from it;

■ the project produces a value-adding outcome as identified in the business case;

■ it has identified and empowered a single project manager to plan, co-ordinate and control the project;

■ it has been able to set and apply escalation conditions for the project manager;

■ it has been able to provide sufficient resources of the necessary quality to allow the plan to be fulfilled.

Project manager

The project manager co-ordinates the project on behalf of the project steering group and makes sure that it produces the required deliverables to the identified standard of quality, on time and within budget. To do this, the project manager develops an approved plan and then makes sure that all the milestones are achieved.

Commonly, a project manager's success is measured by whether the results required have been delivered on time, on budget and to the required standard of quality, but often changes are agreed during a project that may increase the costs or the time span needed to complete it. It would clearly be wrong to judge the project manager according to the original budget and timescale; it is better to measure how well the project manager has managed the changes and the expectations of those with a stake in the project.

Criteria for judging a project manager should include the extent to which:

■ there is an authorised plan that shows progress to date and forecasts for time, cost and quality;

- escalation conditions for time and cost have been agreed with the project steering group and are being applied;
- there is a record demonstrating that changes to scope, timescale, cost and benefits have been approved by those with authority to do so;
- there is a record of risks to the project, together with mitigation plans and actions;
- the project steering group is kept regularly and sufficiently informed through progress reports and forecasts.

Some organisations assign several project managers to the same project, thinking this will lessen the risk. On the contrary, this means work is duplicated, gaps go unnoticed, leadership is unclear and communication becomes confused. The risk of the project failing is increased. The project in Figure 4.2 is doomed to confusion.

The project steering group is responsible for delivering a viable outcome, but who is responsible for developing the project plan? From whom would they expect progress reports? What are the implications of splitting authority between two project managers?

FIGURE 4.2 **A project doomed to confusion**

There should be one project manager who plans, monitors and controls the project. This person should have sufficient experience and personal authority to remove the need to duplicate this pivotal role. Selecting a suitable project manager will depend on factors such as:

■ the value of the project;
■ its timescale;
■ the risks;
■ how critical it is;
■ who is available.

The more demanding a project, the more its project manager should be experienced and competent, so it is helpful to grade them (see Table 4.1 on page 106).

■ PM1 – a project or team leader who would be expected to manage a team within a project, reporting to a project manager.
■ PM2 – a project manager who would be expected to manage a project with minimum supervision.
■ PM3 – a senior project manager who would be able to manage several projects at once and would readily help to develop the organisation's approach to project management.

The list is not definitive and will vary between organisations, but it can be used as a guide when organising the pool of a project's workers, recruiting new project workers or identifying and selecting people suitable for a specific project.

Is the project organisational structure suitable?

Having designed or inherited a project organisation, it is sensible to identify where the in-built risks may lie. Questions to ask include the following:

■ Is there a clear separation of project ownership from its day-to-day management?

- Is there a definable combination of leadership and management capabilities?
- Is there a clearly identified single project manager?
- Has each role been assigned to people with sufficient authority to undertake every responsibility allocated to them?
- Does the project organisation contain the authority within itself to make the decisions necessary to its continued progress?
- Are all three key perspectives (commercial, customer and developer) represented at the project steering group?
- Have the client's aspirations been accommodated?
- Have all responsibilities identified as necessary to the project been assigned to individuals?
- Do all individuals know their responsibilities and are they comfortable with them?
- Has the organisational structure sensibly accommodated its most important stakeholders?

Developing a project management structure

The importance of a suitable project organisational structure as a foundation for its success should not be underestimated. Nevertheless, despite the principles, success depends ultimately on how effectively that structure works in a real company.

Creating a project's organisational structure can be difficult. The following examples are based on fundamental principles but propose very different structures appropriate for the different projects.

Development and implementation of a computer system

Many business projects contain a significant technology component that needs careful consideration based on expert opinion. Few projects, however, are "technology only". In most cases, a business person's behaviour will have to adapt if the full benefit of the change is to be realised. Consequently, the organisational structure should not be designed around the premise that any project involving technology is a technology project; it will be a shared endeavour between the

FIGURE 4.3 **Project structure for development and implementation of a computer system**

technology, user and commercial stakeholders, all of whom should be represented in the project organisational structure.

In this example, a senior executive is sponsoring the project. A case has been made for new technology to be introduced in the hope that it will reduce operating costs in the administration department. The company's internal technology department will source, tailor and implement the computer system.

The senior executive should be the project sponsor and the administration department's manager should be a member of the project steering group, authorising the specification and acceptance of the system his team will have to use. The administration department manager will also be sufficiently senior to provide users to test and help implement the system.

The systems development manager will also serve on the project steering group to advise on the choice of supplier, confirm the suitability of the selected software and provide the technical resources needed to develop the system.

Given the skills, knowledge and experience required, the project manager could come from any team provided that the individual has the ability to plan, monitor and control time, cost and quality. Some knowledge of the project is always advisable, however, especially if the manager can draw on previous similar experience. With this in mind, the project sponsor could choose the candidate from:

- the administration department;
- the technology department;
- a specialist project management agency or department.

There is merit and risk in each choice. By picking a member of the administration team, the sponsor would sensibly place control of the budget and time imperatives in the hands of someone other than the project's suppliers. So the project manager would be known to the sponsor and should be motivated to achieve the organisation's aims. This does not necessarily mean, however, that the individual will have the requisite project management experience.

A member of the technology team may have carried out similar projects many times before and most of his work may have been project based. Even so, although the IT component of the project will be significant, it is more than just about the development and installation of software. There will be training and induction activities, user tests to be planned and conducted, and issues arising from the working practice changes required from the administration department.

If all else fails, the candidate may be sourced from a specialised project management resource provider. The person may have little experience of software development projects, but can draw on the competencies of colleagues to deliver the desired output on time and to budget.

In any of the three possible outcomes, the team is unaffected by where the project manager comes from. A structure for discussion is illustrated in Figure 4.3.

An office move

A company wants to move a team of 100 people from one building to another. The team manager has secured funding for the move, which involves participation from the technology department (which will uninstall, move and reinstall computers and printers) and the facilities department (which will prepare the new office and crate and move possessions).

FIGURE 4.4 **Project structure for an office move**

The project has a champion, the team manager, who will have had to justify the move in commercial terms and so is a candidate to become the project sponsor in the project steering group. The same person may also have specified and approved the layout of the new office and will approve its suitability before the team starts to use it, which means he also represents the customer's views. Therefore, he will be responsible for not only the financial viability of the move but also the fitness for purpose of the new office, two aspects of the project that may conflict.

Two people may be able to represent the developers of the solution the project is to deliver. One may come from the technology department and authorise the provision of technical resources and the most appropriate strategy for delivering a suitable technology service. The other may come from the facilities department and authorise the use of suppliers to make the move and make sure it meets approved standards. Both would be the most senior people in the project to deal with technical issues that could not be resolved by anyone else.

As in the first example, there are several potential sources for the project manager:

- the team that is moving;
- the facilities department;
- the technology department;

- a specialist project management agency or department.

The strongest case may be to identify a project manager from the facilities department because its members will have carried out such projects many times and have a wealth of experience. Their work will have been project based, so they may well have the necessary project management skills. A possible structure for this project is illustrated in Figure 4.4.

A conference

A company regularly holds public conferences. Delegates are invited to hear speakers on a range of topics for which they are charged a fee. Although the commissioning and running of a conference has the characteristics of a classic project, not every conference requires a separate project steering group because managing conferences is business-as-usual for those involved.

There is, however, a particular risk to be addressed. Conference managers are expected to deliver a successful conference. Yet success means different things to different people. To the sales manager, it may mean making a profit. For the head of editorial success may refer to the currency, accuracy and reliability of the conference's content. Meanwhile, to the conference department manager, success may mean having accurate marketing material, effective booking mechanisms and

FIGURE 4.5 **Project structure for a conference**

seeing everyone turn up on the day to hear speakers in the advertised order. Not least of all, the customer services manager will serve as an advocate for the interests of delegates, ensuring that account is taken of their expectations and wishes.

The risk is that with these different measures of success, the conference manager will be unable to secure an important go or no-go decision should the number of delegates be low. Should it fall to the conference manager to negotiate with a sales manager who wishes to cancel the event and the customer services manager who wants it to continue?

A single, carefully selected project steering group may be able to oversee all conference projects, providing the various conference managers with a single, consolidated source of authority, resource provision and decision-making capability to which they can turn. A possible structure for this project is illustrated in Figure 4.5.

A time management solution

An organisation wants to implement a process for recording the time spent by its employees on planned and unplanned activity. A computer system will facilitate this, but employees will be significantly affected because they will be penalised for failing to complete timesheets on time, and will be restricted from undertaking any activity for which a timesheet code does not exist.

The project has been sponsored by the head of operations who wishes to increase productivity through more focused, planned work. The developers will be members of the technology department, but there will also be a small but significant emphasis on the legal matters involved, so human resources will have to ensure that regulations are complied with.

The project is likely to touch every part of the organisation, not only because most people will have to complete a timesheet at the end of each week, but also because the management information arising from the computer system will be used by many departments in a variety of ways.

The project steering group has a clear project sponsor, the head of operations, while members of the human resources and technology

FIGURE 4.6 **Project structure for a time management solution**

departments will represent the interests of the solution developers. Given the potentially large number of users of the solution, however, there is a good case for forming a user forum. This may include anyone who has an interest in the fitness for purpose of the products of the solution – that is, the computer system, the management information it produces or the way it may affect working practices. The project sponsor should identify someone to chair the user forum who can arbitrate on all matters it discusses and present a single consolidated view of requirements.

Although a significant technology component is envisaged, manual procedures could in theory achieve the same end, so the sponsor may wish to select someone from the operations department to manage this project. The project organisational structure could look like that in Figure 4.6.

TABLE 4.1 **Project manager grades**

Skills	Knowledge	Experience	Character	Responsibilities
PM1 – project or team leader				
Project administration	Company business	Application of company approach to project management	Organised	Assist in project planning
Time, resource and quality planning	Company organisational structure	Demonstration of skills	Able to motivate others	Maintain the project change/issues/risk logs
Delegation	Company products and services	Management of people	Problem identification and analysis	Maintain project metrics, including time, cost and quality tracking
Project control	Company approach to project management	Delegation of work	Communicative	Monitor and report progress against plan, identifying variances where relevant
People management	Planning and control techniques	Participation in at least one project environment	Confident	Assist in effective communications with internal and external stakeholders
Communications	Risk management techniques			
	Project tools			
PM2 – project manager				
Project administration	Company business	Application of company approach to project management	Organised	*Develop, and seek approval for, the project initiation documentation*

Skills	Knowledge	Experience	Character	Responsibilities
Time, resource and quality planning	Company organisational structure	Demonstration of skills	*Self-motivated*	*Maintain the project plan within identified constraints*
Delegation	Company products/services	Management of people	Able to motivate others	Manage project changes/risks/issues
Project control	*Company financial environment*	*Management in a matrix environment*	Problem solving	Identify and delegate work packets to project teams
Negotiation	Company approach to project management	Delegation of work	Communicative	*Motivate and co-ordinate the project team and other personnel involved in the project*
Conflict management/ avoidance	*Industry-recognised project management methods*	*Managed at least two three- to six-month projects from start to finish*	*Influential/persuasive*	Monitor, report and control progress against plan, escalating when outside of agreed tolerances
People management	Planning and control techniques	*Induction of new project personnel*	Confident	*Maintain effective communications and expectations with stakeholders (internal or external) and propose solutions to resolve conflicts*
Induction	Risk management techniques		Professional	Maintain project metrics, including time, cost, quality and benefits tracking

Skills	Knowledge	Experience	Character	Responsibilities
Communications	Project tools		*Delivery focused*	*Maintain the business case to allow project steering group assessment of continued project viability*
				Implement and operate effective change management
				Develop, and seek approval for, the project closure documentation
PM3 – senior project manager				
Project administration	Company business	Application and development of company approach to project management	Organised	Develop, and seek approval for, the project initiation documentation
Time, resource and quality planning	Company organisational structure and *personnel*	Demonstration of skills	Self-motivated	Maintain the project plan within identified constraints
Delegation	Company products/services	Management of people	Able to motivate others	Manage project changes/risks/issues
Project control	Company financial environment	Management in a matrix environment	Problem solving	Identify and delegate work packets to project teams
Negotiation	Company approach to project management	Delegation of work	Creative	Motivate and co-ordinate the project team and other personnel involved in the project

Skills	Knowledge	Experience	Character	Responsibilities
Conflict management/ avoidance	Industry-recognised project management methods	Managed at least *three* three- to six-month projects from start to finish	Communicative	Monitor, report and control progress against plan, escalating when outside of agreed tolerances
People management	Planning and control techniques	*Managed at least two concurrent projects*	Inspirational	Maintain effective communications and expectations with stakeholders (internal or external) and propose solutions to resolve conflicts
Interviewing	Risk management techniques	*Facing clients*	Influential/persuasive	Maintain project metrics, including time, cost, quality and benefits tracking
Selection and recruitment	*Project and portfolio tools*	*Working with suppliers*	Confident	Maintain business case to allow project steering group assessment of continued project viability
Induction		*Interviewing potential project personnel*	Professional	Implement and operate effective change management
Communications		*Selection and recruitment of new project personnel*	Delivery focused	*Develop, and seek approval for, the project closure documentation*

Skills	Knowledge	Experience	Character	Responsibilities
Client, account and supplier management		Induction of new project personnel		*Participate in the interviewing, selection and coaching of project practitioners*
Consultancy				*Promote the benefits of the company approach to project management*
Sales			—	*Participate in the development of the company approach to project management*

Note: Differences between levels are shown in italics.

5

Articulating and promoting the vision

ON MAY 25TH 1961, John F. Kennedy, president of America, said:

I believe that this nation should commit itself to achieving the goal, before this decade is out, of landing a man on the moon and returning him safely to the Earth.

This clear, measurable rallying cry galvanised the energy and enthusiasm of a nation and resulted in the extraordinary spectacle on July 20th 1969 of the first manned mission to land on the moon. If the vision statement had been any more verbose than the president's pithy 31 words, it would have lost its power and impact to motivate. However, behind that statement would have been an enormous set of expectations from others, which, if the initiative was to maintain momentum and focus for almost a decade, would require analysis, expression, communication and promotion. If a vision is to be shared, it is only to be expected that people will wish to contribute to it.

Identify the different perspectives of success

Any vision must accommodate and express the wishes of the three groups described earlier: the user, the specialist and those who fund the project. Yet each will already have their own preferred way of articulating what is important to them. At some point, the users will expect to complete a needs statement. On receipt, the specialists will intend to develop a solution outline. And to justify the entire initiative, the sponsor should seek to construct a commercial cost justification (which will be explored in detail in Chapter 6). An effective, well-articulated vision captures elements of each group's perspective and expresses them together in a clear, complete and coherent manner such that the vision itself, and everything that follows, is consistent. When these three perspectives come together, the vision can begin to do more than simply list the needs of the various stakeholder groups. The confluence of expectations allows for the true purpose of the initiative to be developed, even going so far as to explain what cultural shifts are necessary if real change is to be realised.

As a leader – and sponsor – President Kennedy sought for his nation to conquer space and gain political capital and power from so doing. The television-watching public sought pride in its country's achievements and expected to see them played out across the world's media. The scientific community hoped for advances and learning, expecting that experiments would be conducted and materials from the moon returned to Earth. The astronauts would have been comforted by the president's last six words, but may have had expectations of their own. They may have wished to exercise considerable control over the various vehicles in which they were to be transported, that their families would be cared for by the nation in the event of an accident, or simply that they would be able to see outside the spacecraft (famously, early designs had no windows).

In drawing together these expressions, a considerably larger but more complete vision emerges, perhaps lacking the impact of the president's précis, but presenting a fuller picture that allows for the removal of inconsistencies, and accommodates the compromises necessary for a tract that eventually speaks for everyone. In understanding this, a plan may be built which takes account of the vision and seeks to aid its delivery. So, if the vision required that the nation should feel "pride", the plan would have had to help deliver it. This may have meant, for example, ensuring that all significant stages of the journey were televised live. If the scientific community's expectation was for "technological advance", the plan would have needed to allow for a spacecraft design which could accommodate the return of materials to Earth for analysis. And in many more ways, the vision would mould the plan.

To return to what is, literally, the real world, the visions of an organisation may be as complex yet are too often promoted in too simplistic a form. How can the vision be captured and articulated?

FIGURE 5.1 **A project's vision from three perspectives**

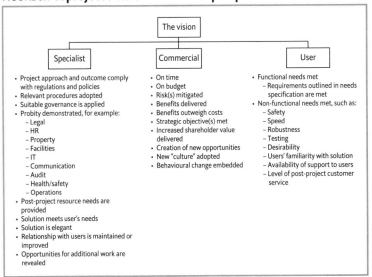

Figure 5.1 outlines the general areas in which people from each of the three groups might be expected to show greatest interest.

Commercial/strategic managers

Matters that will be of greatest interest to this group (represented in the project by the sponsor) will be those that are most likely to affect the commercial and strategic vision for the project, as it is in these precise areas that they are expected to demonstrate greatest competence and enthusiasm. The expression of a commercial vision in the form of a business case or cost justification will be considered in the next chapter. Less easy to capture are statements that describe the behavioural and cultural changes expected, and upon which the realisation of benefits depend. Some examples are included later in this chapter.

Users

Users are most interested in the fitness for purpose of the deliverables the project creates. They are keen that the quality of the project's deliverable is as expected. And if they have trouble expressing what they mean by quality, others will have difficulty developing and delivering it.

"Quality" might be defined as the features and characteristics of a product or service that affect its ability to satisfy stated needs. So the users may express their vision in terms of the features and characteristics they are expecting from the project's main deliverable, commonly captured in a "user needs specification". However, a statement of desired features is hardly a vision and can divert attention from other matters that may be of even greater importance. For instance, the vision for users of a computer system may be to remove their daily dependence on the IT department, which performs a range of technical support activities. So as well as the more usual expectation of certain functional requirements is the aspiration for "user independence", a vision that is harder to define but is no less relevant to the users than the features they expect to be delivered.

Figure 5.1 lists some of the additional features and characteristics that may matter to the people who will use the project's output. It is by no means complete, but it does demonstrate that delivering a product is only a part of what they have in mind.

Specialists

Initially, the vision of the specialists may be to deliver a solution that meets the needs of the users and does so within the prevailing policies and regulations. But probing further into the specialists' expectations, fitness for purpose and compliance may be just their outward projection. Additional and hidden aspirations for the project may also include a wish to build something that is groundbreaking, creative or innovative – something that will cause others to reflect on its elegance or beauty.

Articulate the vision

As the true vision is revealed, it becomes easier to conceive of a plan to meet it or to seek compromises that rein in the expectations of stakeholders. But gaining insight into the various stakeholders' expectations is a separate challenge.

Ask the stakeholders what they are expecting

Having instituted a project steering group (or having at least identified the project's commercial, user and specialist stakeholders), convene a meeting. In preparation, ask them how they would describe their vision for the project. People should describe their vision in a series of concise bullet points (see later examples), not wordy paragraphs from which the vision must be teased.

Sponsors must be especially well briefed since they have an additional responsibility to manage disagreements and confusion. When the group is together, seek to gain mutual understanding of each person's perspective. A set of examples (see later in this chapter) can help to highlight the typical differences between their various perspectives (as identified in Fig 5.1). It is particularly important that people express their expectations fully. The "SMART" approach (that is, statements should be specific, measurable, achievable, realistic and timely) is helpful. Check each perspective (commercial, user and specialist) against these characteristics, then take each one in turn and ask the participants to further develop and refine a list to which they can commit.

Ask the stakeholders what matters most

When the various statements have been pulled together into a single list, one further question is necessary to test understanding and commitment: in what order should these vision statements be prioritised? At the very least, the aim should be to develop a list in which the criteria have been ranked in order of high, medium and low priority. In this way, it is possible to determine not only what matters most, but also in what order parts of the project might be cut should there be a need to change the plan later on. It is far better to have these discussions in the formative stages of the project rather than when it is well under way, as it helps to articulate the vision, provide focus to the plan and serve as a basis against which change-control decisions may be more readily made.

Identify contradictions and broker compromises

A conclusion to any mismatched expectations is needed, so that the project manager may be provided with a clear set of priorities on which to base the plan. The sponsor has the authority to arbitrate and seek compromises; this should not be left to project managers to resolve since they have too little power. In this way, the vision becomes a more realistic and consistent expression of compromises, yet one that unifies the various stakeholders.

Capture and secure the vision

Although many things surrounding a project may change, the fundamental vision should remain relatively stable throughout its lifetime. Even if something happens to cause a substantial rethink, it is important to have an articulated expectation against which to determine the impact of a change.

Obtaining a consistent, prioritised, non-contradictory and SMART vision may not be easy. The risks of failing include the following:

- If the vision is unclear, the project may be unsuccessful in meeting expectations, resulting in a delay to implement the solution or, at worst, a failure to achieve the expected benefits.

- If the commercial vision is unclear, money may be invested in an initiative which might have been better spent elsewhere.

- If the vision is not articulated to a low enough level of detail, it may be misinterpreted, thereby causing a failure to achieve success.

- If priorities are unclear, changes will be considerably harder to manage, resulting in time delays and budgetary challenges.

- If the vision is unclear, it will be more difficult to motivate and direct the team, resulting in the expense of confusion and rework.

The prioritised list of expectations created by this process becomes the vision. A summary paragraph may be developed to sell the project – President Kennedy had his 31 words – but for a robust expression on the back of which a plan may be created, substance is essential.

Many people do not understand why a project generates so much

FIGURE 5.2 **Project organisation for a conference**

documentation, but some written reports are essential in answering the project's most important questions. One of these is the business case, which is often considered a suitable repository for the vision. This important topic is considered in Chapter 6.

An example of a vision

Many companies hold public conferences throughout the year, inviting paying delegates to hear speakers talk on a range of topics. The project organisation for a specific conference is shown in Figure 5.2.

The vision for the project may be described thus:

To deliver a conference on a topic of relevance to delegates which is attractive enough to a sufficient number of them that a profit is made, and that this event enables us to grow the business.

Yet if each member of the project steering group were to be interrogated further, it is likely that a greater and more revealing level of detail could be discovered.

From the commercial (sales manager) perspective:

- the sum of delegate revenues outweighs the total costs of running the conference (by a specific margin);
- the specified budget is not exceeded unless there are revenues which compensate;
- all delegate revenues are received before the event takes place

(that is, there are no "bad debts" or delegates at the conference who have not paid in full in advance);

■ no less than 3% of delegates book on another conference within a year.

Given the second half of the vision statement, the project sponsor is seeing this conference not only as an immediate profit-generating exercise, but also as an opportunity to build future business. This aspiration is translated into a meaningful target (the last criterion) which must be met if the vision is to be fully realised. The project will be completed just after the conference itself has ended. However, it will not be possible to determine whether this final measure of success has been achieved until a year has passed. This carries two consequences:

■ the "benefits realisation" period after the project will last a year, during which the sponsor should retain an interest and ensure that actual benefits are measured;

■ the project manager should make sure that suitable delegate records are kept to allow for the measurement of repeat bookings.

This is the only way in which it will be possible to know whether the vision has been achieved.

From the specialist (head of editorial) perspective:

■ the factual content of the conference material is accurate;

■ conference content is up-to-date;

■ the content of the agenda is not influenced by the commercial interests of the sponsor.

From the specialist (conference department manager) perspective:

■ the conference agenda is organised logically;

■ there are frequent breaks;

■ the most engaging speaker is placed in the agenda slot after lunch;

■ each conference speaker has an understudy;

■ all speakers will have performed well at one of the organisation's previous conferences;

- confirmation of attendance will have been received from each speaker no later than two months before the conference, and no later than two weeks before the publication of the conference marketing materials.

Note that the editorial specialist expects to maintain absolute editorial independence from the sales manager. This may cause conflict between the two parties, but it is better that any disagreements are managed within the jurisdiction of the project, not least so that the project manager can look to a single source (the project steering group) for resolution.

From the user (customer services manager) perspective:

- conference content is as advertised in the marketing materials;
- at least 90% of conference appraisal forms were completed before delegates left the venue;
- at least 40% of those who completed their conference appraisal forms agreed that they would recommend the organisation's conferences to a colleague;
- there are no more than two category 1 complaints arising within a week of the completion of the conference;
- delegates have been provided with an opportunity to network with people they have not previously met;
- delegates have come from industry and social sectors the organisation is seeking to attract;
- at least 60% of delegates mark the quality of the venue and associated facilities as above average;
- at least 70% of delegates agree that they left the conference knowing more than when they arrived;
- at least 85% of delegates consider the conference subject matter to have been relevant;
- at least 75% of delegates consider the speakers to have been engaging and authoritative.

The customer services manager is naturally inclined to consider the project from the perspective of the delegates – that is the manager's day job and focus within the project. The customer services manager is therefore acting as an advocate for the end customer and the criteria listed above provide a detailed interpretation of the delegates' vision to attend a conference that is "attractive".

Promote and share the vision

The vision must carry the authority of those who own it. To begin with, it is the job of the sponsor to articulate it and engage others. Assuming that the organisation buys into the potential value of a project to deliver the changes proposed by the vision, the project steering group (or at least a group of people who see the world from the three perspectives described) may define the vision further, and then share and validate it with other stakeholder communities including – but not limited to – the portfolio management team. Regardless of where in the life cycle of the change one may be, effective communication is central in articulating and promoting the vision.

Without sufficient preparation and planning, communication can be expensive and ineffective at best, and damaging at worst. For example, the CEO of a chain of private hospitals released a regular memorandum to the workforce, describing the changes which they were required to implement in the coming month as part of an ongoing change initiative. The vision – to be the country's premier provider of private health care – was repeated time and time again, as if saying it often enough would make it so. These memos were never supplemented by regular hospital visits by the CEO, nor by any other member of the executive board. This created the very real impression that change was being imposed by a single individual. The absence of any engagement by other members of the executive committee gave the clear impression that there was probable conflict within the leadership team; indeed, the finance director began to privately brief against the CEO. The consequence was the emergence of widespread and destructive cynicism among the workforce, which, once entrenched, became almost impossible to remove.

There are conscious choices to be made about which approach – or combinations of approach – may be applied to the promotion of a vision.

A hierarchical approach

There is value in the use of formal channels of communication such as that described in the example above. It is sometimes important to maintain a sense of control over what may be a complex or confusing message, especially when the size of the stakeholder community may be very large. A hierarchical approach, where information is disseminated to the workforce in a top-down manner, is commonly used in project environments as it fits with the tiered nature of the project's own organisational structure. It may also be suited to the transactional leadership style of a project manager or where an individual demonstrates a directive leadership strategy (see Chapter 2). As an approach, it can help to limit anxiety and add authority to the purpose and method of the change. It may also infer that the information is being distributed fairly; everyone receives the same message. However, when choosing an approach to communication, the disadvantages must also be acknowledged. A hierarchical approach is, essentially, a one-way street for the flow of information. This can have the effect of rendering a stakeholder community voiceless. Without the opportunity or outlet to either articulate or express their views, emotions can easily become inflamed. What may have begun as an attitude of curiosity among members of a group on the receiving end, can very rapidly turn into resentment and anger. When combined with the inference that a message delivered in this way demands conformance, the limitations of this approach are clear – and extremely risky if it has been directed at customers.

A consensual approach

In common with a democratic leadership strategy (see Chapter 2), this approach seeks to involve stakeholder communities by actively lobbying for their views. As a means of limiting resistance – which is a specific objective of a democratic leadership strategy – it may also have the advantage of increasing a community's allegiance to the vision. As the message is shared among stakeholders, the sense of the vision being owned or dominated by a leader is lessened. Indeed, the inferred change may be co-opted and adapted to better suit the needs or nature of the groups in question. However, there are disadvantages here too, not least the fact that in disseminating an expression of the vision in this way, it may lose its clarity, becoming ambiguous, confused or without focus. The great risk is that, rather than being a clear and common expression, it becomes something that everyone interprets differently. Furthermore, it may be assumed by a workforce that a management team that is prepared to give over its vision to others to consider is undecided, insincere, or even incompetent. This approach may also give the impression that the leadership is open to shifting its position or altering its plans, which may in turn undermine a strategic objective. And it assumes that a stakeholder community actually wants to participate. Customers – a stakeholder group often asked to become involved in the development of an organisation's future – may assert that it is the leadership team's job to articulate and promote its vision.

A plan for communication

The communications plan is a tool which can be used to prepare for the engagement of different stakeholder communities on which the leader's vision depends. The communications plan can be used to describe:

- what information must be communicated among the stakeholders;
- who needs to participate in this information exchange;
- what the communication format should be and who should develop or present it.

A stakeholder analysis such as that suggested in Chapter 2 is a useful first step in determining which individuals and communities are to be included. Thereafter, the communication plan can be broken into two parts:

- a table, identifying the information needs and audiences;
- a list of planned communication, with dates or frequencies to explain how those audiences may be engaged.

Figure 5.3 shows a common format for the table noted above. It shows how the methods used in this illustration are a combination

FIGURE 5.3 **Communication methods**

Messages / Audiences	e.g. Our entire workforce	e.g. Our sales force	e.g. Our customers
e.g. "The future prosperity of our organisation is dependent on this change"	Methods: • CEO speaks at annual conference • Message repeated in monthly newsletter • Communications cascade through weekly team briefings • Employee Q + A sessions	Methods: • Sales director solicits insights from key account managers • Key account managers invited to participate in change forum • All account managers invited to regional roadshows	
e.g. "We are changing our organisation structure to be more focused on customer service"		Methods: • Sales Director solicits insights from key account managers • Sales director meets personally with key account managers to advise on new structure, no later than end of quarter 1	Methods: • Key account managers meet personally with key customers within one month following their own briefing • Interactive website to allow customers to engage directly

of those sending information and those receiving it. For example, the repeated use of a message in a newsletter may be effective in presenting a very specifically worded articulation of what the CEO wishes to communicate, and help to promote the vision as a message that everyone will receive in the same way. As an important community of stakeholders, customers may also be told what is about to take place, but may also be expected to have questions or opinions which they may wish to express, and which the management team would be wise to allow. Therefore, the use of an interactive website to enable customers to engage directly with the organisation has been proposed, acknowledging the importance of securing feedback and insight from this key stakeholder community.

Methods of communication

The example in Figure 5.3 shows only a few of what may be a wide range of methods to engage the interest or participation of others. Further techniques include the following:

- **Branding.** This gives the change a look and feel which, when repeated, encourages recognition. As is commonly understood, when done successfully, branding can articulate an essence of something in a very simple way. This applies equally to change initiatives as it does to products and services. Once designed and developed, it may be used to mark and identify all further forms of communication, separating and elevating it from the great volume of traffic which characterises the modern workplace.

■ **Engagement networks.** These encourage informal leaders to participate in the communication of specific messages to groups who recognise their authority or position. For example, there may be a community of local IT managers across the organisation who are key to the success of the change. Recognising them as a distinct community, and attending to their concerns through a tailored engagement network, can demonstrate that their participation is important and valued. Furthermore, when the solution is being implemented these same networks may serve to provide adoption support. Any number of networks may be identified, but it is vital that, once initiated, they are maintained so the relationships are nurtured. Practically, these networks may serve communities which are defined geographically (such as the local IT managers noted above), cross-functionally (such as project managers), and operationally (such as sales managers).

■ **User forums.** These facilitate essential two-way communication needed for audiences who will be affected by the change, and on whom success is dependent. This may appear to be another engagement network, as described above. However, this differs in that it may be formed from a unique and tailored group of those who will use or operate what the project delivers. First identified in Chapter 4, defining and engaging this group into a forum of user representatives who can speak and act on behalf of those they represent is vital, not only in the early stages of change when requirements are being uncovered, but also when the project begins to reveal what it has created, and requires for that output to be tested or proven. Thereafter, the wider user community is to be educated in the use of the project's output; the user forum is a way of facilitating a commitment to the principle and practice of training and education. Ultimately too, the benefits of change will depend on this group (and those it represents) adopting new behaviours or practices. For all of these reasons, a user forum is one of the single most important conduits for effective communication.

- **"Town Halls" and roadshows.** These promote messages physically to geographic groups, solicit responses, promote the benefits and address difficulties. They can create a buzz about a proposed or forthcoming change, and have the benefit of making those who work in the receiving location feel as though they are recognised. However, if this is all that happens, then the outcome can be both expensive and ineffective. But as a supplement to other methods it has the advantage of being able to inject excitement into what might otherwise be a very dry issue. For example, a Town Hall meeting in which all of the staff are involved can create a sense of relationship among the attendees and, with the participation of a sponsor, demonstrate the authority attached to a project. A roadshow may be made quite distinctive and different from the usual cascade and bombardment of other messages, with the inclusion of branded give-aways, competitions, food and drink, and presentations.

- **Tailored written messages.** These may be suitable to promote messages that address the entire range of stakeholders, or just particular communities that have a very specific perspective on the change, perhaps because of their capabilities or roles. The written word can, of course, be transmitted in many forms. The content may be sent physically or digitally. Oddly, in a world dominated by technology, there is value in creating a physical newsletter or pamphlet because it can be noticed. Placed on a desk, it is seen even before digital devices are switched on. Of course, in that same world, the cost or ease of sending such materials to people who may have no permanent place of work, may be prohibitive. A common resort is to use email. However, this too has many disadvantages, not least that it is one of the most common and overused methods of communication. The message really has to be distinctive if it is to rise above and beyond the mass of material that typical workers regularly receive. This explains the rise in the use of alternatives, including social media tools, especially those designed to operate within professional and working environments.

■ **"Live" meetings.** These encourage readiness among those who need to know what they must do or say differently. Strictly speaking, the use of video meetings or conference calls may be of particular value when the change is coming closer; the cost of these meetings can be considerable and it may be an option for achieving a very specific purpose rather than as a more general forum for exchange. However, if the funds are available, a carefully managed virtual meeting can serve as an effective vehicle for overcoming geographic boundaries.

■ **Briefing sessions.** It is vital to engage more senior colleagues who, while understanding the need for the change, also need to address issues being raised by their employees. When a change is initiated, the value of an engaged and participative leadership team cannot be underestimated. Not only is it important that they speak and act with a clear, common and supportive voice, but also that they take responsibility for the effectiveness of communications within their own areas of remit. Commonly, people at such a level may not respond well to being "educated" or by being invited to a training session, so the alternative is to engage them via a briefing. This is often best achieved in two phases: first, to engage individual members of the leadership or management team, and second, to brief them as an entire group. This lessens the risk of the loss of control and allows for individual needs to be accommodated before their exposure in a wider group.

■ **Feedback tools.** Every community needs a means by which it can say how it feels about any part of the change. Commonly, questionnaires are used. These have the advantage of being able to cover a wide scope, and to allow for the creation of reports that reflect trends. However, they also have a tendency to limit feedback by virtue of requiring the responder to answer questions which they may not consider important.

Selecting and using the techniques that are most effective to communicate the vision is important if only to ensure that the project's communications budget is used efficiently. Communication can be especially effective when messages are simple, powerful and repeated, or when they are expressed in the form of a metaphor or story. For example, an organisation that was seeking to gain support for a change to its complex procurement process described it as akin to a journey through a forest, which the hapless traveller had to negotiate without a map, but who was advised by goblins at every turn to touch certain trees if they were to get out successfully. The metaphor helped to communicate the very real sense of bewilderment that users of the procurement process were feeling. Although every participant in the complex ecosystem represented by the forest had a very individual perspective on the importance of their own role within it, the concept of a "frightening" fairy story united them in their understanding of what it must be like to negotiate such a journey. It also served to identify that a useful first step in tackling the challenge might be to develop a map on which everyone could agree.

All opportunities should be used to address any apparent inconsistencies, acknowledging that change is difficult and confusing. This can result in someone's movement from a position of resistance to neutrality, or even support. But by far the most important of all is to recognise that leadership by example can have the most significant of outcomes – good and bad.

No single technique can achieve what every stakeholder community needs. It follows that a tailored combination of methods is necessary to suit the very specific nature of the change, the organisation, and the particular culture of the people in and around it.

In summary, it is crucial that the vision captures the wide range of expectations of the stakeholders of the change and that it is presented in a form that suits the audience. In attempting to pull together and balance people's varied aspirations, it may be necessary to spend longer trying to define what began as a simple premise. In compensation, it is often possible to gain a clearer and more intimate understanding of the true objective. By sharing the vision with others, conflicts and challenges will be encountered, but in dealing with them earlier there will be more opportunity to achieve compromise and engagement. Having taken care over such matters, the governance put in place to manage change will be more suited to the vision, and the plans will be better aligned to it.

6

Planning: risks and rewards

THERE IS ONLY ONE TIME when it is possible to state the cost and end date of a project with certainty: when it is complete. No matter how well supported it is, every assertion until then is an estimate. Even if a customer or supplier wishes to fix a price or the deadline is "of the essence", too much can change for anyone to treat the budget or timescale as anything more than a target. A target and a plan, however, are two very different things. A target is an objective or a goal. A plan should describe how that goal will be met.

Targets such as dates and budgetary figures are easy to set, and because they are, in the desire to meet them a project can become driven by urgency and economy rather than pragmatism and balance. All too often, projects fail because a target was mistaken for a plan.

In cultures where there is an urgency to see results, the benefits of planning are often forgotten until it is too late. In many instances plans are not produced because it is thought there is not enough time to think ahead. A former colleague of the author once ruminated that his organisation never appeared to have the time to plan, yet it always found enough time to do the project twice.

In organisations where projects are small or familiar, there is sometimes a feeling that there is no need to plan. The risk of the absence of a plan is not thought to be great enough to warrant creating one. But this does not recognise the high likelihood of change. Even small or simple projects or those similar to some undertaken previously can be affected by change. The time given to drawing up a plan is time used to understand how different the world is since a similar project was undertaken and how much more it may change during the life cycle of the next.

For many people, including some project managers, planning is either too difficult, too unpleasant or both. Not everyone has a natural aptitude for planning, nor does everyone enjoy it. But project managers must understand the importance and benefits of a plan if they are to fulfil their role competently.

A plan has many benefits. It can confirm whether or not the identified targets are achievable, and if they are not, the plan can provide the evidence for further debate. A plan can be used to express a clear and commonly understood approach to the project. It can help to identify its risks and to establish the factors on which success will depend.

A Monty Python sketch, "The 100 yards for people with no sense of direction" (in *Silly Olympiad*), in which the competitors run off in different directions, illustrates the way in which many projects are conducted. Time is invested in creating a plan, yet when approval is granted to move from initiation into the delivery stage, the plan is abandoned and chaos ensues. A plan has the added advantage of providing a means for keeping a project on track. In short, a well-constructed plan is essential.

The principles of planning

Planning and control

Just what should be planned? How much detail should a plan contain? How long should an average task take? How many stages should a project have? It would be helpful if there were some simple rules of thumb for answering such questions. However, every plan will be different in terms of its detail, the amount of risk it carries, or the way it has been structured. The best way to proceed is to plan what you wish to control. For example, if a manager asks for project progress reports to be provided at agreed intervals, the plan must have identified clear milestones that are delivered at the same frequency otherwise one report will change very little from the previous one.

Refining the plan

How long would it take to landscape a particular site? Perhaps three months would be sufficient. But there are many unknowns: no budget has been suggested; there is no design; the risks of the project have not been considered; and the potential for changes to the specification have not been taken into account. So it would be natural to compose a list (probably a long one) of assumptions and caveats that could be read alongside the estimate. Effectively, they would be guesses in place of facts. Many assumptions are made early in a project because the facts have not yet been revealed. But planning does not take place only at the beginning of the project. It is a continual process of refinement by which guesses are gradually replaced by facts.

Breaking a project into stages

Even before a project has been planned, it is not unusual for some people to wish to set the completion date or budget. This creates a challenge for project managers looking into the uncertain future; and the further into the future they look, the more uncertain it becomes. This is why professional project managers divide their projects into stages.

A project manager will develop two plans: one that covers the whole project, and a much more detailed one that focuses on the next stage only. The first, the project plan, will carry a greater level of risk because it looks further into the future. The stage plan will carry less risk as it covers a shorter, more predictable, planning horizon. Each stage is used as a vehicle to deliver some of the intended deliverables and to increase confidence in the project plan. At the end of each stage, the project manager is able to return to the project steering group with an increasingly reliable project plan.

As well as helping to refine early estimates as the project progresses, breaking the project into stages:

- enables progress to be tracked and measured, providing assurance to the project's stakeholders; and
- allows the justification of the project to be reconsidered, making sure that it continues only if it remains viable.

Building in contingency

Although it may seem sensible to refine the estimates of cost and time required to complete a project as it progresses, some sponsors will wish to fix them as soon as possible so that budgets can be set and people can allocate sufficient time for their role in the project when it is needed. Despite the caveats that may accompany the plan, the targets become fixed in people's minds and the assumptions are forgotten. Even if the emerging plan suggests that the original targets were inappropriate or unachievable, they are now so embedded in the organisation's psyche that to challenge them can look like failure.

It is therefore crucial to add a contingency element to early estimates. Contingency is an estimated amount of time or money, carefully calculated when a project is being planned, to address identified risks and the potential amount of change the project may encounter. As each stage is passed, it should be possible to reduce the contingency element, accounting for what has been learned during the project's progress so far and the reduced risk that should remain ahead. Thus, the contingency element should be ring-fenced in order to prevent resources from being used as a slush fund to bail out the project in the case of poorly-managed time, cost or quality variances.

If the project manager can produce a set of contingency figures based on an audited risk analysis, the project steering group can be confident that the amount of contingency being requested is reasonable. The group may also wish to retain control of the contingency budget. In this way, the project manager can draw on the fund only with the project steering group's approval and only to mitigate a risk for which the contingency was originally identified.

Having a clear and auditable approach to developing a contingency fund has a further benefit. In making public the amount and how it is broken down, there is less likelihood that each layer of management will add an additional percentage, which might take the total project budget to an unacceptable level.

Contingency will be considered again, in Chapter 10, in the context of change control.

Management by exception

At some time during a project something will go wrong or a change will be requested that may risk it missing its time and cost targets. Therefore, project managers should be given authority within specific parameters to carry out their jobs without having to seek approval for changes to costs or deadlines. Agreeing to manage by exception removes the confusion of who is authorised to take charge when problems or changes arise.

Management by exception requires the application of escalation conditions. Project steering groups provide their project managers with a degree of time and budgetary flexibility so that they can act on their own authority within pre-agreed constraints. For example, if the escalation conditions for time and cost have been set for plus or minus two weeks and plus or minus 5% respectively, the project steering group need not be involved in the daily management of the project as long as its forecast end date does not vary by more or less than two weeks and the forecast cost remains within plus or minus 5% of its target.

If at any time the project manager forecasts that the project will not be completed within the agreed escalation conditions, the problem must be taken to the project steering group for a decision on how to proceed.

Escalation conditions do not mean that the project steering group is allowing the project manager to overspend or deliver late. They simply provide the necessary flexibility while underlining the project steering group's ultimate authority if the project should veer too far off track.

A red, amber and green coding system is used to show how the project is progressing. Red denotes that it is outside of one or both of its escalation conditions for time and budget. Amber means that the project is off target but in the designated manager's control. Green means it is on target.

Management by exception can be used to separate any two levels of authority. It can be applied to the relationship between the project steering group and the project manager, the project manager and the project management team, and the project steering group and the portfolio management team. Although only time and cost have been described, the approach can be applied to any date or numeric driven target, such as quantified benefits. Although it may not be immediately apparent, quality is accounted for by the negative figures applied to time and cost. For instance, if a project is forecast to be completed early or under budget, it may suggest that something has been forgotten or removed from its scope and that the output will be substandard.

Management by exception is a technique used to control a project. However, like the other principles described above, it must be considered when planning:

- the benefits of a project;
- the mitigation of risks;
- the quality of the deliverables;
- timescales and costs.

Planning the benefits

In Chapter 5, different perceptions of what constitutes a successful outcome were considered. For businesses, commercial success is the most crucial. However, the benefits of a project are notoriously difficult to articulate and quantify. To strike a balance between the benefits of the project and the investment needed to fund it, both must be considered on equal terms. This means they must be measured in hard currency which, although difficult, is always desirable if the investment is to be justified.

Common examples of (as yet) unquantified benefits include:

- contribution to strategic objectives;
- generation of efficiency improvements;
- provision of access to new customers;
- provision of access to new markets;
- reduction/removal of competitive pressure;
- improvement in customer satisfaction;
- compliance with regulatory imperatives.

Quantifying benefits

Most benefits of a project, including those above, can be quantified in financial terms. It is usually possible to use the "so what?" argument to assist in setting a value. If the benefits are not quantified, the debate with those from whom the project is seeking funding will become one in which emotion is used in place of evidence. Although not always the case, most of the benefits identified above can be quantified in terms of:

■ an increase in revenues/profits;
■ a reduction in overheads;
■ mitigation of risk;
■ enabling activity elsewhere that will deliver one of the above.

Table 6.1 shows the results of quantifying some specific benefits.

TABLE 6.1 **Quantifying benefits ($)**

	Year 0	Year 1	Year 2	Year 3	Year 4
Increased revenues	–	**5,000**	**60,000**	**60,000**	**70,000**
Increased customer satisfaction	–	5,000	10,000	10,000	10,000
Competitor removal	–	–	20,000	20,000	20,000
Customers from new market	–	–	30,000	30,000	40,000
Cost savings	–	**8,000**	**10,000**	**11,000**	**11,000**
Headcount savings	–	5,000	5,000	5,000	5,000
Removal of redundant IT kit	–	3,000	5,000	6,000	6,000
Total	–	**13,000**	**70,000**	**71,000**	**81,000**
Cumulative total	–	**13,000**	**83,000**	**154,000**	**235,000**

But are these benefits anything more than a guess? The future is uncertain and nothing is guaranteed. However, when the project has been completed and the business has waited patiently through the post-project period, those who funded it will want to measure the return on their investment and compare the benefits with the forecast benefits in the business case.

The benefits in the business case must be clearly expressed so they can be measured and quantified financially. For example, customer satisfaction can be measured both before and after the project through a survey. Consequently, the business case may say that "a 5% improvement in customer satisfaction between year 0 and year 1 is envisaged as a direct result of this project. In year 2, it will increase by a further 5% and remain stable during years 3 and 4". This is an unambiguous target. At the end of each year, a measure can be taken of customer satisfaction to see if the targets have been met. Even so, unless the increase in customer satisfaction translates into a financial return, the project's backers would be justified in transferring their sponsorship to one that does.

With this in mind, the increases in customer satisfaction could be related to an increase in revenue. More satisfied customers may spend extra on the organisation's products and services. Thus a 5% improvement may "lead to an increase in sales of $5,000 in year 1 and a further $5,000 in year 2, after which sales will stay at the level of this extra $10,000". These figures can be measured before and after the project to determine whether the forecast was well judged.

Even so, it is often difficult to know that the project in question was directly responsible for delivering the increase in customer satisfaction and revenue because, for example, there may be other projects with similar targets. Forecasts can always change, but at the very least, the business case must present a compelling argument supported by analysis for a judgment to be made on whether to proceed with the project.

Cost/benefit analysis

The benefits of a project should outweigh the costs; however, the point at which the costs are outweighed by the benefits may be some way in the future. How far is a question that a cost/benefit analysis can help to determine.

This simple cost/benefit analysis compares the investment and the intended returns of a project over time. In Table 6.2, the cost/benefit analysis shows a healthy return being made on the investment. In year 2 the benefits outweigh the costs invested to date and "payback" is achieved. In years 3 and 4 the profits grow substantially.

TABLE 6.2 **Cost/benefit analysis ($)**

	Year 0	Year 1	Year 2	Year 3	Year 4
Benefits	–	13,000	70,000	71,000	81,000
Costs	2,500	15,850	64,620	27,400	24,250
Net	–2,500	–2,850	5,380	43,600	56,750
Cumulative	–2,500	–5,350	30	43,630	100,380

What matters now is to consider whether those figures are realistic as initial forecasts are often too optimistic. They should also be compared with the cost/benefit figures for other projects under consideration.

Discounted cash flow

The figures used in Table 6.2 are straightforward and take no account of the time value of money. Money received in the future is worth less than money received today, which can be invested. If the interest rate is 6%, $1 today will be worth $1.06 in a year's time. To put it another way, getting $1 in a year's time is like getting $0.94 today. In other words, the value of the future return on a project must be discounted in the cost/benefit analysis. This approach to forecasting more realistic monetary values is called discounted cash flow.

Table 6.3 adds more detail so the discounted cash flow can be calculated.

The first four rows are identical to those used in the straightforward calculation in Table 6.2. The new rows allow the net figure to be discounted by a number of percentage points. The discount factor is the amount by which the net figure must be multiplied in order to discount it by a specified amount. It is calculated like this:

TABLE 6.3 **Discounted cash flow ($)**

	Year 0	Year 1	Year 2	Year 3	Year 4
Benefits	–	13,000.00	70,000.00	71,000.00	81,000.00
Costs	2,500.00	15,850.00	64,620.00	27,400.00	24,250.00
Net	–2,500.00	–2,850.00	5,380.00	43,600.00	56,750.00
Cumulative	–2,500.00	–5,350.00	30.00	43,630.00	100,380.00
Discount factor	1.00	0.94	0.89	0.84	0.79
Discounted net	–2,500.00	–2,688.68	4,788.18	36,607.40	44,951.32
Net present value	–2,500.00	–5,188.68	–400.50	36,206.90	81,158.22

Note: Figures have been rounded.

$$\frac{1}{(1+i)^n}$$

where "i" is the rate and "n" is the number of years hence. So assuming a rate of 6% and a forecast needed for year 2, the calculation would be:

$$\frac{1}{(1+0.06)^2} \quad \rightarrow \quad \frac{1}{(1.06)^2} \quad \rightarrow \quad \frac{1}{(1.1236)}$$

$$= 0.89$$

The net figure is multiplied by the discount factor to determine a more realistic value called the discounted net, a value which, when accumulated over time, provides what is called the net present value. Thus it could be said of the example in Table 6.3 that this project will yield a net present value of $36,206.90 in year 3. However, the point at which payback is achieved has been pushed one year further into the future, compared with the non-discounted example. This "extra" year for the investment to yield a return is an important consideration for the portfolio management team.

FIGURE 6.1 **Financial dependency network**

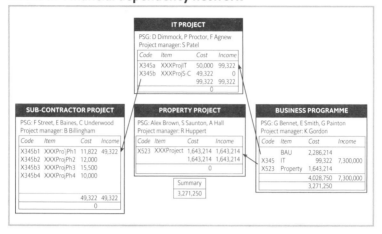

Internal rate of return

The internal rate of return is another measure used to compare one project with another. Calculating it is similar to working out the discounted cash flow, but in reverse. For example, the project yields $36,206.90 based on a discount factor of 6%. A discount factor of 200% would give a yield of –$1,237.41, a negative figure. Somewhere in between these negative and positive figures is a discount factor that would give a zero net present value, in this case, roughly 150%. This is the internal rate of return. Put another way, if all the money that was invested in this project had been borrowed, and the project broke even, the interest rate paid on that borrowed money would be the internal rate of return.

As a rule of thumb, the higher the internal rate of return the better. However, it fails to take into account the size of the project. One with a relatively low investment may have the same internal rate of return as one worth many times more.

Financial dependency network

Sometimes individual projects in a programme are not necessarily expected to show a "profit". What they must do, however, is show how they will use their funding efficiently so that the benefits identified at programme level may be realised (see Figure 6.1).

The business programme on the right shows a forecast cost of $4,028,750 spread across a combination of business-as-usual activity and two projects (IT and property). For this investment, the programme forecasts income of $7,300,000. On balance, this suggests a "profit" of $3,271,250.

The IT and property projects are breaking even, as is the subcontractor project on the left. These projects are expected to deliver benefits that outweigh the investment being made in them, but these benefits are identified at programme level. Thus a different approach is needed to provide incentives for people involved in these sorts of projects. Rather than rewarding them when the benefits are achieved (which, in the case of a programme, might be in many years' time), it may be more effective to reward their ability to contain costs or produce quality deliverables on time. The programme must take care of the benefits management, not the projects themselves.

Planning for the unknown

Donald Rumsfeld, when American defence secretary, famously said:

Reports that say that something hasn't happened are always interesting to me because, as we know, there are known knowns; there are things we know we know. We also know there are known unknowns; that is to say we know there are some things we do not know. But there are also unknown unknowns – the ones we don't know we don't know.

The Plain English Campaign commented: "We think we know what he means, but we don't know if we really know." Despite the complex way in which he expressed himself, what Rumsfeld said is relevant to project management:

- "There are known knowns." Rumsfeld was referring to things that have ceased to be risks because they have happened and thus it is not possible to prevent them. In projects, these are called "issues".

- "There are known unknowns." These are the risks that have been identified and which it may be possible to mitigate, that is, preventing a problem arising or reducing its effect if it does arise.

FIGURE 6.2 **Steps in effective risk management**

- "There are unknown unknowns." These are the risks that have not been identified or anticipated. They are the threats to a project's successful outcome that are not yet even known about.

Thus:

- a risk is something that may place the success of the project in jeopardy;
- an issue is a risk (known or unknown) that has happened;
- an assumption is a guess that, by virtue of being unknown, is a risk.

Risk management rather than issue management is essential to effective project management. Successful project managers seek to identify and mitigate risks, minimise the likelihood of issues occurring and reduce the number of assumptions made during the life of the project.

Any plan is a forecast. Risk management helps reduce uncertainty by using the steps in Figure 6.2.

Identify

Risks have different levels of detail. A high-level risk may be expressed as: "The use of new technology may create some unforeseen challenges during the project." This is non-specific, but early in the project's life cycle it may be sufficient to determine a "sense of riskiness", so some equally high-level mitigating action may be identified or an amount of contingency set aside.

These questions help not so much to identify specific risks but to establish the inherent riskiness in a project:

- Impact on business-as-usual

- Is the benefits realisation phase likely to last long?
- Will the project significantly affect the organisation's business-as-usual commitments, especially sales and operations?
- Are any working practices expected to change as a result of the project?
- Are people's roles and responsibilities likely to change?

■ Stability of requirements

- Is the current burden of change within the business area already high?
- Is there a history of changing requirements in this business area?
- Is the business area subject to external regulation?

■ Governance

- Will a methodical approach to the management of the project be difficult to apply?
- Will a methodical approach to the development of any IT components be difficult to apply?
- Will structured requirements-gathering and approval procedures be challenging to undertake?

■ People

- Is there a difference among senior executives regarding their commitment to this project?
- Are the developers and users likely to have difficulty working in partnership?
- Are those involved in the project relatively inexperienced in the values and practices of the organisation?
- Is easy access to experienced technical competences likely to be a challenge?

■ Novelty

- Is this the first time anything similar has been undertaken by the organisation?

■ Complexity and size

- Will a significant number of customers or users be involved in the project?

- Will any external suppliers be needed?
- Will there be interdependencies between this project and any others?
- Does this project represent a complex technological change?
- Is the project likely to take longer than a year?

There are 20 questions listed. The more are answered "yes", the more likely the project is to experience a significant number of issues or changes. In this case a contingency amount, equal perhaps to one-fifth of that set aside for risk mitigation, should be added. If the answer to half of the questions is "yes", the amount added might be one-tenth of that set aside for mitigating risks. In other words, the estimates are imprecise, but they are at least based on some form of reasoning. An alternative (or additional) technique might be to consider previous, similar projects and assign a contingency amount based upon knowing by how much their final duration and costs varied from their initial estimates.

Changes, as opposed to issues, are those things that may not have been anticipated, yet cannot strictly be considered a problem. If they look to be exceptional, consider justifying them in their own right by means of a business case, or postponing them to a later release of the solution.

If the amount of anticipated change is likely to be high, it is probable that a number of the project's valuable people will spend a good deal of their time understanding the problem or opportunity, identifying a solution, assessing its impact and developing a plan. Not only might this otherwise become an unplanned drain on the project, but it will also divert their energy and expertise from the parts of the project in which they are meant to be engaged. The contingency pot should also include an amount to pay for the administration and management of change, not just the changes themselves. A sum of at least two to three person days might be set aside for each issue or change request that is encountered. If the estimated number of issues or change requests gets into double figures, the cost of change administration and management can become a significant burden.

As more becomes known about the project, the level at which risks are identified and articulated should become more detailed.

One or two people may have to create a high-level examination of a project's risk, but it is sensible to consult more widely when developing a more detailed risk register. This helps to make sure that specific risks are identified and are considered from an appropriate range of perspectives.

This calls for a risk workshop involving people from all parts of the project. No one should be excluded as the objective is to turn "unknown unknowns" into "known unknowns". Participants should be given a clear introduction and background from the project's sponsor. The project manager usually sets up the session, but if the project manager wishes to take part, an external, impartial organiser should be used.

The project manager should provide any relevant documents, including project management documents and reports on lessons learned from previous projects. It is helpful to highlight areas in which risks may be identified, such as:

- funding;
- timing;
- scope of requirements;
- customer expectations;
- supplier capabilities;
- roles and responsibilities;
- technology;
- methods;
- politics.

Participants write down as many risks as they think relevant on "reminder" notes. It is also helpful if they describe a mitigation, but this can be included later.

The way in which detailed risks are articulated matters a great deal. This note is neither helpful nor illuminating:

Risk: No resources
Mitigation: Tell management

A risk should be articulated as a combination of cause and effect like this:

Risk: <u>Key people from the legal team will be unavailable during the summer due to their engagement in other projects ... resulting in an inability to make critical purchase decisions.</u>
Mitigation: Secure the services of an external legal representative. Obtain portfolio management team authority to use legal team in precedence over other projects during the summer.

The underlined sentence shows the cause and its effect.

Many such notes should be produced during the risk workshop. When participants have had time to identify and articulate as many risks as they can, it should be possible to qualify them.

Qualify

It is important to rate and rank the risks to identify which most deserve the scarce resources available to the project.

The reason for writing the risks on reminder notes is to put them on a simple matrix like the one in Figure 6.3.

This matrix rates each risk in terms of:

- likelihood – the probability that it will happen;
- impact – the effect on the project were it to happen.

The scales are not arbitrary because risks are positioned according to the scores in Table 6.4.

The impact list suggests some separation between the values, and the maximum value 11, which is outside the normal scale, suggests an effect on other projects, non-project activity or a client's interests.

Although the likelihood list appears to be no more than a sliding scale, it shows that issues can be identified, qualified and evaluated in the same way as risks. Risks and issues differ only in their likelihood. An issue has happened and scores 10 – a certainty.

FIGURE 6.3 **Impact/likelihood matrix**

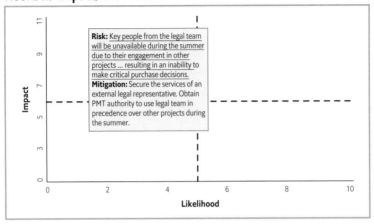

TABLE 6.4 **Impact/likelihood scores**

	Score	Risk
Impact	0	None, the risk has been fully mitigated
	3	Activity may be affected, but work can proceed to sign-off
	5	Deliverable may be compromised, but no effect on project completion
	7	Stage may be compromised, but completion is still achievable
	9	Project completion may be compromised
	11	Business or customer may suffer
Likelihood	0	The risk has passed
	2	Very low likelihood
	4	Low likelihood
	6	Even likelihood
	8	High likelihood
	10	A certainty

Evaluate

Which is the more important, a risk or an issue? To those used to fixing problems, an issue is often more important because it is immediate and must be fixed; whereas those who are risk averse may wish to tackle a potential problem before it occurs. This argument, however, considers only whether it is a potential or actual problem. To properly understand the relative "value" of a risk or issue, it is necessary to assess its impact. When both the likelihood and the impact are considered it is easier to judge whether one specific risk or issue deserves more attention than another.

This is done by multiplying the two numbers to create a risk factor. A risk with a likelihood of 6 and an impact of 7 has a risk factor of 42; whereas an issue with the maximum likelihood of 10 (because it has happened) but an impact of 3 has a risk factor of 30. In this case, it may be more sensible to invest in mitigating the risk even though dealing with the issue seems more immediate.

It is simple to generate a risk factor to establish the relative value of the risk or issue. However, some organisations want to give each risk a financial value. The risk factor is considered in terms of financial exposure, multiplied by the likelihood expressed as a percentage (where 100% makes it an issue). For instance, a supplier who has agreed to a penalty clause may stand to lose $25,000 for late delivery. If the likelihood of this happening is 20%, the financially evaluated risk factor would be $5,000 (20% × $25,000).

Although the risk factor is now expressed in financial terms, it remains a useful way of comparing risks and helps determine whether the cost of mitigating a risk is proportionate. For instance, if it cost the supplier $10,000 to pay extra people to carry out some of the work and finish on time, this might be considered too expensive when compared with the relative $5,000 exposure. However, if the likelihood of a late delivery began to increase, the $10,000 may progressively become the more attractive option.

This approach is useful, but there is a danger that financial quantification will drive project personnel more towards analysis and further away from mitigation. In addition it can be difficult to know when to stop quantifying the exposure. For example, the supplier at

FIGURE 6.4 **Impact/likelihood numeric risk factors**

			IMPACT			
	0	3	5	7	9	11
2		6	10	14	18	22
4		12	20	28	36	44
6		18	30	42	54	66
8		24	40	56	72	88
10		30	50	70	90	110

risk from the penalty clause may be exposed to more than the $25,000 charge. The sum could increase substantially through loss of reputation and other customers changing suppliers. The consequence is a risk matrix with no upper limit for financial impact, making it difficult to compare one risk with another, and almost impossible to cap the amount requested for mitigation.

A simple approach is usually the most effective. Not only is the numeric (non-financial) risk factor helpful in evaluating the relative worth of each risk and issue, but it also helps identify who should deal with it (see Figure 6.4).

A factor of 110 shows that an issue (which, by definition, has taken place) is affecting the business or a customer, so it must be referred to the portfolio management team for mitigation. Risks or issues with factors between 57 and 90 should be handled by the project steering group, and those with a factor between 21 and 56 should be dealt with by the project manager. Those scoring 20 or below should be assigned to team leaders.

This approach makes sure the right people hear about risks or issues for which they have authority to mitigate.

Mitigate

Mitigation is the process of making the likelihood or effect of a potential event less severe but, depending on the risk itself, there may be one or more mitigations available.

These are potential options: **S**hare; **E**ndure; **A**void; **L**essen.

Share

Risks are often shared. Colloquially, this is known as "having skin in the game". It is a common practice as projects have become collaborations which draw on capabilities which the sponsoring organisation itself may not possess. This has led to the creation of partnerships, as opposed to more straightforward client/vendor relationships, depending for their success on mutual commitment. If the client and vendor carry the burden of risk together, there may be greater confidence that both will be encouraged to deliver a successful project outcome. For example, it is quite common to share the risks and rewards of an initiative with a key supplier through penalty and reward clauses in contracts. Specifically, to mitigate the risk of a project going over budget, a customer might insist on compensation for every day by which the supplier exceeds a target completion date. However, sharing the risk does not always transfer the whole burden to someone else. In the film *Jurassic Park*, the venture's sponsor, John Hammond, complained that the lead computer programmer, Dennis Nedry, was untidy and unreliable. Nedry counter-challenged that he considered his achievements to be significant considering that his company won the contract with the lowest bid. So, while Hammond secured a fixed price to develop the fictional park's IT systems and security, he remained exposed to – and arguably increased – the risk of a poor-quality solution, the consequences of which were severe!

Endure

As an assumption is a guess it is therefore a risk. It should be considered in terms of its likelihood and effect, but it may be decided that the project can live with – that is endure – the risk. For example, it might be assumed that everyone on the project will work an eight-hour day but decided that the project will live with the risk that some people may work fewer hours or be called to work on other projects.

Avoid

Some risks can be circumvented. For instance, a project may face a risk that proposed changes to a computer system may be delayed because of other technology priorities in the organisation. This can be mitigated by using a manual alternative.

Lessen

It is possible to reduce the effect and/or likelihood of a risk. The specific mitigation may affect either the impact or the likelihood, or both, so it is important to know what the outcome should be. For example, if the only person able to produce an important report is a novice employee, the likelihood of producing a poor-quality deliverable might be lessened by requiring their manager to set clear expectations at the outset. However, while this action addresses the risk's likelihood, it does little to mitigate the impact if the author continues to deliver a report of poor quality. With this in mind, the report's audience could be warned before publication to lower their expectations; something might still hit the fan, but not so much of it.

At the very least, the likelihood of a risk should be monitored to determine whether it is moving towards becoming an issue. For example, if there is a risk that time will run out before completion of user acceptance testing, the likelihood can be monitored by tracking the number of outstanding defects being recorded every day. If the number rises, so will the likelihood of the risk becoming an issue. If the number falls, the probability is lessening.

The risk register

It should now be possible to put all the information about a project's risks into a risk register to monitor and control them (see Table 6.5 on the following page).

In many of these examples, mitigation carries either a financial or a time cost, so each risk should be quantified financially to allow contingency funding to be provided for the preferred mitigation.

TABLE 6.5 **The risk register**

Risk	Likelihood	Impact	Factor	Mitigations	Cost
Pre-written, packaged software solution will not hold key sales data needed by marketing team, resulting in their inability to work effectively	10	3	30	**1** Continue to use existing sales and marketing system alongside new solution. ACTION: JP to advise sales team to prepare for parallel running.	2 days per month to synchronise systems = $800
				2 Request a specific change from software supplier. ACTION: PT to obtain detailed quotation from supplier.	15 days' additional fees = $6,000
If the live date is missed, legal sanctions may be taken against our business, resulting in damage to reputation and other losses	2	11	22	**1** Identify this project as mandatory to make sure that it has priority over essential resources. ACTION: Sponsor to raise at next portfolio management team session.	Portfolio management team to consider effect on other projects
				2 Commence project early to allow for any slippage. ACTION: Sponsor to raise at next portfolio management team session.	Portfolio management team to consider effect on other projects

Risk	Likelihood	Impact	Factor	Mitigations	Cost
Based on supplier's past performance, delivery of equipment required for implementation will be delayed, resulting in delivery delay to client	6	9	54	**1** Identify an alternative supplier. ACTION: SS to ask Procurement for recommendation. **2** Instigate a penalty/ reward clause in the contract ACTION: JP to ask legal department for guidance.	$10,000 premium $5,000 reward provision
Key people from the legal department will be unavailable during the summer because of their engagement in other projects, resulting in an inability to make critical purchase decisions	6	9	54	**1** Secure the services of an external legal representative. ACTION: Ask legal department for a recommendation. **2** Obtain portfolio management team's authority to use legal team in precedence over other projects during the summer. ACTION: Sponsor to raise at next portfolio management team session.	$1,500 premium
Total risk-based contingency budget					Maximum $23,300

Planning: quality

A PLAN IS A FORECAST. Many people think that a project forecast is expressed in terms of a completion date and a total budget, but neither can be predicted adequately until what the project has to deliver is known. Thus a forecast is better described as a probability assessment based on skill and experience of the time and resources required for the successful delivery of a specified end product.

The specified end product will not be produced by chance. It must be defined, planned, built, tested and accepted before it can be used for its intended purpose. This means that a successful outcome will mean different things to different people. The sponsor may consider as successful a project that delivers a low-cost, high-income-generating solution, whereas customers may expect it to provide something that works and is robust and reliable. For the developers, a successful project must deliver an output that is supportable since it may have to be maintained and managed over a long period.

When a project has been completed questions will be asked about its success. Posing them at the beginning of the project forces participants to identify success criteria, which might be:

- Does the new computer system process twice as many trades per day as the previous one?
- Does the new office provide each of the 350 staff with at least 36 square feet of desk space?
- Were all new staff recruited by the end of June?
- Have the new facilities been secured within their quoted budget?

- Have the new office operating procedures been made available to the Tokyo office as a priority?

These questions describe the quality of the project's intended outcome, but it is also essential to measure the quality of the project's output as it progresses. Only by having clearly defined and agreed measures is it possible to know whether a step in the project has been completed successfully.

Consequently, before creating a project time schedule or a resource plan, it is helpful to know what the project must deliver at periods in its lifetime and at its end. These are the project's milestones or "products".

If an activity fails to deliver or contribute significantly to the delivery of a product, it is reasonable to ask why time and effort were spent on it. This means it should be possible to show that all project activity contributes clearly to the delivery of specified products. Examples of products could include a:

- piece of tested software;
- marketing plan;
- test schedule;
- design document;
- "business case";
- presentation;
- conference;
- trained user.

Products result from activities; for example, training is the activity that delivers a "trained user" (the product). When planning a project that involves training, how long should be allowed and what is an appropriate investment? It is possible to answer such questions only when more is known about the product itself. The standard expected of the trained user must be defined. In the same way that success criteria have been described for the project, so is it possible to describe success at product level. In the example above, if the users have been trained to drive a car, these are some of the ways an examiner might judge their fitness to do so:

- Can they perform an emergency stop without stalling the engine?
- Can they reverse around a corner without hitting the kerb?
- Can they correctly identify and interpret road signs?
- Do they use their rear-view mirrors before every manoeuvre?

If time and cost were the only things worth planning, the roads would be full of drivers who had completed their training when their budgets and instructors' patience had run out. If the expectations of a project's products are clearly described:

- fewer activities will be forgotten;
- more activity will be focused on delivering the intended outcome;
- the suitability of estimates for timescale and cost will be improved;
- it will be possible to know when an activity has been "finished";
- expectations of a fit-for-purpose output will be commonly understood, thus reducing confusion and reworking.

The technique of product-based planning puts quality at the heart of planning, enabling the:

- products of the project to be clearly identified;
- products to be ordered into a reliable delivery sequence;
- quality of products to be described.

Product-based planning was first described as part of the PRINCE approach to project management (see Chapter 1) and has become a widely practised, robust and reliable technique. It does not remove the need to plan a timescale and a budget, but it ensures that when developing the schedule and resource plan, they are based on a far better understanding of the intended outcome and approach.

Product-based planning produces the:

- product breakdown structure;
- product flow diagram;
- product description.

A simplified version of this valuable technique is described below. Details of enhancements can be found in the book *Managing Successful Projects with PRINCE2*.*

The product breakdown structure

This seeks to identify all products to be generated by the project to confirm the scope of what it is required to deliver.

It starts with the single product that the project is intended to deliver, which is the sum of a list of components. For example, a desktop computer comprises a screen, a keyboard, a mouse and a processing unit, which is itself the sum of smaller components, such as the hard drive, the motherboard, the power supply and the case.

Figure 7.1 shows a training course as a collection of component products. The training course is a "starter" product, but everyone's expectations of it may be different. To understand these better, break this high-level, poorly defined product into ever smaller component parts until it has been expressed as the entire set of building blocks needed throughout the whole project.

Initially, the training course can be split into three smaller components: the specified course, the prepared course and the delivered course. It may be possible to estimate the development time and cost of each of the three products but there is unlikely to be enough information about them, so the specified course is decomposed into the gathered requirements and the course definition document. These are difficult to subdivide further, so this "root" stops there. The prepared course can be subdivided into many further products, each of which becomes redundant as those below it describe it better. For instance, there is no need to describe delegate materials – they are the sum of exercise briefs, sample solutions and copies of slides.

Planning should be a team effort, so it is wise to involve interested stakeholders in creating a product breakdown structure. A facilitator, usually the project manager, should lead the process. It can help to post reminder notes on a board as products are identified.

The facilitator should recap frequently what has been described

---

* Axelos Limited, The Stationery Office Books, 2017.

FIGURE 7.1 **A training course as a collection of component products**

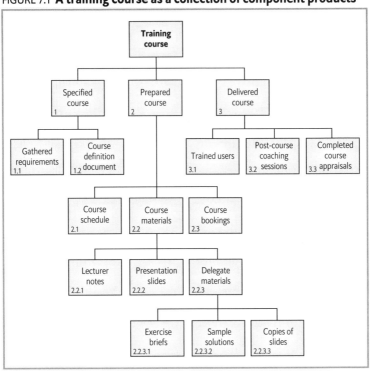

so that everyone has a clear and common understanding. There are usually differences about products that should be in or out of scope. For instance, some may wish to include post-course coaching sessions (product 3.2) at which delegates meet the lecturer after the event; others may disagree. Each product identified will take time and money to develop and deliver, so a conclusion must be reached when the plan is created. If a product is to be excluded from the project but its development is still necessary to it, it remains on the product breakdown structure as an "external" product that must be accommodated in the plan eventually.

What began as a single deliverable is now much better defined as a list of component parts that together describe the scope of the project. The starter product has been decomposed into:

- 1.1   Gathered requirements
- 1.2   Course definition document
- 2.1   Course schedule
- 2.3   Course bookings
- 2.2.1   Lecturer notes
- 2.2.2   Presentation slides
- 2.2.3.1 Exercise briefs
- 2.2.3.2 Sample solutions
- 2.2.3.3 Copies of slides
- 3.1   Trained users
- 3.2   Post-course coaching sessions
- 3.3   Completed course appraisals

How detailed should a product-based plan be? The answer is the same regardless of whether the plan focuses on products or activities. As the plan will be used to delegate and control the delivery of products, the products that make up the end product should be subdivided only so far as the project manager can monitor their progress regularly and frequently. Project managers should ask themselves – and their project steering groups – how long they would be prepared to wait to discover whether a product had been completed or not. A good rule of thumb is 2–3 weeks.

Figure 7.2 shows some common errors in a product breakdown structure.

The product flow diagram

Once the product breakdown structure has been developed satisfactorily, it should be possible to produce a product flow diagram as illustrated in Figure 7.3 to show the sequence in which products must be developed.

Everyone involved will have an opinion on the best sequence and the process of creating a product flow diagram can help draw into the project a wide and varied range of expertise. It is sensible to involve the people who helped develop the product breakdown structure

FIGURE 7.2 **Some common errors in a product breakdown structure**

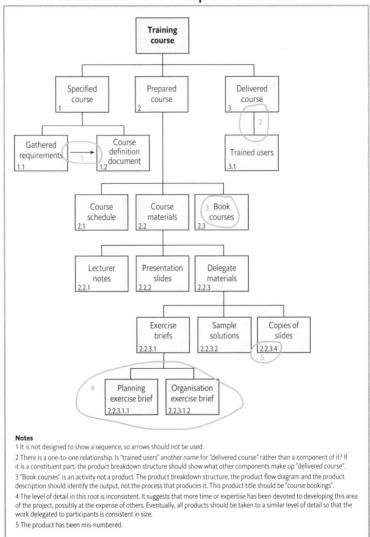

Notes

1 It is not designed to show a sequence, so arrows should not be used.

2 There is a one-to-one relationship. Is "trained users" another name for "delivered course" rather than a component of it? If it is a constituent part, the product breakdown structure should show what other components make up "delivered course".

3 "Book courses" is an activity not a product. The product breakdown structure, the product flow diagram and the product description should identify the output, not the process that produces it. This product title should be "course bookings".

4 The level of detail in this root is inconsistent. It suggests that more time or expertise has been devoted to developing this area of the project, possibly at the expense of others. Eventually, all products should be taken to a similar level of detail so that the work delegated to participants is consistent in size.

5 The product has been mis-numbered.

in drafting the product flow diagram. And it is desirable that senior managers take part as their views will be valuable. As everyone will be asked to estimate the time and investment needed to deliver each

FIGURE 7.3 **Product flow diagram**

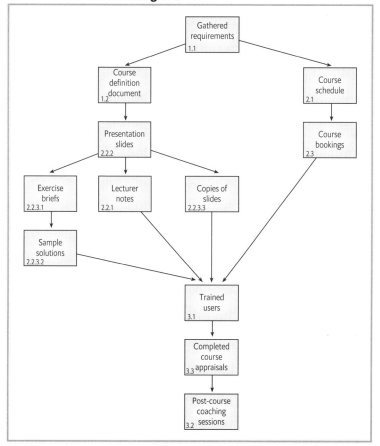

product, involving them early helps them to understand the project and the emerging approach.

In constructing the product flow diagram the redundant, higher-level products should be removed and the remaining products should be placed in an order defined by their dependence. This can be time-consuming, but planning is a difficult and demanding process; it is better to identify the challenges and deal with them before it is too late or they become too costly to fix.

It is a good idea to use the same facilitator and to nominate a note-taker because products will be taking shape during this process and some of their characteristics will need recording.

At the outset, identify the start and end products, noting that there may be many products with no prior dependency. The sequence should flow from top to bottom and the remaining products should be positioned until most of them are on the board. To reduce misunderstandings, all products should retain the same names as on the product breakdown structure. The facilitator should regularly review how things stand and challenge them, and if appropriate change the order. It is important to allow debate, but the facilitator should not become so involved in the debate as to lose the chance to listen out for new products, which should be added to both the product breakdown structure and the product flow diagram. When all products are on the board, the arrows between them should be added, but only in pencil. It is normal for discussion to flare up again when the slightest change is made to the product flow diagram.

If the project is large or teams have already been formed, groups of products can be allocated to smaller teams. These teams may develop their own product flow diagrams, which are consolidated after debate. Alternatively, to improve the product flow diagram, they may work independently on the same products and then meet to identify and resolve differences.

Participants should not be allowed to express the plan in their own way on the product flow diagram. This can confuse others and introduce errors that will find their way into the time line and the resource plan. Every product should have at least one successor apart from the final one and at least one predecessor apart from the first ones.

A common mistake at this stage is to give the product flow diagram a timescale. This comes later in the planning process. Therefore, two products appearing next to each other (for example, presentation slides and course bookings) does not mean that they will be delivered at the same time. Indeed, the words "at the same time" should be avoided when discussing a product flow diagram. This allows the project to be discussed without preconceived and unsupported constraints, and matters relating to quality can be articulated first so that time and cost expectations can be more effectively managed.

Some common construction errors are shown in Figure 7.4.

FIGURE 7.4 **Common construction errors**

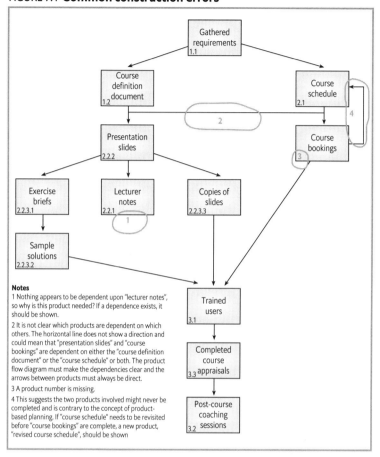

Notes

1 Nothing appears to be dependent upon "lecturer notes", so why is this product needed? If a dependence exists, it should be shown.

2 It is not clear which products are dependent on which others. The horizontal line does not show a direction and could mean that "presentation slides" and "course bookings" are dependent on either the "course definition document" or the "course schedule" or both. The product flow diagram must make the dependencies clear and the arrows between products must always be direct.

3 A product number is missing.

4 This suggests the two products involved might never be completed and is contrary to the concept of product-based planning. If "course schedule" needs to be revisited before "course bookings" are complete, a new product, "revised course schedule", should be shown

A robust plan means the same thing to everyone who reads it. Throughout the process so far, it is highly likely that questions will have been raised about each product and it is unlikely that everyone will have a clear and common understanding. The titles of the products are open to misinterpretation and do not fully describe their content, format and purpose.

FIGURE 7.5 **The product description**

Product title	Course definition document
Purpose	To ensure that the proposed course meets the client's needs such that approval may be granted for creation of the materials.
Composition	1. Introduction 2. Course duration 3. Course objectives 4. Instructional strategy 5. Prerequisites 6. Deliverables 7. Logistics 8. Timetable 9. Syllabus
Derivation	Course requirements
Format	A4 spiral-bound document, hardback and transparent cover bearing client's logo Colour
Audience	Customer sponsor
Quality criteria	1. Does it satisfy each item from the course requirements? 2. Is the volume of course content achievable within the timescale? 3. Has at least 30 minutes been devoted to risk management? 4. Is the course based around a case study? 5. Has a maximum number of delegates per course been stated?
Quality method	1. Quality review by supplier before presentation to client 2. Quality review by customer's internal quality review panel

The product description

It is often sensible to start the planning process with the product breakdown structure. The product flow diagram and the product descriptions are often developed together because the latter provides a definitive description of each product so that everyone has a clear and common understanding of it. While the product breakdown structure and the product flow diagram are being developed, the facilitator should challenge and capture the views of the participants on the character of each individual product through the product description (see Figure 7.5).

Title

This should be simple and clear.

Purpose

This section is not a repository for everything known about the product but a specific description of why it is needed, ideally in a single sentence. If the purpose cannot be articulated, it is worth asking if the product is required at all.

Composition

This section should read like a table of contents. If the product is a document, the composition should list the section headings to appear in the end product. The content of each section can be expanded as this helps develop expectations of what the product will contain. Products are not always documents. "Trained user" is a product and its composition may be simply described as "a course delegate". Qualifying what standard that delegate must achieve comes later.

Derivation

This section is the equivalent of a list of sources. As well as listing the immediate preceding products needed from which to develop this product, it can also contain directions to any other materials or information necessary in its development. For example, the course definition document can only be developed once the course requirements have been completed. Additional information may be gleaned by interviewing a colleague who has had training elsewhere and is listed here to guide the person developing the course definition document to a further source of information. This section is also often used to list any standards to which the product developer should refer.

Format

This describes the physical characteristics of the product. In Figure 7.5 it is a document and its "look" has been described. If the product was "architectural plan", the format may be "Ao blueprint".

Audience

This important section lists the users of the product. It is important to know who they will be so that the next section can encompass their varying expectations.

Quality criteria

Because quality criteria define the characteristics of the product that would make it fit for its purpose, this list is the most important part of the product description. Just as the project has success criteria, so does each individual product and, in the same way, they are expressed as questions. If each question asked in this section were answered positively, the product would be fit for its purpose and could be approved and signed off. The more sophisticated and elaborate the list of quality criteria, the greater the expectation of the quality of the end product.

This list not only confirms that the developed product is complete, but also steers the product developer towards getting it right first time. Knowing the audience and describing their expectations before development starts minimises the potential of developing a series of failed prototypes.

Creating a list of quality criteria can be helped by:

- arranging quality criteria in order of those who will use the product (the audience);
- asking everyone in the audience to prioritise the quality criteria relevant to them;
- checking all product quality criteria for consistency with project success criteria;
- asking whether the rest of the product description has been followed;
- expressing quality criteria as measurable and unambiguous questions to which "yes" or "no" are the only options;
- avoiding adjectives such as "effective", "clear" and "suitable" because each member of the audience will interpret them differently;

FIGURE 7.6 **Quality method**

Product title	Course definition document
Purpose	To ensure that the proposed course meets the client's needs such that approval may be granted for creation of the materials.
1	To provide a basis for change control
	To show how long the course will take to deliver
	To describe the objectives of the course
Composition	1. Introduction
	2. Course duration
	3. Course objective
	4. Instructional strategys
	5. Prerequisites
	6. Deliverables
2	7. Something about logistics
	8. Timetable
	9. Syllabus
Derivation	Course requirements
Format	A4 spiral-bound document, hardback and transparent cover bearing client's logo
	Colour
Audience	Customer sponsor
Quality criteria	1. Does it satisfy each item from the course requirements?
	2. Is the volume of course content achievable within the timescale?
	3. Has at least 30 minutes been devoted to risk management?
	4. Is the course based around a case study?
	5. Has a maximum number of delegates per course been stated?
3	6. Is the document fit to be placed in front of a client?
	7. Is it long enough?
	8. How clear is the content?
Quality method	1. Quality review by supplier before presentation to client
4	2. Quality review by everyone else

Notes

1 There are multiple purposes listed, some of which duplicate what has rightly been included in the composition section.

2 This is unclear. The person charged with developing and delivering this product will need to know what is meant by this phrase.

3 These three examples are bad for different reasons. "Is the document fit to be placed in front of a client?" is subjective. The client's criteria need to be identified and written here instead. "Is it long enough?" is a closed question but begs the question "how long is long enough?". If the length of the document really matters, a better quality criterion would be: "Is the document less than ten pages long and more than five?" "How clear is the content?" is not a closed question, so any response will be a subjective judgment and of little value.

4 The product description has to answer the difficult questions as early in the project as possible. Proposing that a quality review will be carried out by everyone else suggests that either little thought has gone into deciding who should review the document, or that everyone really does need to review it. This will affect the number and fitness of the quality criteria.

■ checking the composition section and determining the quality criteria for each item listed. This will help if identifying quality criteria for the overall product is causing difficulties.

The number of quality criteria does not just indicate the product's prospective quality; it shows the quality of the product description itself.

Quality method

There are many ways of testing a product, including:

- examination;
- informal/formal review;
- inspection;
- demonstration.

In all cases, the product description is the yardstick against which the product itself is tested, and approval for the formal completion of the product can be sought only when the product is deemed fit for its purpose.

There are many opportunities to introduce errors into a product description (see Figure 7.6).

Using product-based planning

Product-based planning is at the front end of the traditional planning process. It provides a means to articulate one of the three parts of a plan that is too often forgotten – quality – so that the time and cost components may be more reliably developed. The more that is known about the products of the project, the more robust the plan will be, so product descriptions should be developed as planning proceeds and greater clarity is gained.

It is highly desirable to involve the emerging project team in the planning process. It not only results in a better and more clearly defined output, but also promotes the involvement of senior stakeholders from whom approvals will be needed, and from team members who will be required to estimate the time and cost needed to deliver the project's products.

The people who have the task of delivering the project's products should be those who know them best. The project manager can never be an expert in every area of the project, so it makes sense for the product-based plan (particularly the product descriptions) to be developed in co-operation with the experts. The project manager should delegate creating some product descriptions to specific team members.

Having drawn up a product flow diagram, the team may be worried that a product description is needed for every product in it. However, in developing product descriptions, it makes sense to prioritise products that are critical, new or confusing, or all three. Producing proper product descriptions will lessen the risk of delivering something that is unfit and will need reworking.

TABLE 7.1 **Product outlines**

Title	Audience	Purpose	Composition	Quality criteria

Gathered requirements	Developer	To capture the needs of the customer such that a solution may be described.	1 Introduction
			2 Purpose of training
			3 Scope
			4 Audiences
			5 Training needs
			6 Logistical requirements:
			  – timing
			  – numbers
			  – locations
				1 Have all current project practitioners been included in an audience group?
				2 Have training needs been prioritised?
				3 Does the scope include all departments within the division?
				4 Does the timing avoid bank holidays and the month of August?
				5 Have locations been specified that enable all delegates to participate without incurring overnight accommodation costs?

Course definition document	Customer	To confirm that the intended course satisfies the customer's needs such that approval may be granted for the creation of materials.	1 Introduction 2 Course duration 3 Course objectives 4 Instructional strategy 5 Prerequisites 6 Deliverables 7 Logistics 8 Timetable 9 Syllabus	1 Does the document satisfy each item listed in the gathered requirements? 2 Is the volume of course content achievable within the allotted timescale? 3 Has at least 30 minutes been devoted to the study of risk management? 4 Is the course based on a case study? 5 Has a maximum number of delegates been stated?

FIGURE 7.7 **Product breakdown structure for fitting out and marketing a new factory**

Many organisations have a library of product-based plans and there is every reason to benefit from those drawn up for previous projects. This does not mean that a plan can be transferred from one project to another with a little tailoring, as all projects are unique. However, this is a great opportunity for the planners of the present to learn from planners of the past.

Another way of managing the potential number of product descriptions is to focus on the characteristics of the product that matter most. By shrinking the number of sections, it is possible to reduce the workload needed to create them. This can be achieved by replacing a number of product descriptions by a single table of product outlines (see Table 7.1).

Table 7.1 shows only five of the possible eight ways of characterising a product, but the loss of value arising from the absence of the remaining sections is balanced by creating an expression of quality that is more likely to be digested by the project steering group.

The product breakdown structure, the product flow diagram and the product descriptions will go through a number of changes, so maintaining robust control of the versions of the plan is important. New

FIGURE 7.8 **A risk highlighted by placing "factory employees" in the product flow diagram**

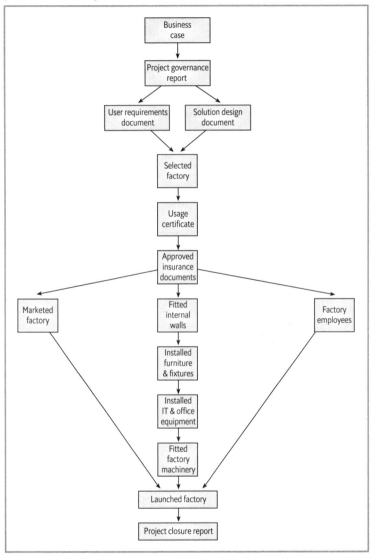

FIGURE 7.9 **Refining "factory employees" on the product breakdown structure**

products will be identified, existing products will be considered too detailed or too high-level, and some products will become redundant as knowledge improves and the plan is rationalised further. For instance, when developing a product flow diagram, there may be suggestions that the product breakdown structure has identified products that have not been fully broken down. Figure 7.7 shows the product breakdown structure for fitting out and marketing a new factory.

The product "factory employees" may be described as "paid employees, working in the factory", but placing it in the product flow diagram highlights a risk (see Figure 7.8).

The risk is that employees may be in place before the factory installations are completed and are being paid before they can do productive work. If factory employees really means "staff who have been offered a role with the company", the plan is missing the original output, "paid employees working in the factory", which remains an essential project milestone. Factory employees needs refining on the product breakdown structure, as shown in Figure 7.9.

Figure 7.10 shows the revised product flow diagram. The reconsideration of one product has changed the plan significantly.

The product flow diagram contains no timescale or budgetary

FIGURE 7.10 **Revised product flow diagram**

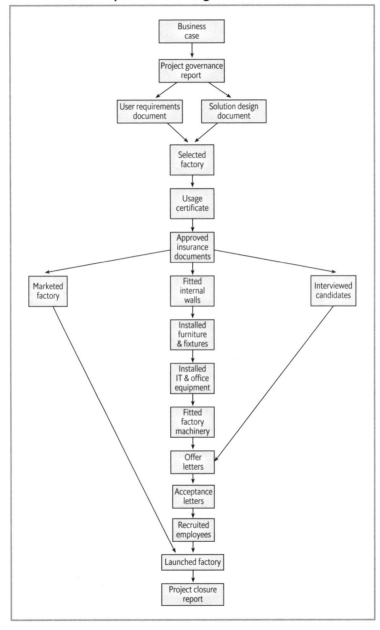

FIGURE 7.11 **A product flow diagram with stages**

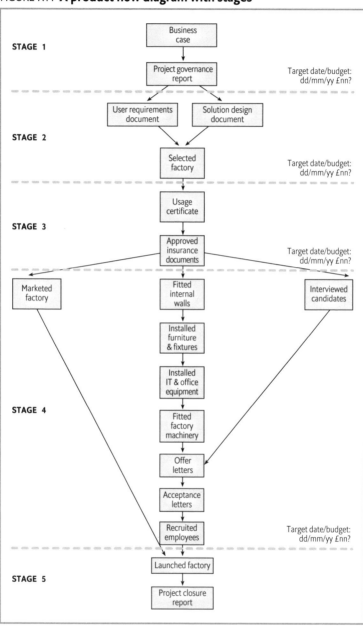

information. This means a draft can be produced relatively swiftly and the basic plan presented to senior managers so that they can consider the project's content without the usual pressure to debate time and cost. Until the products and their delivery sequence have been agreed, time and cost expectations will be largely unsupported by evidence and the product flow diagram describes the project without the need to commit too much advance resource.

If the timescale is brought up during discussion, the product flow diagram can accommodate it by dividing the project into stages against each of which a target date and budget may be placed. This should not mean that the date or investment has been promised, but this new expression begins to show how quality, cost and time expectations may need playing off against each other. Looking at Figure 7.11, the project steering group will see what must be delivered to meet a deadline that, on reflection, may cause them to realise that compromises are necessary.

A means to an end

For a product-based approach to planning to succeed, there is no absolute requirement for each of the three parts of the technique to be applied. The technique is a means to an end. Ultimately, a plan will be more robust if it contains an expression of what the principal stakeholders will get for the time and money they invest in the project. However, all too often this is unclear, which is why a product-based approach is recommended.

The creation of a product breakdown structure, a product flow diagram and product descriptions means the plan is well under way. However, the inevitable questions remain: how long will it take to deliver these products and how much will it cost to complete the project? Now is the time to answer them.

Planning: time and cost

The link between products and tasks

The importance of knowing what must be delivered cannot be under-estimated, but there comes a point when estimates of time and cost must be produced. To do this, you need to know what tasks will be necessary to deliver each product.

Many products begin life in draft form using the product description as a guide. Once the draft has been completed, it is usual for a review to take place. This is where one of the quality methods referred to in the product description will be employed. As the product is compared with the product description, reviewers identify errors, which they note and to which the developer must attend. Once the amendments have been made, it should be possible to submit the product for final approval.

The process can be summarised as:

- develop draft product;
- review product;
- amend product;
- approve product.

When drawing up a plan, it is helpful to know the relationship between products and tasks. Products are created as a result of the tasks above or any others considered essential. Therefore, a sequence of tasks must be performed to deliver each product on the product flow diagram. When imagining the list of things that must be done to complete the project, it is sensible to think of a sequence of products (the product flow diagram) in which each has a life cycle. The list will look like this:

Product 1	**Product 2**
■ Draft	■ Draft
■ Review	■ Review
■ Amend	■ Amend
■ Approve	■ Approve

and so on.

This important relationship will be revisited when the time schedule is developed. But before that something must be known of the techniques available to assist in estimating how long these products will take to develop and how much their development will cost.

Estimating techniques

An estimate is a probability assessment based on skill and experience of the time and resources required for the delivery of a specified product that has been considered at length during product-based planning. Knowing the product in greater detail makes estimating time and cost much easier. For example, how long is a piece of string (the product)? Once you know that the piece of string must be able to run twice around a package measuring 1m × 1m × 1m leaving enough to form a double knot, the question can be answered.

Various techniques assist in estimating time and cost. They fall into two broad categories:

■ Those that may be used without reference to any stored data or prior experience, for example:
  – top down and bottom up;
  – Delphi technique;
  – analogy.
■ Those that require estimation data from previous projects, for example:
  – work distribution;
  – standard project/product.

FIGURE 8.1 **A top-down estimate**

Top down and bottom up

Top-down and bottom-up estimates are created at different points in a project's life cycle. A top-down estimate takes the whole project and applies an overall timescale and cost. It is created at the beginning of the project and breaks down time and cost across its stages, but it is unlikely to go into further detail because in the early days of the project, no further long-term detail will be available. Despite this, demands to know how long the project will take and how much it will cost will still be made and a response is necessary. Given the high-level nature of a top-down estimate, it is usual to add some contingency to allow for whatever risky assumptions have to be made. An example of a top-down estimate is shown in Figure 8.1.

Figure 8.1 contains expressions of time, cost and quality, but if the project steering group is to approve the plan, it will need something extra to give its members confidence that the first stage has at least been estimated to a lower level of detail (see Figure 8.2).

In Figure 8.2, the feasibility study report (the first product in this project) has been decomposed by a product breakdown structure into a set of smaller products so that a better estimate can be made of the time and cost they will consume in their development. When added together, these estimates should match the top-down estimates. If they do not, the project manager should provide the project steering group with refined top-down estimates and a formal request to amend the proposed budgets and timescales. This is bottom-up estimating, a technique supported by the product-based approach to identifying deliverables.

As each stage is completed, the process is repeated. As more becomes known about the project, the amount of contingency requested at each

FIGURE 8.2 **A top-down and bottom-up estimate**

		Stage 1	Stage 2	Stage 3	Stage 4	Stage 5
T O P D O W N	Time	8 weeks	8 weeks	10 weeks	15 weeks	15 weeks
	Cost	$20,000	$25,000	$45,000	$65,000	$5,000
	Quality	Feasibility study report	Needs analysis report	Design report	Developed solution	Tested, implemented solution
B O T T O M U P	Quality	Gathered data	Drafted report	Reviewed report	Amended report	Approved report	Presented report
	Cost	$3,000	$8,000	$2,000	$4,000	$2,000	$1,000
	Time	1 week	2 weeks	2 weeks	1 week	1 week	1 week

stage should be reduced and confidence in the overall estimate for the end of the project should increase.

Top-down and bottom-up estimating allows planning to take place at both project and stage levels, and helps overcome the challenge of the future becoming more uncertain the further ahead you look.

The Delphi technique

Named after the Oracle of Delphi, which the Greeks consulted before all major undertakings, this technique seeks to develop a consensus about an estimate through meetings, questionnaires and surveys. It was developed by the Rand Corporation in the late 1940s to forecast the impact of technology on warfare. Experts submitted their views on the likelihood, frequency and impact of potential attacks by the enemy. Other experts provided anonymous feedback and the process was repeated until a common view emerged.

Many projects have a considerable specialist aspect to them and project managers cannot be expected to be expert in every one. They can use the Delphi technique, carefully adapted, to obtain estimates in which they can have some faith.

Having used the experts to assist in creating product descriptions, the project manager asks them to state how much effort or budget would be needed to deliver these products. When the replies are received, feedback is obtained, usually anonymously. The experts are then encouraged to revise their earlier estimates in the light of these other views. During this process the range of the estimates should shrink as the experts home in on a figure they can all agree to. If complete agreement is impossible, average scores can be used to obtain what will still be a more reliable estimate than might otherwise have been produced.

This process takes time and should be reserved for areas in which the project manager has little expertise or where the range of initial estimates provided by experts is wide.

Analogy

Comparing the project, or aspects of it, with something similar is one way in which estimates can be developed. For example, physical and computer models are used to test different aspects of an aircraft's performance without the need to construct a life-size version in advance. The method also encompasses the application of historical data to a present project. For example, a firm knew that it had previously taken them a week to train 10 people how to operate a new piece of machinery. They used that knowledge to create an accurate estimate of how long it would take to train double the number of people when a device of a slightly more complex design was introduced.

Work distribution

This technique is similar to analogy in that it assumes that some types of project, such as the development of computer software or building new houses, are repeated within organisations. Much of the activity is repeated every time the project is undertaken so it would be foolish not to use past experience to improve estimates for the future. The work distribution technique relies on data gathered from previous, similar projects, which it apportions across the standard project life cycle to arrive at the proportions of effort or budget required by each stage (see Figure 8.3).

The success of such a model depends on the reliability of data from previous projects and the projects themselves being similar. However, if such data can be recorded (and improved over time), the

FIGURE 8.3 **The work distribution technique**

FIGURE 8.4 **Spreading the proportions spent on projects across different types of resource**

model can be used quite flexibly. For instance, if a budget has been set aside, it is a straightforward task to apportion it across the different stages of a project to get some sense of the amounts available for each. Alternatively, if the first stage has been completed and used a certain amount of the budget, the amounts likely for the future stages can be calculated.

Another method is to spread the proportions traditionally spent on projects across different types of resource (see Figure 8.4). Once again, this works best where the projects are similar and therefore the data are reliable.

Standard project/product

The standard project technique also depends on data from previous projects. In it a table is drawn up that applies two measures of the project so that an estimate for effort or cost can be calculated (see Figure 8.5).

FIGURE 8.5 **Standard project/product technique**

Size \ Complexity	Low	Medium	High
Small	1	2	4
Medium	3	5	9
Large	5	10	15

This is similar to a rate card used by sales people to arrive at a price. In this case, the numbers (showing the effort in days needed to complete the exercise) have been refined over a period during which many standard projects have been repeatedly carried out. This produces a matrix that can be used to work out the effort required for future projects.

Figure 8.5 illustrates that this technique can be used not only for projects but for products as well. Many people who work on projects or business-as-usual do repeatable work that delivers essentially the same products every time which vary only in size or complexity. The table allows them to determine the effort needed on their next task simply by estimating its relative size and complexity. As long as both scales mean something measurable, the estimates can be extremely accurate.

For example, a department supporting computer users in a large organisation was responsible for moving people's desks and computer equipment to a new location and used a form of the table in Figure 8.5. For them, small in size meant that fewer than 10 users were to move, medium indicated between 10 and 19, and large referred to 20 and above. Low complexity meant that the users would be moving somewhere else on the same floor of the building, medium indicated that they would be moving to a different floor, and high meant a move to another building. Therefore, when someone wished to book a team move, an early estimate could be provided using the standard project technique.

Productivity

People are often called "human resources", but they are not robots and treating them like an inanimate resource underestimates the risk they pose to a project. These free-thinking, emotional, unpredictable human resources are, above all, different from each other. Rules of thumb when creating estimates about people's productivity include the following:

- **People will not be 100% productive.** The results of a workforce survey* are summarised as follows:
  - Global office workers spend 60% of their time on tasks that do not directly contribute to a productive outcome, including the search for information, priority management, project status communications and meeting attendance;
  - 167 hours every year are spent in meetings, two-thirds of which are considered to be unnecessary;
  - Only 27% of their time is devoted to the role for which they were hired;
  - Workers spend 4½ hours every week engaged in work that has already been done.

  Project managers, therefore, should allow for non-productive time if estimates are to be realistic. This is not to suggest that they should unquestioningly allow for extreme levels of non-productive time, but they should take account of sickness, training and annual leave. Most organisations have a standard productivity rate, which can vary between 65% and 80%.

- **Productivity does not always increase when more people are allocated to a task.** Sometimes the reverse is true. Creating a document is often best left to one person; to assign an additional person may double the duration as they discuss it between them. The quality may well be improved, but that is only one outcome. If the target is economy, it is often preferable to identify the best person for the job and allow him to tackle it alone.

* https://asana.com/resources/anatomy-of-work

■ **People have different productivity rates.** Choosing the best person for the job, or the fastest, may not always be possible. As people work at different rates, a person's experience and speed must be a factor when creating an estimate. A junior member of the team might take two days to deliver a specific product, whereas a more senior member could do the same work in half the time. When thinking about how long something will take to deliver, it is usual to think of ourselves. This "halo" effect assumes that everyone else is as good as we are. But everyone has a unique complement of skills, knowledge, experience and competencies, so an estimate should be tailored to the person who will actually deliver the product. A series of factors can be developed to account for different work rates. Alternatively, named individuals or skill sets should be identified before estimating the effort required to deliver each product.

■ **Productivity increases are usually temporary.** Frederick Herzberg, an American psychologist, showed that even after increasing workers' salaries, the motivational and productivity improvement lasted for a relatively short time, after which they reverted to what he called the "Potter Line", a rate of productivity which, for them, was normal.

Here are some ways a project manager can increase the likelihood that estimates will be dependable:

■ **Let people estimate their own work.** The halo effect can be used to the project's advantage. If someone estimates for themselves, they know best the speed at which they work and what else they have to do during the same period of time. There is an added advantage that once team members have estimated their own work, they have created a form of contract with the project which makes it difficult to suggest that the estimates are unreasonable or unachievable.

■ **Make planning assumptions clear.** Once the planning assumptions are documented, they are available for questioning and challenge. In this way, the project management team can

FIGURE 8.6 **A simple product flow diagram**

assure themselves that the estimates are based on reliable and robust planning conditions.

- **Agree product descriptions.** The product is intended to be the output that satisfies its intended audience. This target should be agreed before development begins, not only to increase the likelihood of a successful delivery, but also to ensure that both the delegator and the person being delegated have the same product in mind. Once the output is agreed, any debate about timescale or budget is more rational.

- **Look at metrics from previous work.** If a team member suggests it will take ten days to complete a product when it took 20 to fulfil a similar objective, the project manager has useful evidence for improving the reliability of the estimate.

- **Negotiate penalty/reward clauses.** Estimates can be made to appear more reliable when penalties drive up the standard of performance and productivity, at least temporarily. Offering a reward can have a similar effect. Much depends on the person or team since everyone is motivated by something different.

Planning timescales and budgets

The product flow diagram is a necessary foundation for planning time and cost. Although it does not include a timescale, it does provide a clear delivery order for the products. Figure 8.6 shows a simple product flow diagram that can be used to produce a timescale and budget for the project.

Because effort has gone into developing the product flow diagram, the dependencies should be reliable. If they are not, the costs and timescales may be flawed.

The duration and costs of development for each product must be estimated. It is usual to create an estimating sheet containing most of the information on which the Gantt chart (see Figure 8.7) and resource plan will be based. A sample estimating sheet might look like Table 8.1.

The estimating sheet is product-based, but the tasks required to deliver the products will be estimated. This is why they appear in the next column. The third column requires the project manager to suggest who should undertake the task. As the plan is not yet anywhere near complete, it is unlikely that the project steering group would allocate any people to the project other than the project manager. Therefore, the names or initials in the third column indicate the people the project manager wishes to secure. If names are not known, it may be sufficient to state what skill type is required, for instance, a junior analyst or a senior business specialist.

Human resources are not the only cost that must be identified. Although people may be the most significant investment, other costs attributed to the project must be included, such as travel, accommodation, materials and equipment. In a larger project, it is usual to have many human and non-human costs, so knowing the person or resource type and having some robust prior knowledge about the product (the product description) make it possible to estimate these costs.

In Table 8.1, the fourth column (identifying the planned costs) is a mixture of two expressions of cost: financial (the cost of going to the trade show) and effort (every other figure). Since the project steering group will want a set of financial figures, these two forms of expression will need to be combined into one single financial figure. This will happen soon when the resource plan is developed, but the non-financial effort figure is needed first because it will not be possible to calculate the duration without it.

Duration is a period of time, measured in hours or days. Effort is the time it would take a single, average person to complete the task if able to work at 100% productivity all the time, unfettered by any other work or distraction. Effort is measured in person-hours but people are rarely, if ever, able to sustain periods of any significance in which they can work at 100% productivity. Furthermore, many people are assigned multiple tasks, sometimes combining other project and business-as-usual work. Therefore, allowing for a productivity rate of 80%, the duration allocated for a four person-day task would need to be five days, provided that person has no other concurrent tasks.

TABLE 8.1 **Sample estimating sheet**

Product	Tasks	Resources	Cost	Assumptions
Product 1	Develop	PR	0.8	PR took this long on previous project
	Review	ST/MW	0.5/0.5	Constrained to half-day as slot for teleconference is already booked
	Amend	PR	0.25	PR took this long on previous project
	Approve	PSG	0.1	Assuming PSG will approve via e-mail
Product 2	Develop	AK	0.5	Based on 0.1 per item x 4 items, plus contingency of 0.1
	Review	PR/MW	0.1/0.1	Estimate based on MW experience
	Amend	AK	0.25	Based on need to rework half original
	Approve	PSG	0.1	Assuming PSG will approve via e-mail
Product 3	Develop	PR	0.8	PR took this long on previous project
	Review	ST/MW	0.5/0.5	Constrained to half-day as slot for teleconference is already booked
	Amend	PR	0.25	Assuming quarter of product to be reworked, plus contingency
	Approve	PSG	0.1	Assuming PSG will approve via e-mail
Product 4	Develop	AK	0.8	AK estimate based on experience
		Train fare	$100	Costs to visit trade show
	Review	ST/MW	0.25/0.25	ST estimate based on experience
	Amend	AK	0.25	Assuming quarter of product to be reworked, plus contingency
	Approve	PSG	0.1	Assuming PSG will approve via e-mail

Understanding effort in this way allows work to be spread across a number of people. For instance, four person-days do not necessarily

FIGURE 8.7 **Gantt chart based on Table 8.1**

need to be delivered by one person. They could be shared and, potentially, reduce the duration of the task.

The last column of the estimating sheet is where planning assumptions, which often remain in the project manager's head, are logged. The plan, of which the estimating sheet is a part, must be able to stand on its own without needing a project manager to present it. It must be self-contained so that anyone reading it has all the information they need.

Now there is sufficient information to create one of the most familiar depictions of a project plan, a Gantt chart. This describes the plan's duration and was developed by Henry L. Gantt in 1910. He produced many different charts which caused others to take an interest in what was a revolutionary way of communicating a message, but the type of chart commonly used today was refined in 1942. Figure 8.7 is an example based on the estimating sheet.

Information from both the product flow diagram and the estimating sheet has been combined with the products and tasks shown on the Y axis. The human resources are shown next to the tasks, and the dependencies from the product flow diagram are shown by arrows linking the products (task dependencies are also shown to indicate the order in which they should take place). Even though it may have

FIGURE 8.8 **Duration of product 4**

been a challenging exercise, the time taken to develop the product flow diagram will have been well spent. The dependencies shown in the Gantt chart are based on the skills, knowledge and experience of everyone who participated in the product-based planning workshops, rather than the instinctive view of the project manager.

The X axis represents information not present on the estimating sheet. The timescale or duration is estimated using the various information sources. They are:

- the product descriptions;
- knowledge of the people and other resource types to be employed;
- the effort intended for those resources;
- knowledge of estimating techniques and experience in using them.

Figure 8.8 shows how the duration of product 4 was determined.

From the estimating sheet, it is known that AK is required to devote 0.8 person-days to the development of product 4. Two days have been planned for the duration of this task to allow for AK's rate of productivity and any other tasks he may be undertaking. ST and MW are both asked to deliver a quarter of a day's effort during one day. Whether they are required to work in sequence or in parallel, they are not expected to exceed the quarter of a day's effort they will charge to the project's budget or to finish any later than at the end of day 9. The approval of the product, sought from the project steering group in the final task, requires a small investment of their time: 0.1 of a day's effort. Yet how sensible is it to provide them with half a day in which to complete the task? Members of the project steering group are busy people, so there is a risk that their signatures will not be forthcoming on the afternoon of day 10 unless the project manager has been particularly effective in alerting them in advance. With this risk in mind, it may be sensible to allow the project steering group more time, perhaps a week, in which to complete approval, no matter how small the effort.

The emerging plan contains an expression of quality, an illustration of the duration and an inference of what the costs may be. Now the budget needs to become more coherent so that everyone can see when the various financial commitments will be made.

There now is sufficient information from which to compile the resource plan, the third and final component of the forecast (see Table 8.2).

TABLE 8.2 **The resource plan**

	Day 1	Day 2	Day 3	Day 4	Day 5	Day 6	Day 7	Day 8	Day 9	Day 10	Total
PR	0.80	0.35		0.80		0.25					2.20
ST		0.50			0.50				0.25		1.25
MW		0.60			0.50				0.25		1.35
AK	0.50	0.50	0.25				0.80			0.25	2.30
PSG		0.10	0.10			0.10				0.10	0.40
Total	1.30	2.05	0.35	0.80	1.00	0.35	0.80		0.50	0.35	7.50

Note: Costs are in person-days when not monetary.

This view is essential if the project manager is to have any hope of forecasting, monitoring and controlling the project's costs. It contains the person-day effort figures from the estimating sheet, but presented over time. These figures can be summarised in several ways. If an important event, such as the end of a financial month, falls at the end of day 5, the project manager would be able to show that the effort forecast during the current month is 5.5 person-days, and 2.0 in the next. Additionally, the figures can be summarised horizontally to give the project manager the total figure to be negotiated with the resource pool managers, who will have to provide the people. For instance, AK is not required for 100% of the time, but he must devote 2.3 days in total for which the project must budget.

What this resource plan does not show is financial information; in particular, the $100 cost of visiting the trade show is missing, but so too is anything to indicate what the eventual cost of the project will be. To calculate this, a rate is needed for each of the various people who are working on the project which, when multiplied by the number of person-days, will cost their input (see Table 8.3).

TABLE 8.3 **Resource plan with financial information**

Human	Day 1	Day 2	Day 3	Day 4	Day 5	Day 6	Day 7	Day 8	Day 9	Day 10	Total
PR	0.80	0.35		0.80		0.25					2.20
$300/d	$240	$105		$240		$75					$660
ST		0.50			0.50				0.25		1.25
$200/d		$100			$100				$50		$250
MW		0.60			0.50				0.25		1.35
$200/d		$120			$100				$50		$270
AK	0.50	0.50	0.25				0.80			0.25	2.30
$200/d	$100	$100	$50				$160			$50	$460
PSG		0.10	0.10			0.10				0.10	0.40
$400/d		$40	$40			$40				$40	$160
Total human	1.30	2.05	0.35	0.80	1.00	0.35	0.80		0.50	0.35	7.50
	$340	$465	$90	$240	$200	$115	$160		$100	$90	$1,800
Non-human travel							$100				$100
Total	$340	$465	$90	$240	$200	$115	$260		$100	$90	$1,900

Below each person's name is a rate; for instance, PR costs $300 per day and is needed for 2.2 person-days, giving a total investment in PR of $660. The whole cost of the project is $1,900, including the non-human costs shown beneath the total human element.

Many organisations split their resources into three main types:

■ human revenue;

FIGURE 8.9 **Resource plan for resource pool managers**

- non-human revenue;
- capital.

The first two have been identified already, but the capital costs, such as buying a building or a piece of computer hardware for the project, have not. Thus, many organisations will express the budget in terms of revenue and capital.

The plan now shows what needs to be delivered, when and how much it will cost. This is the heart of what a good project plan should be. However, to determine whether this plan is achievable, the project manager needs to know that the resources he proposes employing are available, particularly if he has particular participants in mind. Without this, the plan is little better than an aspiration. The project manager must negotiate with the resource pool managers who nominally "own" these people to secure them for the period indicated by the project plan. It follows, therefore, that the resource pool managers also need a plan, showing which of their resources are engaged in what type of work, where, to what extent and for how long. An example is shown in Figure 8.9.

Here two people, resources 1 and 2, are being used across five projects. The top half of the figure shows when each person is due to be engaged in each of the various projects; the bottom half shows the person-days commitment. On the basis of the timeline at the top, resource 2 appears to have two projects to work on during week 2, which, without knowledge of the relative effort needed for each, might be thought achievable. Indeed, without the bottom half of the plan, resource 2 might be encouraged by a resource pool manager to "do his best" to carry out projects 4 and 5 at the same time. The bottom half of the plan, however, shows that resource 2 is required to put in seven person-days' effort in five working days. Without overtime or lowering quality standards, this cannot be achieved. This message, together with everything else shown in Figure 8.9, needs to be made available to the project manager so he can see the effect on his own project plans.

Using the flexibility of the plan

Initially, most plans have a degree of flexibility. For instance, the duration or start and end dates of some tasks may be changed. So too might the number of people assigned to tasks, or the quality of the output might be negotiated. But any change made to one aspect of the plan usually has an effect elsewhere, so taking advantage of the potential flexibility in a plan is not always straightforward. The activity network illustrates this point.

This is a way of looking at the project's timeline to gauge the effect of moving tasks or products. For instance, Figure 8.10 is a summary of the Gantt chart in Figure 8.7.

Product 1 is slightly different in character from the others. It can slip on the timescale for a limited period without affecting the end date of the project itself. If its end date moves beyond day 6, product 4 will be affected because it depends on product 1 and will slip by the same amount. However, until product 1 affects product 4, the flexibility for it to move may be helpful. The activity network identifies tasks and products where there is potential for movement and explicitly identifies those where there is none. It looks like the product flow diagram laid on its side (Figure 8.11).

Figure 8.11 describes some of the time-related characteristics of each product, with an example box identifying what is meant by the numbers:

FIGURE 8.10 **Summary of Gantt chart in Figure 8.7**

- EST – earliest start time. The earliest point at which the task or product may commence.
- EFT – earliest finish time. The earliest point at which the task or product may be completed.
- LST – latest start time. The latest point at which the task or product may commence before it affects others.
- LFT – latest finish time. The latest point at which the task or product may be completed before it affects others.
- DUR – duration. The number of working days between the EST and the EFT, or the LST and LFT.
- FL – float. The difference between the EST and the LST or the EFT and the LFT. This is the amount by which the task or product may slip before it affects others.

In the example, product 1's capacity to slip is shown because it has a float of 4, but all the others have none. Because of their zero float,

FIGURE 8.11 **The activity network**

FIGURE 8.12 **The effect of starting product 1 later**

products 2, 3 and 4 are on the critical path; any slippage by any task or product on this path will result in an identical slippage in the project's end date.

A project may have more than one critical path and any of them might change during the course of the project as the float capacity is consumed by slipping tasks. Therefore, the critical path(s) is an area of risk in the project.

The fact that product 1 has some float may be helpful to the project manager. What would the effect be if product 1 were started later?

In Figure 8.12, product 1 has been allowed to start later with no effect on the project's end date. If managing the timescale and quality were the only things that mattered, this might be an acceptable change. However, since the project manager must also manage the budget, the effect of this change on the resource plan also needs to be determined. It may have been impaired already because PR is scheduled to develop both product 1 and product 3 at the same time.

As suspected, the effort planned for days 1 and 2 has shuffled across to days 4 and 5, and PR has become overcommitted on day 4. The likely consequence is that the project will slip, or the quality of product 1 will suffer as PR tries to keep within the deadline.

TABLE 8.4 **The effect on the resource plan of starting product 1 later**

	Day 1	Day 2	Day 3	Day 4	Day 5	Day 6	Day 7	Day 8	Day 9	Day 10	Total
PR				1.60	0.35	0.25					2.20
ST		0.50			0.50				0.25		1.25
MW		0.60			0.50				0.25		1.35
AK	0.50	0.50	0.25				0.80			0.25	2.30
PSG		0.10	0.10			0.10				0.10	0.40
Total	0.50	1.70	0.35	1.60	1.35	0.35	0.80		0.50	0.35	7.50

Resource levelling

Time, resource and quality are linked in the project plan, so change to one is likely to have an impact on another. Such challenges can arise at any time, but they come to light particularly when comparisons are made between what the resource pool managers are able to supply and what the project manager wants. This must be resolved through resource levelling.

The resource plan in Table 8.4 contains an example of a resourcing peak, which is circled. This is where the effort required from people exceeds their capacity to deliver it. Equally, there are examples of resourcing troughs, where people appear to be unproductive. Resource levelling aims to smooth the peaks and troughs so that resources are being used as effectively as possible. This is more easily done in a project where the resources have been assigned full-time, since the troughs are gaps in which people could be more productive rather than periods when they could be engaged in another project. This removes much of the need to negotiate with resource pool managers. However, because the opposite is true where the resources are assigned only for part-time engagements, it is significantly more difficult to level the resource plan.

Shifting tasks is one way of moving effort from one part of the plan to another and can work in a project's favour, for example where a peak is resolved by shifting the task with float to a point where a trough is filled. However, there are often more creative options available. These will be used not only at the end of the planning process, but also when

FIGURE 8.13 **PERT diagram**

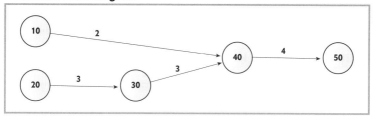

the plan has been approved and is in operation. Further techniques to level and control the plan will be discussed in later chapters.

Project evaluation and review technique

Another way to express the duration of the project is shown in the project evaluation and review technique (PERT) diagram. Developed during the 1950s by the US Department of Defence, it helps identify the critical path and establish the earliest and latest start and finish times, duration and floats. The product flow diagram for the example above would look like Figure 8.13.

The circles represent milestones and 10, 20, 30 and 40 are equivalent to products 1, 2, 3 and 4. They are numbered in tens so that additional milestones may be added if necessary. In this example, 50 represents the end of the project. The numbers in between are the duration of activities.

There are some important differences between this expression, the product flow diagram and the Gantt chart, as well as some limitations. For instance, the PERT diagram shows five milestones where the product flow diagram showed four. This is because the project evaluation and review technique requires each milestone circle to consume no time and require no resources. Therefore, the duration associated with each milestone is shown on the line that succeeds it. Thus the duration between milestone 40 and the end of the project, milestone 50, is four days. From a product-based perspective, milestone 50 might be questioned. What are its success criteria? Are they any different from those of milestone 40? If they are, might extra time be needed to achieve them?

This is not a technique to be used in addition to the approach described during this chapter, but as an alternative. Although it makes reference to milestones that may be considered "products", the emphasis on the quality definition of the products is far less. Furthermore, PERT is intentionally a means of representing a time schedule. It is rarely used to develop budgets.

Ready to go?

The planning process described here and in Chapter 7 has followed the sequence:

- **P**roducts
- **R**esources
- **E**ffort
- **T**imescales

The creation of a project plan is a process that should begin with a reasonable understanding of what the project has to deliver: its products. It should then be possible to determine what resources will be needed and what effort and costs will be expected. Only then will it be possible to produce a timescale. This is a sensible approach to planning, yet all too often the process begins with a Gantt chart, with no reference to deliverables, quality or resources.

At the end of these steps, the plan will contain expressions of how expectations of quality, budget and durations are to be met. They will be consistent because the right amount of money to deliver the specified products in the proposed timescale will have been calculated. It may well be that the plan fails to meet expectations in one or more respects, but any change to one aspect of the plan usually has an impact on another, so the process should be reapplied to any changes. In this way, the plan is refined to a point at which it satisfies as many stakeholders' expectations as possible, ideally all of them.

The four words above spell PRET, which means "ready" in French. Only by covering these steps in this order is the plan ready to be submitted for approval.

9

Initiating projects

EXCEPT FOR THE PORTFOLIO MANAGEMENT TEAM, which normally should be in place before the organisation undertakes a large number of projects, most of the project-specific roles emerge as a project gets under way. Some organisations would prefer that there were rules governing when a project steering group or project manager should be officially in place, but that depends on who is available and the political, strategic, legal and commercial priority of the project.

Consequently, initiating a project can be a hit or miss affair and rules will only partially succeed in regulating the chaos common when a project begins. What follows is a recommended approach. Those managing this process should remember that, at this time more than any other, the organisation may be uncomfortable with the proposed degree of governance, and therefore the need to sell the principles underpinning the whole approach to project management is likely to be greatest.

The project life cycle

Most people appreciate that a project should have a clear start and end, but it also requires structure around what happens between these points. Figure 9.1 shows the life cycle used throughout this book to describe the key deliverables and approval points. Note that, while the key management deliverables and events are intended to be common to all projects, there are variants in the way specific, specialist deliverables are created during the "delivery" phase. This is because there are many product and service development approaches. Agile development is one of the most common, and is explored in greater detail in Chapter 11.

FIGURE 9.1 **The project life cycle**

PRE-PROJECT	PROJECT				POST-PROJECT
IDENTIFICATION	INITIATION	DELIVERY		CLOSURE	*BENEFITS REALISATION*

There is an important point to make before considering this life cycle in more detail. Figure 9.1 shows the progression of an idea (described in the project outline) to the realisation of the forecast benefits (described in the benefits realisation report). However, only the initiation, delivery and completion stages fall within the life of the project. It is during these stages that the portfolio management team (or, in their absence, the company's senior management team) have delegated project ownership to the project steering group. They are responsible for steering the project to a successful conclusion so that the benefits will be realised when the main deliverable is used in earnest. During identification and benefits realisation, the project should be firmly in the hands of the wider business. In practice, initiation sees the project handed over from the portfolio management team to the project steering group, so it is normal for a period of transition to exist while the management environment emerges.

Once the project outline has been approved, the idea of a project is now on the roster and a budget has been set aside for its initiation. Ideally, a strict order should be imposed on the activities taking place during initiation; however, most organisations have their own approach to handling budgets, committing resources and decision-making, so it is more useful to consider the outcomes expected from initiation.

A common claim during the initiation stage is that there are too many unknowns to enable the business case and a project governance report to be created. This is a strange argument since the purpose of the initiation stage is to resolve the unknowns. The planning process must resolve as many unknowns as is possible so that the project steering group is clear about the risks. So although it is a difficult stage, it is the only opportunity to develop effectively the project's management environment.

The success of this stage can be judged against the following criteria:

■ Is there a well-balanced project steering group?

■ Has a project manager been identified and recruited?

■ Does the business case propose an acceptable margin between costs and benefits?

■ Have the customer's requirements been clearly and fully articulated?

■ Does the solution design document address the customer's requirements?

■ Does the project governance report, including the project plan, show how it will meet the targets set out in the business case?

■ Have all products from this stage been approved by the appropriate authorities?

The business case

The business case underpins any project because it describes success in terms of measurable benefits. To forecast the intended benefits, much thought is needed and the results must find a place in the business case. The sponsor is best placed to develop the business case because it is the sponsor who will be charged with delivering the successful outcome and will probably have pushed for the project to be funded so far. Once completed, the business case should be submitted to the portfolio management team to be approved. If they do so, they should also provide the budget requested.

In practice, it is not unusual for the project manager (if one has been identified) to help to develop the business case, not only because it is an ideal way to become familiar with the project itself, but also because creating the document should be planned, monitored and controlled. However, this document must not be owned nor signed off by the project manager; if this happens, what clearer demonstration could there be of the business's lack of interest or dereliction of responsibility?

The success of a business case should be judged against the following criteria:

- Does it show the difference over time of the costs of the project compared with its intended benefits?
- Are all identified risks accompanied by a mitigation?
- Where alternative solutions exist, does it propose a preferred option?
- Can it be easily compared to other business cases when setting priorities?
- Does it consider not just the project costs alone, but also those that may be incurred beyond its closure?
- Does it enable a clear approval decision to be made?

Table 9.1 lists what should be included in a business case.

TABLE 9.1 **The business case**

Opportunity or problem	A description of the opportunity or problem that has led to the need for what this project is intended to deliver.
Strategic fit	Shows what contribution the project will make to the organisation's strategic direction.
Interdependencies	An analysis that illustrates the way in which this project may affect, or be affected by, others.
Success criteria	A set of measures by which to describe a successful project outcome.
Options considered	An overview, with supporting analysis, which describes the alternatives to the chosen solution. This should include the "do-nothing" option.
Selected option	A complete analysis of the selected option, including the following:
– Risks	What are the risks of the venture?
– Benefits	What are the merits of the venture?
– Costs	What will be the whole-life costs of the venture?
– Cost/benefit analysis	How well, and when, will the benefits outweigh the costs?
– Deliverables and timescales	What are the key deliverables and their due dates?
– Planning assumptions	What assumptions have been made in developing the business case?
– Benefits realisation plan	How will the benefits be measured and delivered?
– Management by objectives	What incentives will be offered (if any) to encourage a successful outcome?

How the business case is developed is largely up to the individuals, but what it should look like is more readily described.

Opportunity or problem

Opportunities may include the chance for commercial gain, such as a new market, or the chance to develop and sell a new product or service. However, business cases often describe a problem that must be overcome to avoid the organisation being exposed to risk. This section, therefore, provides an introduction to the risks and benefits sections under "Selected option", which provide greater detail.

Strategic fit

This section shows how the project will contribute to the strategic aims of the organisation. This is an opportunity to describe whether the project contribution to each of the balanced scorecard quadrants is direct, indirect, partial or absent and adds a dimension to the business case that is not purely commercial.

Interdependencies

The project may be part of a wider portfolio or programme of work, so it will be helpful to show the principal dependencies with those other initiatives. This not only helps those who will have to manage those dependencies; there are also cases where knowledge of a project's interdependencies will help to justify it, for instance where it provides little measurable benefit other than in allowing dependent, benefit-generating projects to take place.

Success criteria

This section should describe fully and clearly what success looks like. This topic was described in Chapter 5, and examples were provided.

Such statements can be drawn together for the project steering group to agree the final list. This will guide the project manager in developing the project governance report.

Options considered

Most problems or opportunities have a range of solutions, more than one of which may be compelling. The business case must successfully outline the solutions most likely to satisfy the need so that only one is selected for full expression. Here are some examples of alternatives for consideration:

- The business case to justify a new building for a company might consider the merits and risks of staying put, moving to a new, preconstructed building or commissioning a purpose-built office.
- An operational inefficiency may be overcome by introducing a new computer solution. As well as living with the inefficiency, the

business case could consider whether pre-packaged software or a system developed in house would provide the best answer.

In both examples, the do-nothing option must feature. It is an essential part of any business case; not only does it provide a point of reference for other considered options, but it also often presents a compelling argument in favour of the project. Below are some examples of projects where the do-nothing option justified the eventual project:

- **Software upgrade project.** Many organisations depend on key applications and software that they buy or license from specialist providers. Occasionally, it becomes no longer economically or strategically sensible for a software provider to continue to maintain an application – or a version of it – that has come to the end of its natural life. The customer is faced with a choice of continuing to use software which, in time, will no longer be supported by the supplier, or to upgrade or purchase an alternative. While it may appear sensible to justify the investment in a new solution by quantifying the benefits of its features and functions, the more common and successful argument is based on the evaluated risk of continuing to use an application which, if and when it fails, will not be fixed by the supplier.

- **Regulatory and legal changes.** Companies such as banks are heavily regulated to avoid the risk that money is mishandled. When a bank is informed of a regulatory change that carries a legal penalty for failure to comply, it has little choice but to accommodate it in its systems and operating procedures. The only option may be when to adopt the change.

- **Year 2000 date change.** During the late 1990s, it became necessary to amend the way in which many computer systems recorded calendar dates. Since many systems held only the last two digits of the year, there was real concern that some computers would fail to differentiate between the year 2000 and the year 1900. The change initiative was not justified by the benefits it would bring. Instead, projects went ahead because they would mitigate the risk of not amending the date. Millions were spent worldwide to avoid planes crashing, sewage plants flooding and hospital equipment failing.

Selected option

The selected option is the one that provides the most compelling argument in its favour. The use of the word compelling is intentional. Although the heart of the business case is formed from a balance of costs and benefits, during the early days of a project much of the debate will be emotional. It is important to avoid becoming either too driven by the stark numbers, or too persuaded by the power of an eloquent but unsubstantiated argument. The words and numbers used to describe the selected option must compel the organisation to put in a calculated figure, to face certain risks and to foresee the likelihood of a return on the investment. The costs, risks and benefits subsections must be expressed robustly.

Selected option: risks

A risk is a possible future event that may have adverse consequences. The business case should identify the risks to a project as well as its benefits from the outset. Although the project outline may have contained a high-level risk assessment, the sponsor will have been focused on selling the idea, so this may be the first opportunity to consider the risks properly. An early example of the risk register might look like Table 9.2.

The risk register identifies things that may have an untoward effect on the project and the mitigations that may be possible.

Since the business case is, by definition, not a plan, it is not expected that the costs (in money or time) of mitigation will have been fully assessed. When the project manager starts to create the project plan, these risks (and any others identified) will be subjected to a fuller assessment to determine more precisely their effect on the time, cost and quality expectations of the project. However, a rudimentary assessment will be necessary if the cost of mitigation is likely to increase substantially the timescale or significantly affect the costs/net benefits of the project.

The risk assessment also allows the project's effect on others in

TABLE 9.2 **Example of a risk register**

Risk	Likelihood	Impact	Mitigations
Pre-written, packaged software solution will not hold key sales data needed by marketing team, resulting in their inability to work effectively	High	Medium	1 Continue to use existing sales and marketing system alongside new solution. 2 Request a specific change from software supplier.
If the live date is missed, legal sanctions may be taken against our business, resulting in reputational and other losses	Low	High	1 Make this project mandatory to ensure it has a priority call on essential resources. 2 Commence project early to allow for any slippage.

TABLE 9.3 **Benefits over time ($)**

	Year 0	Year 1	Year 2	Year 3	Year 4
Increased revenues		5,000	60,000	60,000	70,000
Increased customer satisfaction		5,000	10,000	10,000	10,000
Competitor removal			20,000	20,000	20,000
Customers from new market			30,000	30,000	40,000
Cost savings		8,000	10,000	11,000	11,000
Headcount savings		5,000	5,000	5,000	5,000
Removal of redundant IT kit		3,000	5,000	6,000	6,000
Total		13,000	70,000	71,000	81,000
Cumulative total		13,000	83,000	154,000	235,000

the portfolio to be seen. The second example in Table 9.2 shows how a choice made at this stage may affect the provision of resources to, or the duration of, other projects.

Selected option: benefits

This section should describe clearly each benefit in turn, including how they are to be measured and quantified in financial terms.

In preparation for the cost/benefit analysis, it is necessary to show the benefits over time (see Table 9.3).

TABLE 9.4 **Costs over time ($)**

	Year 0	Year 1	Year 2	Year 3	Year 4
Resources	1,300	12,250	16,820	12,600	19,850
Consumables				1,000	
Hardware			28,000		
Software			17,000		
Environmental				11,000	
Accommodation	500	1,200	1,200	1,200	1,200
Expenses	700	2,400	1,600	1,600	3,200
Total	**2,500**	**15,850**	**64,620**	**27,400**	**24,250**
Cumulative total	**2,500**	**18,350**	**82,970**	**110,370**	**134,620**

Selected option: costs

Every cost associated with the project should be identified so that it can be quantified. Costs should not be only those expected up to the point of project closure; they should also include the operational, maintenance and support of the deliverable the project is producing. There is a good reason for this. The benefits of a project are unlikely to be realised until some time after it has been closed, yet running costs will be incurred while waiting for those benefits. Consequently, they must be shown over the same time period for a realistic comparison of costs and benefits to be made.

Budgets may be needed in:

■ company personnel;
■ external contract staff;
■ consultants;

- hardware;
- software;
- licences;
- property;
- expenses (accommodation, travel, and so on);
- maintenance contracts;
- environment and operations.

To aid the cost/benefit analysis, the costs shown over time should be presented in the same form as the benefits (see Table 9.4).

Selected option: cost/benefit analysis

This will show whether the project is forecast to deliver a successful outcome and when. It provides a single view of the costs and benefits (see Table 9.5).

TABLE 9.5 **Costs and benefits ($)**

	Year 0	Year 1	Year 2	Year 3	Year 4
Benefits	0	13,000	70,000	71,000	81,000
Costs	2,500	15,850	64,620	27,400	24,250
Total	**–2,500**	**–2,850**	**5,380**	**43,600**	**56,750**
Cumulative	**–2,500**	**–5,350**	**30**	**43,630**	**100,380**

Payback will be achieved in year 2 but it may also be desirable to show the discounted cash flow (see Table 9.6).

If the project is part of a wider programme, it may be appropriate to include a financial dependency network to show the relationship between the different parts of the programme, and identify this specific project, like this example from Chapter 6 (Figure 9.2).

FIGURE 9.2 **Financial dependency network**

TABLE 9.6 **Discounted cash flow ($)**

	Year 0	Year 1	Year 2	Year 3	Year 4
Benefits	0.00	13,000.00	70,000.00	71,000.00	81,000.00
Costs	2,500.00	15,850.00	64,620.00	27,400.00	24,250.00
Net	−2,500.00	−2,850.00	5,380.00	43,600.00	56,750.00
Cumulative	−2,500.00	−5,350.00	30.00	43,630.00	100,380.00
Discount factor	1.00	0.94	0.89	0.84	0.79
Discounted net	−2,500.00	−2,688.68	4,788.18	36,607.40	44,951.32
Net present value	−2,500.00	−5,188.68	−400.50	36,206.90	81,158.22

Note: Figures have been rounded.

Selected option: deliverables and timescales

The business case has yet to describe what the project will deliver; so far, it is no more than a commercially focused response to a problem or an opportunity. This section presents a chance to describe what the project will produce during its initiation, delivery and closure stages, and when. This will give readers an early understanding of the project's outcome from a non-commercial perspective, identifying target dates by which key milestones should be met.

This is not a plan. A separate set of materials will be produced to describe how, if at all, these dates are to be met. Until the project plan is produced, the high-level deliverables and timescales listed here are only aspirations. However, unrefined as they may be, they are probably an improvement on what was included in the project outline and describe another important dimension of the management environment. Table 9.7 shows what this section may look like.

TABLE 9.7 **Deliverables and timescales**

Product	Target completion date	Status
Project outline	dd/mm/yy	Complete
Business case	dd/mm/yy	Under way
Project governance report	dd/mm/yy	
User requirements document	dd/mm/yy	
Solution design document	dd/mm/yy	
Developed solution	dd/mm/yy	
Tested solution	dd/mm/yy	
Approved solution	dd/mm/yy	
Project closure report	dd/mm/yy	
Lessons learned	dd/mm/yy	
Benefits realisation report	dd/mm/yy	

Selected option: planning assumptions

None of the numbers or dates in any of the examples in this chapter has been explained. There is no audit trail to describe how they were derived or calculated. Although it is dangerous to make assumptions, by its nature, planning is educated guesswork. Those considering the business case will wish to know how the numbers and dates quoted were arrived at, so a list of planning assumptions must be included that fully describes the calculations in the business case.

Example planning assumptions include the following:

Benefits
- "Redundant kit" has been valued on the basis of a saving on the monthly lease rate.
- "Competitor removal" has been valued on the basis that the company will gain 30 new clients per month when its closest competitor is removed.

Costs
- People participating in the project will work a standard eight-hour day.
- A flat cost rate has been applied to all internal resources.
- A flat cost rate plus a margin of 30% has been applied to all external resources.
- 20 days' holiday per person have been included.
- No activity is expected during the 14-day Christmas and New Year period.

Selected option: benefits realisation plan

This section describes how the intended benefits will be measured, tracked and delivered. This is discussed in detail in Chapter 13.

Selected option: management by objectives

The last section of the business case recognises that most people need some form of incentive to achieve demanding targets. The business case itself is a series of targets including dates, budgets and "profits", and those engaged in delivering the project may be encouraged if their remuneration is linked to its success.

It is not unusual for the project steering group, and the sponsor in particular, to have their personal reward packages linked to the project delivering payback on the planned date. However, the eventual profitability of the outcome is only partly in the project manager's control, so it is unusual to reward the project manager if the project achieves payback. Rather, project managers should be rewarded on their ability to manage change. They should be offered incentives to apply an effective change control process, maintain the plan against which changes will be measured and apply management by exception so that the right people take the right decisions at the right time.

The business case – a summary

The business case is the single most important document in the project, so it follows that it should be robust, clear and decisive in its recommendation. Yet despite the energy invested in creating it, the organisation may not be much nearer knowing how the targets identified in the business case are to be met. This is the purpose of the project governance report (which includes the all-important project plan). It, too, must be completed by the end of the initiation stage if the essential questions are to be answered before the project moves into the delivery stage.

The project governance report

As soon as the initiation stage has begun, questions will be asked about the project's future. The business case seeks to answer the question: Why is this project necessary? Four more questions must now be answered:

- Who will be involved in the management of the project?
- What will the project deliver?
- When will it deliver it?
- How much will it cost?

The answers are contained in the project governance report. As these challenging questions are posed, the project governance report gradually accommodates ever more detail about the emerging project. At the end of this stage, these questions must have been answered to the full satisfaction of the senior management team so that the portfolio management team can delegate responsibility to the project steering group.

Some organisations attempt to mandate the point at which development of the project governance report should begin. Although there will be many gaps in it at the beginning of the initiation stage, this is not necessarily a bad thing. The gaps demonstrate what remains

TABLE 9.8 **Project governance report**

Organisation	
Organisation chart	What are the reporting lines?
Roles and responsibilities	Who are the chosen incumbents and what are their responsibilities?
Communications plan	How will the project's stakeholders be engaged?

Project plan	

Quality plan
  – Deliverables
  – Responsibilities
  – Standards
	What must the project deliver?

Planning assumptions	What caveats have been attached to the plan?
Time schedule	When is the project intended to deliver its milestones?
Resource plan	What resources are to be used and when?
Risks	What are the possible challenges that the project may face, and what mitigations are proposed?
Project controls	How will the project be kept on track?
– Control cycle	What interventions have been planned?
– Escalation management	How will problems (real or forecast) be escalated?
– Change control	How will changes be considered?
– Configuration control	How will control be maintained over the project's products?
– Quality control	How will products be tested?
– Risk and issue management	How will risks and issues be managed?

unknown and thus what needs to be resolved before the project can move confidently into the delivery stage. So, in practice, the project governance report is best begun as soon as the project manager is in place. Even if the business case has yet to be completed, the project governance report is crucial and serves to remind everyone what questions remain to be answered.

Table 9.8 lists what should be included in the project governance report.

The success of the project governance report can be judged against these criteria:

■ Does it identify and describe the roles and responsibilities of those who will form the project's management team?

■ Does it show how time, cost and quality targets identified in the business case may be met?

■ Are the time, cost and quality components of the plan consistent with each other?

■ Does it describe how the project will be kept on track?

■ Does it enable a clear approval decision to be made?

Consequently, it should include the following components.

Organisation

Organisation chart

This should identify the roles in the project and the reporting lines between them. As people are identified for each role, their names should be placed clearly in the appropriate boxes. It can be all too easy to deny knowledge of involvement, so this demonstration of their participation is a further means of informing the people chosen, and others, of their role. Something similar to Figure 9.3 is required, replacing the question marks with the names of the participants.

Roles and responsibilities

A title can be misunderstood or misinterpreted, so for each role in the chart, the responsibilities must be described fully so that all incumbents are clear about what their own roles, and those of the others, entail.

Communications plan

First seen in Chapter 5 where the communications plan was used to engage different stakeholder communities in the leader's vision, the project communications plan follows the same format and can be used to describe:

■ what information must be communicated throughout the project and beyond;

■ who needs to receive this information;

■ what the communication format should be and who should develop or present it;

■ when it is needed.

FIGURE 9.3 **Organisation chart**

Within the context of an ongoing project, it focuses on those communications necessary to ensure that the project's stakeholders remain sufficiently engaged. Principally, this means maintaining suitable lines of communication with the project's management and delivery teams. However, analysis during earlier periods (such as when the vision was being articulated and promoted) may also have identified important stakeholders outside the immediate project environment, so the plan should accommodate their communication needs too.

FIGURE 9.4 **Communication plan table**

Information needs / Audience	Continued project viability	Suitability of management environment	Initial time, cost, quality, expectations	Current time, cost, quality targets	Notification report	Project	Implementation plan
PMT	A	B		E	H		
PSG	A		C	F	H		
PM		B	D	G	H		
Delivery teams			D	G		I	K
Customers						J	L
Developers						J	L

PMT = Portfolio management team
PSG = Project steering group
PM = Project manager

As noted in Chapter 5, a communication plan can be broken into two parts:

- a table, identifying the information needs and audiences;
- a list of communication types, with dates or frequencies, by which those audiences may obtain the information they need.

The table may look like the one in Figure 9.4. The letters (see Table 9.9) provide a key to the form of communication and when it should occur.

TABLE 9.9 **Key to communication table**

A	Business case will be updated and presented by the sponsor at each and every stage during the project
B	Project governance report will be developed and submitted during the initiation stage by the project manager to describe the project's management environment
C	The project plan component of the project governance report will be used to accommodate the project steering group's expectations of timescale, cost and quality
D	The project plan component of the project governance report will be used by the project manager to show delivery teams how expectations of time, cost and quality can be met
E	The project forecast report will be used by the project manager to communicate progress and issue a revised forecast every two months
F	The project forecast report will be used by the project manager to communicate progress and issue a revised forecast every month
G	The project forecast report will be used by the project manager to communicate progress and issue a revised forecast every week
H	A notification report will be produced immediately by the project manager if at any time the project is forecast to be completed outside the pre-agreed escalation conditions for time and budget
I	A project overview will be created as a slide show to be presented to the delivery team by the project manager at the end of the initiation stage. This presentation will be sent via e-mail to anyone joining the project after it has begun
J	A project overview will be created as a slide show to be presented to customer and developer stakeholders by the project steering group at the end of the initiation stage
K	A detailed implementation plan will be produced by the project manager early in the delivery stage to obtain the delivery team's commitment to the approach being taken
L	The implementation plan will be presented by the project manager as a slide show to customer and developer stakeholders to ensure they understand the implications for their business-as-usual activity during implementation

Project governance report – project plan

This is a living document that describes how the targets set in the business case can be met.

The project plan contained in the project governance report is a snapshot taken when the initiation stage is about to be completed. It is used by the project steering group to confirm that they are confident of the plan's forecasts of timescale, budget and quality and of taking control from the portfolio management team. This snapshot will be retained as a yardstick for measuring progress. It should never be altered because that would undermine the project manager's ability to manage change. Instead, a copy of the project plan is used to record progress and changes and to show what effect they have had on time, cost and quality expectations.

The project plan must spell out how these time, cost and quality expectations are to be met. It may also suggest at any point in the project's life cycle that they cannot be met. In either case, the project plan provides the evidence. It supports debate between the project steering group and the project manager and helps to prevent the project being driven by emotion alone.

The project plan is based on four components:

- quality management and deliverables;
- costs (resources and budgets);
- timescales;
- controls.

Quality plan

This describes how the end product will be developed and delivered to an acceptable standard, on time and to budget.

Quality plan: deliverables

This section must describe the project's deliverables. This means not merely the specified end product, such as a building, a computer

FIGURE 9.5 **Product breakdown structure for fitting out and marketing a new factory**

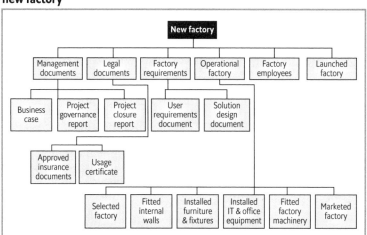

system or a set of working practices, but also all other deliverables that must be produced throughout the life of the project and that lead to that specified end product. This is one way of describing the scope of the project and the product breakdown structure from Chapter 7 (reproduced here as Figure 9.5) helps to illustrate it.

Each deliverable must be described so that those investing in the project can see what they will get for their investment. This is best described through product descriptions. However, since there may be many of them, they can be put in an appendix, or better still, included in the main document but tabulated to make them more palatable (see Table 9.10).

This section can also benefit from showing the order in which the deliverables must be produced. Although this will not include a timescale, it will show the internal and external dependencies in the project. This is best shown as the product flow diagram developed in Chapter 7 and reproduced here as Figure 9.6.

Quality plan: responsibilities

This section describes who will be responsible for which aspects of quality management within the project. It is not a regurgitation of the

TABLE 9.10 **Product deliverables**

Title	Purpose	Composition	Quality criteria
Project outline	To describe the idea of the project such that a decision may be made to fund the initiation stage	Sponsor Title Objective Benefits Scope Key products Timescale Investment Investment needed for next stage Planning assumptions Risks	Does the document provide sufficient information from which to make a funding decision? Have the benefits been quantified in commercial terms? Are the expressions of timescale and cost consistent with each other? Are the estimates quoted each supported by planning assumptions? Has a specific figure been included for the funding needed for the next stage?
Business case	To confirm the commercial viability of the project so that a go/no-go decision may be made to fund its continuation	Opportunity or problem Strategic fit Interdependencies Success criteria Options considered Selected option – Risks – Benefits – Costs – Cost/benefit analysis – Deliverables and timescales – Planning assumptions – Benefits realisation plan – Management by objectives	Does the document provide sufficient information from which to make a go/no-go decision? Has the margin between the costs and benefits been explicitly identified? Have all calculations been subjected to discounted cash flow analysis? Are all success criteria measurable? Has it been made clear why options have been discounted? Have all risks been evaluated for likelihood and effect? Are the estimates quoted each supported by planning assumptions? Is there clear evidence to support the chosen option?

Title	Purpose	Composition	Quality criteria
Project governance report	To describe the management environment of the project such that it may be managed to a planned conclusion	Organisation – Organisation chart – Roles and responsibilities – Communications plan Project plan – Quality plan – Deliverables – Responsibilities – Standards – Planning assumptions – Time schedule – Resource plan – Risks Project controls – Control cycle – Escalation management – Change control – Configuration control – Quality control – Risk and issue management	Does the document clearly show whether and how the targets for time, cost and quality set in the business case can be met? Are all risks supported by a mitigation plan? Have all risk mitigations been assessed for their effect on the plan? Have all key deliverables been described by means of a product description? Are all incumbents identified in the organisation section aware of their responsibilities? Are the plans for time, cost and quality consistent with each other? Are the project controls adequate for the type, size and criticality of project?

roles and responsibilities section but specifically identifies the things that named individuals must do to ensure that quality is:

- specified;
- planned;
- built;
- tested;
- accepted.

Consequently, this section may contain statements such as the following:

- The project steering group will agree a set of success criteria from which all expressions of quality will be derived.

FIGURE 9.6 **Product flow diagram**

- The sponsor will approve time, cost and benefit expectations throughout the project.

- The customer representative will approve the user requirements document on behalf of all end users of the key deliverable.

- The development team representative will approve the solution design document on behalf of the development team(s).

- The project manager will make sure that all key deliverables have been defined in a product description.

- The project steering group will approve all product descriptions before development work starts.

- The project manager will co-ordinate activity according to the plan, taking account of all quality standards to be applied.

- The project manager will make sure that all key deliverables are tested against their quality criteria and according to the method identified in the product description.

- The project steering group will approve all key deliverables once evidence of a satisfactory quality review has been established.

- The customer and developer representatives will decide how many levels of testing are desirable.

- The project manager will accommodate the desired level of testing in the project plan.

- The developer representative will approve the completion of all specialist testing.

- The customer representative will approve the completion of user acceptance testing.

- The project steering group will approve the completion of the project and the release of its deliverable into the operational environment.

Quality plan: standards

In any project, there may be prescribed standards that must be met. These may include documentary or procedural standards for:

- specifying the output;

- designing the output;
- building the output;
- testing the output;
- operating the output;
- managing the project.

This section must describe the standards that must be met for this project.

TABLE 9.11 **Sample estimating sheet**

Product	Tasks	Resources	Cost	Assumptions
Product 1	Develop	PR	0.8	PR took this long on previous project
	Review	ST/MW	0.5/0.5	Constrained to half-day as slot for teleconference is already booked
	Amend	PR	0.25	PR took this long on previous project
	Approve	PSG	0.1	Assuming PSG will approve via e-mail
Product 2	Develop	AK	0.5	Based on 0.1 per item x 4 items, plus contingency of 0.1
	Review	PR/MW	0.1/0.1	Estimate based on MW experience
	Amend	AK	0.25	Based on need to rework half original
	Approve	PSG	0.1	Assuming PSG will approve via e-mail
Product 3	Develop	PR	0.8	PR took this long on previous project
	Review	ST/MW	0.5/0.5	Constrained to half-day as slot for teleconference is already booked
	Amend	PR	0.25	Assuming quarter of product to be reworked, plus contingency
	Approve	PSG	0.1	Assuming PSG will approve via e-mail
Product 4	Develop	AK	0.8	AK estimate based on experience
		Train fare	$100	Costs to visit trade show
	Review	ST/MW	0.25/0.25	ST estimate based on experience
	Amend	AK	0.25	Assuming quarter of product to be reworked, plus contingency
	Approve	PSG	0.1	Assuming PSG will approve via e-mail

Note: Costs are in person-days when not monetary.

FIGURE 9.7 **Gantt chart based on Table 8.1**

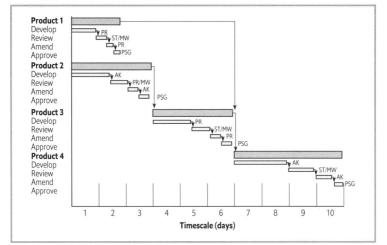

Planning assumptions

Any planning assumptions made should be listed here. The estimating sheet compiled in Chapter 8 and reproduced here as Table 9.11 may also be included.

Time schedule

This should not be regarded exclusively as a project plan because it does not show how cost or quality expectations will be met. A Gantt chart like the one in Chapter 8 and reproduced here as Figure 9.7 may be used in this section.

An alternative form of graphic can be used to show the project's timing. For instance, the product flow diagram can be adapted to show some of the same information as the Gantt chart (see Figure 9.8).

Resource plan

This shows how and when the project is likely to incur its costs. Here reproduced as Table 9.12 is an example from Chapter 8.

FIGURE 9.8 **Product flow chart**

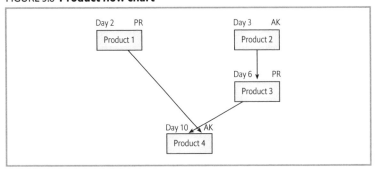

TABLE 9.12 **Resource plan with financial information**

Human	Day 1	Day 2	Day 3	Day 4	Day 5	Day 6	Day 7	Day 8	Day 9	Day 10	Total
PR	0.80	0.35		0.80		0.25					2.20
$300/d	$240	$105		$240		$75					$660
ST		0.50			0.50				0.25		1.25
$200/d		$100			$100				$50		$250
MW		0.60			0.50				0.25		1.35
$200/d		$120			$100				$50		$270
AK	0.50	0.50	0.25				0.80			0.25	2.30
$200/d	$100	$100	$50				$160			$50	$460
PSG		0.10	0.10			0.10				0.10	0.40
$400/d		$40	$40			$40				$40	$160
Total human	**1.30**	**2.05**	**0.35**	**0.80**	**1.00**	**0.35**	**0.80**		**0.50**	**0.35**	**7.50**
	$340	**$465**	**$90**	**$240**	**$200**	**$115**	**$160**		**$100**	**$90**	**$1,800**
Non-human travel							$100				$100
Total	$340	$465	$90	$240	$200	$115	**$260**		$100	$90	$1,900

Risks

This section should further develop the risks identified in the project outline and the business case. The risk register presented in Chapter 6 and reproduced here as Table 9.13 should be included.

TABLE 9.13 **The risk register**

Risk	Likeli-hood	Impact	Factor	Mitigations	Cost
Pre-written, packaged software solution will not hold key sales data needed by marketing team, resulting in their inability to work effectively	10	3	30	**1** Continue to use existing sales and marketing system alongside new solution. ACTION: JP to advise sales team to prepare for parallel running.	2 days per month to synchronise systems = $800
				2 Request a specific change from software supplier. ACTION: PT to obtain detailed quotation from supplier.	15 days' additional fees = $6,000
If the live date is missed, legal sanctions may be taken against our business, resulting in damage to reputation and other losses	2	11	22	**1** Identify this project as mandatory to make sure that it has priority over essential resources. ACTION: Sponsor to raise at next portfolio management team session.	Portfolio management team to consider effect on other projects
				2 Commence project early to allow for any slippage. ACTION: Sponsor to raise at next portfolio management team session.	Portfolio management team to consider effect on other projects

Risk	Likeli-hood	Impact	Factor	Mitigations	Cost
Based on supplier's past performance, delivery of equipment required for implementation will be delayed, resulting in delivery delay to client	6	9	54	**1** Identify an alternative supplier. ACTION: SS to ask Procurement for recommendation. **2** Instigate a penalty/ reward clause in the contract ACTION: JP to ask legal department for guidance.	$10,000 premium $5,000 reward provision
Key people from the legal department will be unavailable during the summer because of their engagement in other projects, resulting in an inability to make critical purchase decisions	6	9	54	**1** Secure the services of an external legal representative. ACTION: Ask legal department for a recommendation. **2** Obtain portfolio management team's authority to use legal team in precedence over other projects during the summer. ACTION: Sponsor to raise at next portfolio management team session.	$1,500 premium
Total risk-based contingency budget					Maximum $23,300

Project controls

Clear controls are needed to describe how the project will be kept on track so that it stands a greater likelihood of meeting its stakeholders' expectations. The project controls section describes the following measures.

Project controls: meetings and reporting

This section describes the way in which various control mechanisms will be used to make sure that progress and forecast information is

TABLE 9.14 **Meetings and reporting**

Control	Participants	Timing	Input	Output
Project initiation meeting	PMT, PSG, PM	At end of initiation stage	Agenda, business case, project governance report, user requirements document, solution design document, next stage plan	Record of actions and decisions, including approval to continue
Team meeting	PM, team leaders	Every week	Agenda, timesheets or records of progress, draft project forecast report	Record of actions and decisions, project forecast report
Scheduled project steering group meeting	PSG, PM	Just before end of each stage	Agenda, business case, updated project plan, next stage plan	Record of actions and decisions, including approval to continue
Unscheduled project steering group meeting	PSG, PM	Exceptional circumstances	Agenda, business case, notification report, revised project plan, revised stage plan	Record of actions and decisions, including approval to continue
Project closure meeting	PSG, PM	At end of closure stage	Agenda, business case, project closure report	Record of actions and decisions, including approval to close project
Lessons learned review	Varies	After closure stage	Agenda, project closure report	Lessons learned report, action plan
Benefits realisation review	PMT, PSG Sponsor	As described in business case	Agenda, draft benefits realisation report	Record of actions and decisions, benefits realisation report

clearly communicated and that corrective action can be taken when necessary.

Although the communications plan will have identified that some meetings and reports will be necessary, this section must describe how they will keep the project on track.

It is usual for the section to include a table (see Table 9.14).

Project controls: escalation management

This section describes what constitutes a significant issue and what actions should be taken if one arises. Escalation conditions for time, cost and benefits margin should be described.

Escalation conditions

The project steering group will be subject to the following escalation conditions:

- Time   +/− 4 weeks
- Cost   +/− 50,000
- Margin +/− 100,000

If a breach of these escalation conditions is forecast, the project steering group must immediately alert the portfolio management team and present a notification report on which corrective decisions will be based.

The project manager will be subject to the following escalation conditions:

- Time +/− 2 weeks
- Cost +/− 20,000

If a breach of these escalation conditions is forecast, the project manager must immediately alert the project steering group and present a notification report on which corrective decisions will be based.

The team leaders will be subject to the following escalation conditions:

- Time +/− 1 week
- Cost +/− 5,000

If a breach of these escalation conditions is forecast, the team leader must immediately alert the project manager and present an action plan on which corrective decisions will be based.

The notification report should describe:

- the circumstances that have caused the project to be forecast being outside the agreed escalation conditions;
- options to address the variance;
- the effect of each option on the project plan/business case;
- the preferred option.

Change control

Baseline

The basis on which any requests for changes to requirements or functionality will be assessed are the following documents:

- Business case v1.0
- Project governance report v1.0
- User requirements document v1.0
- Solution design document v1.0

Contingency

A contingency fund has been identified as follows:

Risk mitigation	23,300[a]
Change management	1,000[b]
Approved changes	52,000[c]
Total	**76,300**

a Identified from the risk register.
b Based on 3 person-days needed to assess the effect of any changes during the life of the project.
c Based on an assessment of the changes applied to previous, similar projects.

Process

Should anyone consider a change to the baseline (described above) is needed, the matter will be subject to this change management process. Any item raised in this way will be referred to as a change request. Problems that have arisen will be treated in the same way. New and existing change requests will be reviewed at the weekly meeting between the project manager and the team leaders.

These four steps will be taken, using the organisation's standard pro-forma for identification, assessment, effect and conclusion:

- Change request identification. A change request may be identified by anyone inside or outside the project.
- Change request analysis. The change request will be described fully by the person who has raised it. If further supporting information is needed, this may be provided by a developer, a customer and/or the project manager.

- Change request impact assessment. The change request will be measured against the baseline to decide whether or not it represents a deviation. The contingency change management fund will pay for the necessary assessment.
- Conclusion and decision. The conclusion must clearly and unequivocally state whether:
    - the change request is a deviation from the baseline;
    - its inclusion would take the project outside the escalation conditions.

If the change request is considered worthy of inclusion and can be accommodated within the agreed escalation conditions and approved changes to contingency funds, the project manager can approve the change.

If the change request is considered to be worthy of inclusion but causes the project to be forecast to be completed outside the agreed escalation conditions, the project steering group can approve the change, drawing on the approved changes contingency fund.

If the change request is considered to be worthy of inclusion and falls outside the project steering group's escalation conditions, it must be referred to the portfolio management team.

Responsibilities

This change management process will be facilitated by the project manager. All other responsibilities are identified above.

Project controls: change control

This section describes how changes will be dealt with if and when they arise (see section on page 229).

Project controls: configuration control

This section describes how the project will maintain control of the products it creates. These questions are a guide to what should be included:

- Which products are to be subject to control?
- Who owns them?

- Where will the products be held?
- How will back-ups be taken?
- How will security be ensured?
- How will the products be distributed and redistributed?
- How will versions be controlled?
- Which version will constitute the baseline?
- How will checks be made to make sure that all products are where they should be?

Project controls: quality control

This section describes the tests that will be conducted to increase the likelihood of delivering an output that meets expectations. It can be broken into two:

- **Product quality tests.** This section will describe any special tests to be conducted on particular products. For instance, the solution design document may need a formal review by the solution design committee to make sure it conforms to the organisation's strategic objectives. The form of special tests should also be described more fully. For example, the formal quality review process may be outlined so that senior managers know its depth and value before committing the money necessary to fund it.
- **Project quality tests.** This section describes tests that will be conducted at stages on large projects or ones that involve many products. For instance, a new computer system may undergo system testing, operational acceptance testing and user acceptance testing. The approach to such tests should be described and the project steering group given the opportunity to decide whether they are prepared to allow the time and money needed to accommodate these quality controls.

Project controls: risk and issue management

This section describes how risks and issues will be managed. It must adequately describe:

- how risks and issues will be identified and prioritised;
- the criteria for assigning ownership;
- how mitigating actions will be planned;
- how progress will be monitored and controlled;
- the process by which contingency funds may be drawn.

The user requirements document

This is used to describe the customer needs that the project's output must satisfy. Its content will depend on the nature of the project. If the project has to deliver a computer system, it may contain a list of functional and non-functional requirements. If the project is to deliver a new office building, the document should describe graphically the user's vision.

Whatever form it takes, it must provide an adequate means for the project's customers to set out what they want so that their expectations can be met.

The solution design document

This is used to describe how the needs of the users are to be met. It too will depend on the nature of the project. This document might describe the design of a computer system or it could be an architect's blueprint. Whatever form it takes, it must provide an adequate means for the developers to describe the solution so that it is based on a sound design.

Risk and issue management

Risk and issue identification

Risks will be identified first during the creation of the project outline. An initial risk identification meeting will be held during the initiation stage. The results will be included in both the emerging business case and project governance report as a risk register.

Issues may be identified at any time and by anyone. They will be documented and processed in the same way as a change request.

Risk owners

Risks will be ranked according to their risk factor (see page 146). Those with a factor of 110 will be assigned automatically to the portfolio management team; those with a factor between 57 and 90 will be assigned to the project steering group; those with a factor between 21 and 56 will be assigned to the project manager; and those with a factor of 20 or below will be assigned to the project team.

Risk mitigation

Mitigations will be identified for every risk. Mitigations will be assessed for their potential cost in terms of money and/or time. The summary of all mitigation costs will be included in the contingency budget (see the section on change control).

Risk management

The risk register will be reappraised at every project controls management meeting. The reappraisal will:

- identify new risks/issues;
- reassess existing risks/issues.

Use of contingency funds

The contingency budget may be drawn upon to mitigate risks, provided those risks have had a contingency sum set aside for mitigation.

The importance of the initiation stage

The initiation stage has the potential to set the foundations for the successful delivery and closure of the project. Despite the governance described above, it may feel chaotic because the project is in the early stages of formation and no amount of due process will ever replace the importance of allowing people to express their views. Nevertheless, it is essential that the success criteria are established by the end of this stage if the project is to have any chance of being successfully steered through its remaining stages.

Project delivery

DELIVERY IS THAT STAGE in the life of a project in which the deliverables are built, tested, approved and released for use. In addition to the more commonly understood deliverables from a project, such as a new product, service or system, the project must also produce informed and enabled communities of people who are to use and operate them. So the delivery stage must succeed not only in preparing the solution for the organisation, but also in preparing the organisation for the solution.

It is to be hoped that during the periods of planning described in previous chapters, thought will have been given to the education of affected communities so that they may begin to understand and demonstrate the new behaviours from which truly successful change will follow.

Before the deliverable is released, it is important that the community of users has been given sufficient opportunity to know as much about it as possible. This reduces the risk that something will impede their adoption of it. Furthermore, since the project is in an active state, the machinery of management may be used to address any misunderstandings or misuse which arise when the project's product is first encountered by the people who are to inherit it.

Preparing the organisation for the solution

It is common to assume that education is achieved through training. However, this is not the only way to encourage confidence and new capabilities. Education can foster empowerment and participation in the change, so that when the time comes to adopt a new set of behaviours, there is already less resistance. Thought of in this way, an educated stakeholder community may be created through a variety of ways.

Shared insight of future state

This can serve to encourage understanding and acceptance of the vision. As described in Chapter 5, exposure to the leadership's vision can be a powerful way of ensuring a more intimate understanding of why the change is necessary. This complements the emergence of knowing how the change is to be achieved. For example, in presenting the vision of a new organisational structure to a team of managers, they can begin to form in their own minds the manner in which it may be made to work.

A role in the change programme

This demonstrates a commitment to the stakeholders in question, and draws on their capabilities. As described in Chapter 4, a commitment to change may first develop through a role in the project. With the intention that this leads to a workforce that is better informed about the project's deliverable, this commitment may be fostered by the project's senior-most users and specialists, both of whom may find themselves and their representatives becoming accountable for its eventual use and operation. If, during the life of the project so far, they have both had the opportunity to participate to design, build and test the project's product, then they will likely have gained a reasonable working knowledge of it, which they can pass on to others.

Stated "minimum standards"

The vision is expressed as a set of norms that will become second nature to the organisation and against which future performance may be judged. A minimum standard is a straightforward set of statements that define – and remind everyone – what the desired behaviours or values look like. If these can have been described as soon as possible in the project's life cycle – and certainly before its closure – there is the opportunity to foster the organisation's familiarity with them. For example, when seeking to implement a more methodical approach to project management, it may be helpful to state simply what standard must be met. A clearer statement of "what good project management looks like" will help to ensure that the workforce shares a common understanding of what to expect. In addition to setting out a framework for education, a minimum standard can:

- provide a target to help direct the implementation of new behaviours;
- serve as a yardstick against which performance may be judged;
- communicate and promote a common language;
- engage those who may not normally participate in the immediate area of interest.

Training

People are provided with the skills and knowledge they will need to participate in the new way of doing things. As noted earlier, this is one of the more commonly used educational methods, and one of the most expensive. When considering whether or how to train a workforce in new ways of working, there are several further considerations, such as whether the training is required to impart new knowledge or skills or both, or whether it must result in a commitment to new behaviours and values. Considering such questions will help to determine the form of training required. For example, if behaviour needs to change it may be necessary to engage trainees in face-to-face training, possibly over a long or intense period. If, alternatively, trainees just need to be able to use a new computer system, short modules of computer-based training may suffice. Such conclusions may be considered and captured in a training needs analysis, an example of which is contained in Chapter 14.

Educational materials

This provides a permanent record of what skills, knowledge and procedures are required to operate the project's key deliverable, such as a computer system or a piece of equipment. These may complement the training noted above, and may include books, videos and handouts.

Beta releases

Features of the change are previewed, exposing them to discrete groups and key users. Such people may not only test the release's suitability, but commence its promotion to the wider community, hastening and encouraging their education.

Iterative development

The project provides frequent and periodic releases of new features or functionality. As noted elsewhere, this has the advantage of providing stakeholder communities with the means to learn about the changes more gradually, learning through an evolutionary rather than revolutionary manner.

Leadership coaching

This helps to ensure that those to whom others report are aware of their responsibilities in the change programme, have the capabilities required, and feel sufficiently confident to promote the change to others. On the surface, this may appear similar to training, described above. However, it is helpful to take account of the nature of an audience that may feel that training is inappropriate for senior members of the organisation. One-to-one leadership coaching or briefing sessions may require a larger investment of time and money. However, if successfully persuaded, a single member of the leadership team may in turn be able to change the behaviours of many more – and do so by example.

User journeys

It is helpful to understand the change from the perspective of those who will be directly affected by it. When articulated, a user journey can help to describe the experience of undertaking a role. While useful as an educational tool to the incumbents themselves, this can be especially helpful to those members of the project team who are responsible for designing and implementing new ways of working. In creating a user journey, the new role (or the revised experience of it) may be challenged without the difficulty and expense of having already implemented it. For example, it is common to describe how a customer's journey may change as a result of implementing a new procedure. Without doing so, it will not be possible to anticipate or appreciate the customer's reaction to change when it is eventually introduced.

Mentoring and role modelling

This can help employees understand new roles and behaviours that they may be required to adopt. If a role is to change substantially it may be helpful for the present incumbents to practise it. For example, a "model office" may be created to allow customers, suppliers and members of the workforce to see or try new or revised roles in an environment that appears life-like. Alternatively, people may be invited to work with a mentor or buddy who can demonstrate new practices and behaviours.

Owning problems and solutions

During the delivery stage, there is the opportunity to engage the powers of creativity and innovation that exist within the leadership team and the wider workforce, and encourage the shared ownership of issues and opportunities that must be addressed. As long as the project remains in place wider communities will look to it to address every challenge or barrier which arises. This is both a problem and an opportunity. It is a difficulty so long as accountability for fixing any implementation issues is seen to belong to anyone other than those who are ultimately to use or operate the solution. It is an opportunity if this period can be used by the project to progressively hand over more of the use and operation of the emerging deliverables to the business-as-usual environment that will eventually own it. For example, where a new computer system is to be developed it will be helpful for the project to fully engage the existing help desk in the administration and management of user acceptance, training and frequently asked questions. In this way the help desk will be more ready, willing and able to adopt new behaviours when the system is eventually released.

Preparing the solution for the organisation

In all likelihood the project will have been planned to deliver a combination of products. These will include those that are to be used

FIGURE 10.1 **The control cycle**

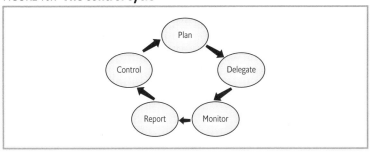

or adopted when the project has completed and – as noted above – the educated communities who are to use them. Whatever it is that the project has been initiated to deliver, its managers must make sure it remains on track. The control cycle illustrated in Figure 10.1 is no different from that applied to business-as-usual.

As the plan reveals what needs to be done and by whom, the work must be delegated. As the work is carried out, the management team must continue to know how well the team is performing and whether the project is forecast to deliver according to the time, cost, quality and benefit expectations. Usually, having monitored these elements, some reports are produced to record the findings. They are circulated not merely for information, but to ensure that, where necessary, corrective action is taken to bring the project back on track. Only on completion of the control step can the plan be updated with the actions taken so that the cycle can be repeated.

Anyone who has to manage an aspect of the project should know this cycle and follow it to keep control of the work for which they are responsible.

One feature that ensures the cycle works effectively is the way it depends on escalation management. Projects quickly descend into chaos without rules governing who is authorised to make which decision, so there must be a way of determining who has control of the project at any time. The concept and practice of escalation management was described earlier.

Plan

The plan provides the road map that describes how the project will achieve its targets. It identifies the deliverables that must be produced and shows to whom the work will be delegated.

Delegate

The portfolio management team delegate responsibility to the project steering group for delivering a commercially or strategically beneficial outcome. The project steering group delegate responsibility to the project manager for delivering the products on time, on budget and to specification. In turn, the project manager will usually have to delegate most of the responsibility for developing those products to the teams working on the project.

When delegating any form of work, care must be taken not merely to describe what is required, but also the constraints within which the work must be carried out. The relationship between the delegator and the delegatee depends on knowing both what must be delivered and the degree of authority within which the delegatee may operate. Therefore, whenever work is delegated, the agreement (formal or informal) must take account of both aspects.

Both parties must agree on the following:

■ Product description – to describe what is expected from the delegatee.

■ Planned start/finish date – to ensure that the work does not commence until a specified date and when it must be finished.

■ Planned effort/cost – to clarify what is involved in developing the product and how much budget is available.

■ Dependencies – to ensure that the delegatee is aware of who and what else is dependent on the product(s) to be delivered, and what will be required to produce them (a product flow diagram is helpful here).

■ Prerequisite products – to allow the delegatee access to previously developed products which may be needed to develop a required new product (for instance, to develop a course definition document, the developer will need the "gathered requirements").

This list focuses on the outcome expected from the delegatee. However, as the delegator remains accountable for the success or failure of the work being undertaken, care must be taken to agree a further set of terms that describe how the delegated work will be controlled:

- Timesheet code – to allow the delegatee to charge hours or costs to the appropriate project account so the delegator can monitor spending.

- Skills/experience required – to make sure the delegatee sufficiently understands the competencies required by the individual(s) who are to do the work (for instance, it may have been specified that the work could be suitable for a trainee).

- Roles – to explicitly describe the responsibilities of each party so that there is no confusion about who is accountable for the work. The delegator remains accountable despite having given some limited authority to the delegatee.

- Reporting arrangements – to make clear when and how the delegator and delegatee will monitor and report progress.

- Escalation conditions – to make sure that the delegatee knows the terms for escalation as soon as any risk to the timescale or budget is identified, thus enabling the delegator to intervene well in advance of the targets being breached.

- Techniques, processes, procedures – to describe any approaches or standards to which the delegatee should conform.

Some projects require a structured approach to delegation, particularly where external suppliers are to do some of the work. In such cases, the arrangement between the delegator (the client) and the delegatee (the supplier) should be set out in the contractual terms of reference and cover the points identified above. Even when not using external suppliers, many organisations use terms of reference to describe the relationship and commitments between client and supplier departments. In large companies especially, these enable project managers to monitor and control the packets of work for which they remain accountable.

Monitor and report

Monitoring is the observation and supervision those in the management team must do to know the condition of their projects. It is not easy to monitor a project or portfolio without a report. Each level in the management hierarchy will need information in a form and at a frequency that will allow the exercising of control without encroaching on the responsibilities of other levels. The worst that can happen is that all levels of management become involved in every corrective decision.

It is also critical that such reports show the extent to which the project is likely to meet its completion expectations, taking account of any revision to those set out in the original project plan.

The reports must be designed to satisfy the need of each tier of management for the timely and accurate information necessary for decision-making or corrective action.

Portfolio management team

The portfolio management team oversees the wider portfolio of projects. As the portfolio progresses through the year, individual projects will be completed, new projects will be proposed and others will slip or vary in some way. The portfolio management team is ultimately responsible for the state of its portfolio, so the team must meet regularly to evaluate the portfolio's health and answer the question: Is the portfolio on track to deliver its commercial and strategic imperatives?

It is normal for a portfolio management team to meet every month, but also to have a process in place for dealing with exceptional matters at short notice. The regular meeting should have a standard agenda that takes into account the following:

- **Prospects** – where project outlines will have been submitted, suggesting a potential but as yet unproven opportunity. The portfolio management team must decide whether there is sufficient budget to fund the initiation stage in which the business case and project governance report would be developed.
- **Initiated projects** – where newly completed business cases and project governance reports are considered to determine whether

the project should continue into the delivery phase, and that the identified project steering group can adopt ownership.

- **Notifications** – where red flags (signalling that the project is likely to breach a key parameter) have been raised.

- **Completions** – where projects have closed but have not yet delivered any benefits.

- **Realisations** – where benefits realisation reports have been submitted to determine the extent to which completed projects have delivered the intended benefits.

Reports from a project register should be used at these meetings so that the state of the portfolio is known at any time. Such a report might look like the one in Table 10.1, although there is no recognised standard.

The essential data are as follows:

Background
- ID – the project's identifying code.
- Last assessment date – when the project was last subject to a health check or audit.
- Assessor – who undertook the health check.
- Project start date – when the project was started formally.

Stakeholders
- Sponsor – the person charged with delivering a commercially successful outcome.
- Customer representative(s) – the people charged with authorising the definition and acceptance of the project's output from a user's perspective.
- Developer representative(s) – the people charged with authorising the design and development of a robust and reliable solution that will meet the user's needs.
- Project manager – the person charged with planning, monitoring and controlling the delivery of milestones to time, cost and quality expectations.

TABLE 10.1 **Project register**

	Project	First project	Second project
Background	ID	1	2
	Last assessment date	Jan 12th	
	Assessor	Pete Robbins	Maggie Jones
	Project start date	Dec 10th	Sep 10th
PSG	Sponsor	Brad Somerville	Mark Knowles
	Customer representative(s)	Kevin Quinn	Helen Smith
	Developer representative(s)	Mark Johnson	Bupinda Patel
PM	Project manager	Will Stevens	Harry King
Time	Baseline end date	May 31st	Jun 10th
	Forecast end date	May 31st	Sep 30th
	Variance (weeks)	0	−16
	Escalation conditions (weeks)	2	2
	Within escalation conditions?	Yes	No
Cost	Baseline budget	$2,026,971	$101,923
	Forecast budget	$2,026,971	$115,000
	Variance	$0	−$13,077
	Escalation conditions %	10	10
	Within escalation conditions?	Yes	No
Benefits	Baseline benefits	$2,703,836	$200,101
	Forecast benefits	$2,703,836	$200,101
	Variance	$0	$0
	Escalation conditions %	10	10
	Within escalation conditions?	Yes	Yes
Business case	Baseline profit	$676,865	$98,178
	Forecast profit	$676,865	$85,101
	Variance	$0	−$13,077
	Escalation conditions %	10	10
	Within escalation conditions?	Yes	No

Time
- Baseline end date – when the project will end as stated in the project governance report.
- Forecast end date – when the project will end as identified in the current project plan, taking account of any actual or forecast variances.
- Variance (weeks) – the difference between the baseline end date and the forecast end date.
- Escalation conditions (weeks) – the amount against which variance is compared to determine whether it should be referred to the portfolio management team.
- Within escalation conditions? – a yes/no response.

Budget
- Baseline budget – the project's intended budget as stated in the project governance report.
- Forecast budget – the project's budget as identified in the current project plan, taking account of any actual or forecast variances.
- Variance – the difference between the baseline budget and the forecast budget.
- Escalation conditions % – the amount against which variance is compared to determine whether it should be referred to the portfolio management team.
- Within escalation conditions? – a yes/no response.

Benefits
- Baseline benefits – the project's intended benefits as stated in the business case.
- Forecast benefits – the project's benefits as currently envisaged, taking account of any actual or forecast variances.
- Variance – the difference between the baseline benefits and the forecast benefits.

- Escalation conditions % – the amount against which variance is compared to determine whether it should be referred to the portfolio management team.
- Within escalation conditions? – a yes/no response.

Business case
- Baseline profit – the project's intended profit (the difference between project/operational costs and benefits over a defined period) as agreed in the business case.
- Forecast profit – the profit as identified in the current business case, taking account of any actual or forecast variances of costs and/or benefits.
- Variance – the difference between the baseline profit and the forecast profit.
- Escalation conditions % – the amount against which variance is compared to determine whether it should be referred to the portfolio management team.
- Within escalation conditions? – a yes/no response.

Table 10.1 shows that project 1 seems in good condition with no variances, but project 2 is forecasting variances for both time and cost that will breach the escalation conditions. Although the benefits remain unchanged, the forecast variance for the forecast budget indicates that the intended profit may not be achievable. These multiple forecast variances provide the portfolio management team with the alerts they need to intervene.

The detail in the project register can be summarised further for those organisations undertaking several projects at the same time, giving the portfolio management team an overview of the portfolio on a "corporate dashboard" (see Figure 10.2). It is essential, however, that any report clearly indicates where and what corrective action must be taken. Thus the corporate dashboard also indicates where escalation conditions have been breached so that further detail can be obtained from the project register.

This view has the added advantage of showing how the portfolio is contributing to the organisation's strategic imperatives. The bar

FIGURE 10.2 **A corporate dashboard**

Project costs	Baseline budget	$2,128,894	No. of projects	2
	Forecast budget	$2,141,971	Breaching TIME escalation conditions	1
	Variance	–£13,077	Breaching COST escalation conditions	1
Project benefits	Baseline benefits	$2,903,937	Breaching BENEFIT escalation conditions	0
	Forecast benefits	$2,903,937	Breaching PROFIT escalation conditions	1
	Variance	$0		
Business case	Baseline profit	$775,043		
	Forecast profit	$761,966		
	Variance	–$13,077		

chart in Figure 10.3 illustrates how the projects measure up to the balanced scorecard of targets. The vertical axis identifies the percentage contribution being made by the sum of all projects to each of the four parts of the balanced scorecard. Therefore, the four bars should add up to 100. Ideally, they will be balanced, demonstrating that the projects are contributing evenly across the four measures. In the example, a greater proportion of projects are focused on the financial quartile. Although this is not a particular problem, success may be at the expense of investment in developing customer satisfaction, processes and intellectual growth. This portfolio contribution is usually considered quarterly.

FIGURE 10.3 **Business balance**

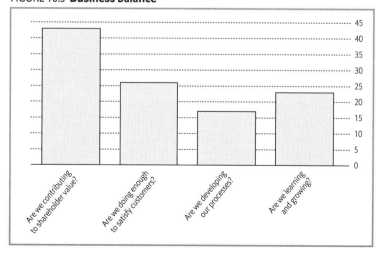

Project steering group

Each project steering group directs an individual project. To do so, it needs a control cycle that regularly tells its participants the status of the project. The project steering group members must also be able to assure themselves that if something exceptional happens to breach the forecast targets, the project manager will alert them immediately.

To maintain a level of control that both supports and gives the project manager his own degree of authority, the project steering group can intervene through:

- project initiation and closure;
- holding meetings at the different stages of the project;
- holding unscheduled meetings;
- holding scheduled meetings;
- project forecast reports.

Project initiation and closure

See Chapters 9 and 13.

Stage meetings

The project steering group is required to deliver a successful outcome measured by the extent to which the project's realised benefits outweigh the actual costs. It follows that the balance between forecast costs and benefits will vary throughout the life of the project as estimates and actual spend vary. Therefore, the project steering group should schedule a meeting at the beginning of every planned stage of the project to confirm that it remains viable. At the same point, the group can consider the performance of the project during the previous stage and review and approve the plan for the next stage.

A typical agenda for such a meeting would be as follows:

- Review of previous stage, where the project manager shows how the previous stage performed compared with the plan so that the project steering group can formally approve its closure.
- Review of project plan, where the project manager presents an updated project plan to show the effect of changes and variances

during the previous stage and thus whether the project steering group's expectations will still be met. If the escalation conditions appear to have been breached, this is an opportunity to alert the portfolio management team.

- Review of business case, where the project steering group considers the updated business case to determine the extent to which the project can deliver a profitable outcome. If the escalation conditions appear to have been breached, this is an opportunity to alert the portfolio management team.

- Review of next stage plan, where the project manager presents the plan for the next stage so that the project steering group can provide formal approval for the project manager to assume continued control of the project within defined constraints.

- Approval of controls, where the project steering group confirms the escalation conditions that will apply to the next stage. This provides an opportunity to limit or increase the project manager's authority.

- Approval to proceed, where the project steering group approves the plans so that the project manager can resume control.

Unscheduled project steering group meetings

These should be necessary only if a breach of the escalation conditions is forecast. Escalation conditions can be put on timescale, costs, quality and benefits so the project steering group can be sure that it will be alerted to extreme matters arising between scheduled meetings. The agenda for the meeting is similar to that of a stage meeting, but the review of the previous stage is replaced by a presentation from the project manager outlining:

- what has happened to require notifying the project steering group;
- the effect on the plan;
- the options available to correct or accommodate the matter;
- the recommended solution and its effect on the plan.

FIGURE 10.4 **Progress management**

Scheduled project steering group meetings

Some managers are uncomfortable with the concept of management by exception. For them, no news does not always mean good news. Consequently, regular project steering group meetings are held, often every month, although this will depend on the duration of the project and the project steering group's need for contact with their project manager. Given that the meeting is not event-based, the agenda is commonly based around the review and approval of the latest project forecast report from the project manager.

Project manager

The project manager is required to plan, monitor and control time, cost and quality. It is probable that during the life of the project there will be pressure from stakeholders to amend one or more aspects of the project as their expectations or needs change. There will also be the unremitting burden of risk – potential problems that may or may not have been identified. The project manager must also motivate the people in the project team to deliver on time, on budget and to the required standard of quality.

These monitoring and reporting mechanisms are the bare essentials for a project manager.

Project team progress meetings

Often the project manager is responsible for a team of people who must be subjected to a regular and repeatable process of delegation, monitoring, reporting and control. Assuming that the project steering group meets every month, it may still want progress reports every two weeks. Figure 10.4 shows how progress data can be gathered, processed, reported and acted on.

This is the agenda for the weekly progress meetings:

- Delivery highlights during previous period – to identify the products started or completed.

- Delivery highlights during next period – to identify the products planned to be started or completed during the next period.

- Timescales – to scrutinise progress and identify variances against the time plan, clarifying the reasons for those variances so that corrective actions can be considered.

- Budgets – to scrutinise progress and identify variances against the cost plan, clarifying the reasons for those variances so that corrective actions can be considered.

- Quality – to scrutinise progress and identify variances against the quality plan (especially where products have been delivered that fall short of the quality criteria) so that corrective actions can be considered.

- Risks and issues:
  - Dependencies – to examine the known dependencies with other projects or outside parties, consider the risk of their being honoured and, where necessary, consider a mitigation plan.
  - Risk mitigation progress – to monitor the progress of agreed mitigating actions so that further corrective actions can be considered.
  - Risks for closure – to determine which risks, if any, are of such little significance that they may be considered closed. (It is sensible to let such risks remain on the risk register in case the likelihood of their occurring or their effect changes.)
  - New risks – to identify, qualify and evaluate any new or previously unrecognised risks.

■ Actions and decisions – to review and assign the actions and decisions taken during the meeting.

For the meeting to be effective, reliable and trustworthy management information is essential. This commonly comes in a project forecast report.

Project forecast reports

These are an important way for the project manager to communicate with management stakeholders, the project steering group and the portfolio management team. They are snapshots of the project, taken at regular and frequent intervals throughout its lifetime so that all the project's managers (the project manager included) are aware of both progress and the forecast of completion.

For most members of the project steering group, a summary of key project management information should be sufficient, with the option of being able to scrutinise detail as necessary. A summary project forecast report like the one in Figure 10.5 is usually sufficient for them.

The project manager should have enough detailed information to monitor the progress of individuals in the project team. It is not enough just to show the information in the summary project forecast report; the project manager needs the report on which it is based so that he can identify specific instances of variance where it occurs and the reasons for it. The project plan and the business case should provide that detail and therefore the core data in them must be up-to-date and accurate.

Since the project manager must control timescales, costs, quality and risks, the project forecast report should reflect that content at a level of detail commensurate with the plan. Furthermore, the project steering group may wish the project manager to maintain the business case on their behalf in between project stages. Consequently, in addition to the summary shown in Figure 10.5, it would be usual for a project manager to consider a more detailed report every week or two during the project's lifetime.

These are some of the terms used in Figures 10.6–10.13:

■ **Baseline.** This is the original set of data agreed by a recognised authority that should be used as a stable foundation against which

FIGURE 10.5 **A summary project forecast report**

Project Name:	Company Annual Seminar
Project Steering Group:	
Sponsor:	Howard Smith
Customer rep.:	Annie Ownes
Developer rep.:	Rafiq Shamsal
Project Manager:	Danny Frost
Report Date:	Monday, February 12

Highlights

Progress to date has been per plan. The Project Outline, Business Case and Project Governance Report have been completed.

The User Requirements Document has commenced with completion expected to plan.

Some budget has been committed to secure the venue and some speakers, and to obtain vital resources for the programme.

Lowlights

The dates for the Draft Programme and Speaker Invitations have been delayed owing to a diary conflict. However, this will not cause a knock-on delay elsewhere. There will be a delay in obtaining the venue logo as this is being redesigned.

Timescale Summary

There are 22 identified deliverables or milestones.

There are 19 **GREEN** milestones.

There are 3 **AMBER** milestones. The PM should remain in charge, but the PSG should know of these variances.

There are 0 **RED** milestones which should be managed by the PSG.

The intended end date is 20/4

The forecast end date is 20/4

The variance is 0 days and is **GREEN**

Benefit Summary

The intended benefits were $100,000

The forecast benefits are $100,000

The variance is 0% **$0** and is **GREEN**

Budget Summary

The intended budget was $72,250

The forecast budget is $73,000

The variance is –1% **–$750** and is **AMBER**

Business Case Summary

The intended gross margin was $27,750

The forecast gross margin is $27,000

The variance is –3% **–$750** and is **AMBER**

Quality Summary

There are **0 GREEN** quality measures.

There are **0 AMBER** quality measures which should be managed by the PM.

There are **5 RED** quality measures which should be managed by the PSG.

Risk Summary

There are **4** identified risks.

There are **2 GREEN** risks which should be managed by the team.

There are **2 AMBER** risks which should be managed by the PM.

There are **0 RED** risks which should be managed by the PSG.

to track variances. There may be a baseline end date, a baseline budget and a baseline benefit, which were all agreed when the business case and project governance report were approved at the end of the initiation stage. The baseline should not be changed, so the effect of changes can be measured reliably. There are, however, rare circumstances when it is necessary and sensible to amend the baseline; these will be considered later.

- **Actual to date** (ATD)**.** This is a range of measures that should increase as the project progresses. For instance, if $300 of a baseline $500 budget has been spent, the actual to date is $300.

- **Estimate to complete** (ETC)**.** This is a crucial set of information in any project report because it is the latest and most recent estimate. This figure represents the amount to come on top of the actual to date. For instance, if the actual to date is $300 and the baseline was $500, it does not follow that the estimate to complete is $200. The costs may have increased since the baseline was approved and the project forecast report must record this. If the estimate to complete is $400, the new total is $700.

- **Forecast at completion** (FAC)**.** This is the sum of actual to date and estimate to complete – $700 in the example above.

- **Variance.** This is the difference between the baseline and the forecast at completion. In the example above, it is –$200 (the baseline $500 less the forecast at completion $700). When compared with the agreed escalation criteria, this figure enables the red, amber and green alert markers to be created.

- **Box colours.** Grey boxes must be completed whenever a new project forecast report is being produced.

Project forecast report: time forecast

The time forecast (Figure 10.6) lists every product or milestone from the plan and shows the progress made in achieving targets and the extent to which the forecast end date is likely to be met.

Start dates are sometimes excluded, but they have some value; if the development of a product is seen to be starting later, there is a reasonable chance that it will be completed behind schedule too.

FIGURE 10.6 **Project forecast report: time forecast**

Project name: Company annual seminar
Project manager: Danny Frost

ESCALATION

	From	To
Off track, requires project steering group's intervention RED=	6	100
Off track, but within project manager's control AMBER=	1	5
On track to deliver on intended delivery date GREEN=	0	0

ID	Milestone	Team member responsible	Baseline Start	Baseline End	Forecast/actual Start	Forecast/actual End	TIME Variance/ R/A/G	Reason
1	Completed and internally approved project outline and business case	PR	03/02	09/02	03/02	09/02	0	
2	Completed project governance report	JK	10/02	10/02	10/02	10/02	0	
3	Completed user requirements document	JK	11/02	14/02	11/02	14/02	0	
4	Draft agenda and topics	JK, PR	15/02	15/02	15/02	15/02	0	
5	Identified venue	SP	15/02	15/02	15/02	15/02	0	
6	Reserved venue	LA	11/02	19/02	11/02	19/02	0	
7	Marketing plan	LA	15/02	19/02	15/02	19/02	0	
8	Confirmed date	DK	19/02	19/02	19/02	19/02	0	
9	Agreed speakers	LA	10/02	19/02	10/02	19/02	0	
10	Draft programme	PR	10/02	01/03	10/02	03/03	2	Diary conflict
11	Approved speaker invitations	JK	01/03	05/03	01/03	08/03	3	Diary conflict
12	Despatched speaker invitations	LA	19/02	21/02	19/02	21/02	0	
13	Completed speaker confirmations	DK	21/02	10/03	21/02	10/03	0	
14	Received venue logos	SP	15/02	15/03	15/02	19/03	4	Logos being redesigned
15	Booked and paid venue	PR	15/02	20/03	15/02	20/03	0	
16	Completed delegate packs	LA	15/02	25/03	15/02	25/03	0	
17	Approved marketing materials	LA	15/02	25/03	15/02	25/03	0	
18	Printed and despatched marketing materials and invitations	DK	25/03	04/04	25/03	04/04	0	
19	Received speaker speeches	PR	10/03	04/04	10/03	04/04	0	
20	Produced and despatched running plans	SP	04/04	15/04	04/04	15/04	0	
21	Final approval meeting	LA	16/04	16/04	16/04	16/04	0	
22	Event	ALL	20/04	20/04	20/04	20/04	0	

FIGURE 10.7 **Project forecast report: cost forecast by type**

Project name:	Company annual seminar
Project manager:	Danny Frost
Summary variance	-$750.00

	ESCALATION	FROM	TO
Off track, requires project steering group's intervention	RED =	-3,000	-1,000,000
Off track, but within project manager's control	AMBER =	-1	-3,000
On track to deliver to intended budget	GREEN =	0	0

				COST								
		Baseline			Actual to date			Estimate to complete					
ID	Resource	Items	Unit	TOTAL	Items	Unit	TOTAL	Items	Unit	TOTAL	Forecast	Variance/ R/A/G	Reason
1	Marketing team (10 person days @ $300 per day)	10.00	$300	$3,000	10.00	$300	$3,000	0.00	$0	$0	$3,000	$0	
2	Technology team (5 person days @ $350 per day)	5.00	$350	$1,750	4.00	$350	$1,400	2.00	$350	$700	$2,100	-$350	One extra day needed to source kit
3	Marketing materials	1.00	$5,000	$5,000	1.00	$5,000	$5,000	1.00	$0	$0	$5,000	$0	
4	Copywriting fees	1.00	$3,000	$3,000	1.00	$3,000	$3,000	1.00	$0	$0	$3,000	$0	
5	Editing in house	1.00	$3,000	$3,000	1.00	$3,000	$3,000	1.00	$0	$0	$3,000	$0	
6	Fulfilment	1.00	$1,500	$1,500	1.00	$1,500	$1,500	1.00	$0	$0	$1,500	$0	
7	Transportation	1.00	$500	$500	1.00	$800	$800	1.00	$0	$0	$800	-$300	Estimates failed to include supplier price increase
8	Stationery	1.00	$1,200	$1,200	1.00	$1,300	$1,300	1.00	$0	$0	$1,300	-$100	Estimates wrongly based on last year's figures
9	Signage	1.00	$300	$300	1.00	$300	$300	1.00	$0	$0	$300	$0	
10	Airfares	5.00	$600	$3,000	0.00	$600	$0	5.00	$600	$3,000	$3,000	$0	
11	Venue	1.00	$20,000	$20,000	0.00	$20,000	$0	1.00	$20,000	$20,000	$20,000	$0	
12	Hotel accommodation	60.00	$400	$24,000	0.00	$400	$0	60.00	$400	$24,000	$24,000	$0	
13	Audio visual	1.00	$3,000	$3,000	0.00	$3,000	$0	1.00	$3,000	$3,000	$3,000	$0	
14	Food and drink	60.00	$50	$3,000	0.00	$50	$0	60.00	$50	$3,000	$3,000	$0	
	TOTAL			$72,250			$19,300			$53,700	$73,000	-$750	

FIGURE 10.8 **Project forecast report: cost forecast by product**

Project name:	Company annual seminar
Project manager:	Danny Frost
Summary variance	-$750.00

			ESCALATION	From	To
	Off track, requires project steering group's intervention	RED=		-3,000	-1,000,000
	Off track, but within project manager's control	AMBER=		-1	-3,000
	On track to deliver on intended delivery date	GREEN=		0	0

ID	Milestone	Team member responsible	Baseline	ATD	ETC	TIME FAC	Variance/ R/A/G	Reason
1	Completed and internally approved project outline and business case	PR	$1,200	$1,200	$0	$1,200	$0	
2	Completed project governance report	JK	$300	$300	$0	$300	$0	
3	Completed user requirements document	JK	$700	$700	$0	$700	$0	
4	Draft agenda and topics	JK, PR	$700	$0	$700	$700	$0	
5	Identified venue	SP	$760	$0	$760	$760	$0	
6	Reserved venue	LA	$10,000	$10,000	$350	$10,350	-$350	One extra day needed to source kit
7	Marketing plan	LA	$1,200	$0	$1,200	$1,200	$0	
8	Confirmed date	DK	$300	$0	$300	$300	$0	
9	Agreed speakers	LA	$3,790	$3,790	$0	$3,790	$0	
10	Draft programme	PR	$3,500	$3,310	$190	$3,500	$0	
11	Approved speaker invitations	JK	$700	$0	$700	$700	$0	
12	Despatched speaker invitations	LA	$900	$0	$900	$900	$0	
13	Completed speaker confirmations	DK	$7,000	$0	$7,000	$7,000	$0	
14	Received venue logos	SP	$400	$0	$400	$400	$0	
15	Booked and paid venue	PR	$17,800	$0	$17,800	$17,800	$0	
16	Completed delegate packs	LA	$12,300	$0	$12,300	$12,300	$0	
17	Approved marketing materials	LA	$700	$0	$700	$700	$0	
18	Printed and despatched marketing materials and invitations	DK	$8,900	$0	$9,300	$9,300	-$400	Increase in prices from suppliers
19	Received speaker speeches	PR	$100	$0	$100	$100	$0	
20	Produced and despatched running plans	SP	$300	$0	$300	$300	$0	
21	Final approval meeting	LA	$700	$0	$700	$700	$0	
22	Event	ALL	$0	$0	$0	$0	$0	
	TOTAL		$72,250	$19,300	$53,700	$73,000	-$750	

FIGURE 10.9 **Project forecast report: project quality forecast**

| Project name: | Company annual seminar |
| Project manager: | Danny Frost |

ESCALATION

On track to deliver as intended   GREEN= | 100,000%
Off track, but within project manager's control   AMBER= | 99%
Off track, may require project steering group's intervention.   RED= | 74%

| | | | | | METRICS |
ID	Quality measure	Baseline	Actual to date	Success/ R/A/G	Reason for variance
1	Speaker acceptances	7	2	29%	Ahead of schedule - none expected at this stage
2	Employee registrations	300	0	0%	On plan - invitations not yet sent
3	Number of external press attending	3	0	0%	Event not yet completed
4	No shows	30	0	0%	Event not yet completed
5	Evaluation forms completed	200	0	0%	Event not yet completed

Using the same columns to represent forecast and actual dates is simply explained: if the date is before the date of the report, it is an actual date. If it is after the date of the report, it is a forecast date. Once an actual date has been entered, there should be no reason to change it.

Project forecast report: cost forecast

There are a number of ways of reporting the costs of the project. Figures 10.7 and 10.8 show two different ways of expressing the same data. The cost forecast (Figure 10.7) lists the resource types, including all the people and non-human costs.

Figure 10.8 lists the costs by product. This is important if an earned value analysis is to be carried out. This example identifies a matter that may interest the project steering group: despite the project having started only a few days ago, money has been committed to some products that have been reported elsewhere as not started (reserved venue, agreed speakers and draft programme).

An alternative used by many organisations is to separate the capital and revenue costs and show them as two summarised rows. However, this may lead to difficulties when attempting to discover the reason for a variance.

Project forecast report: project quality forecast

The project quality forecast (Figure 10.9) identifies the intended success criteria and shows how close the project is to meeting those expectations. It will be particularly important to the project steering group because they want to know that the project is likely to meet not only its time and budget targets, but also its quality targets. They set these targets, so they should take a keen interest in seeing the progress towards meeting them. However, ultimately the project manager will be measured on his ability to balance, control and meet the project steering group's expectations for time, cost and quality. Thus, the project quality forecast provides a means of knowing how near to or far from meeting its target the project is, and, importantly, what should be done to manage any variances.

FIGURE 10.10 **Project forecast report: product quality log**

Project name: Company annual seminar
Project manager: Danny Frost

A Approved
ASTA Approved subject to amendments
RAR1 Revise and reschedule – product unready
RAR2 Revise and reschedule – product needs significant change
RAR3 Revise and reschedule – insufficient reviewers
RAR4 Revise and reschedule – unqualified reviewers
RAR5 Revise and reschedule – unprepared reviewers

ID	Milestone	Quality reviewers	Approval authority	Draft complete	Invitation sent	Baseline review	Review complete	METRICS						Observations
								Outcome	Number of changes	Changes complete	Approved FFP	Baseline approval	Variance RAG	
1	Completed and internally approved project outline and business case	PR, TC, US	PSG	05/02	03/02	07/02	07/02	ASTA	12	08/02	09/02	09/02	0	
2	Completed project governance report	PR, TC, MM	PSG	10/02	05/02	10/02	10/02	ASTA	8	10/02	10/02	10/02	0	
3	Completed user requirements document	MM, SP, TC	PSG	13/02								14/02		
4	Draft agenda and topics	MM, SP, TC	PSG	15/02								15/02		
6	Reserved venue	PR, TC, MM	PSG	18/02								19/02		
7	Marketing plan	MM, SP, TC	PSG	18/02								19/02		
9	Agreed speakers	MM, SP, TC	PSG	18/02								19/02		
10	Draft programme	PR, TC, US	PSG	02/03								01/03		
11	Approved speaker invitations	MM, SP, TC	PSG	07/03								05/03		
15	Booked and paid venue	MM, SP, TC	PSG	19/03								20/03		
16	Completed delegate packs	MM, SP, TC	PSG	24/03								25/03		
17	Approved marketing materials	PR, TC, US	PSG	24/03								25/03		
18	Printed and despatched marketing materials and invitations	MM, SP, TC	PSG	03/04								04/04		
19	Received speaker speeches	PR, TC, US	PSG	03/04								04/04		
20	Produced and despatched running plans	PR, TC, MM	PSG	14/04								15/04		

FIGURE 10.11 **Project forecast report: benefits forecast**

Project name:	Company annual seminar
Sponsor:	Howard Smith
Summary variance	$0	0%

	Escalation	From	To
Off track, may require project steering group's intervention. RED=		−50%	−100,000%
Off track, but within project manager's control AMBER=		−1%	−49%
On track, project manager remains in control GREEN=		0%	0%

	Baseline	Actual to date	Estimate to complete	Forecast	Variance $	%
1 Increased employee satisfaction resulting in reduced staff wastage	$100,000	$0	$100,000	$100,000	$0	0%
2						
3						
4						
5						
6						
7						
TOTALS	$100,000	$0	$100,000	$100,000	$0	0%

FIGURE 10.12 **Project forecast report: risk register**

| Project name: | Company annual seminar |
| Sponsor: | Howard Smith |

0 None	**0** None
2 Very Low	**3** Activity may suffer
4 Low	**5** Product may suffer
6 Medium	**7** Stage may suffer
8 High	**9** Project may suffer
10 Certainty	**11** Business may suffer

Green – anyone can be assigned ownership

Amber – project manager assigned ownership

Red – project steering group assigned ownership

Green	
1	20
Amber	
21	56
Red	
57	110

Share – allow a partner to share the burden of risk

Endure – accept that the risk may become an issue

Avoid – prevent the risk from transpiring

Lessen – reduce the likelihood and/or impact

ID	Risk	Likelihood	Impact	Factor	Mitigation
1	Employees do not sign up in sufficient numbers resulting in loss of benefit	4	9	36	Sponsor to send personal invitation
2	Food poisoning incident from last year is repeated resulting in bad will and potential legal sanctions	2	9	18	New caterers have been identified
3	Venue is lost to a competitor resulting in last minute attempt to secure an alternative	4	9	36	Venue is secured with payment much earlier than usual
4	Speakers say something controversial resulting in company position being compromised	6	3	18	Speeches to be pre-vetted

FIGURE 10.13 Timesheet

Project name:	Company annual seminar
Team member name:	Jackie King
Date:	12/01

ID	Milestone	TIME					COST				
		Original		Forecast/actual		Reason	Original effort	Actual to date	Estimate to complete	Forecast	Reason
		Start	End	Start	End						
1	Completed project governance report	10/02	10/02	10/02	10/02		1.0	1.0	0.0	1.0	
2	Completed user requirements document	11/02	14/02	11/02	14/02		1.0	0.0	1.0	1.0	
3											
4											
5											
6											
7											
8											
9											
10											
TOTAL							2.0	1.0	1.0	2.0	

Project forecast report: product quality log

The product quality log (Figure 10.10) lists the key deliverables or milestones and shows the status of each with regard to their fitness for their purpose. It provides a more detailed means of monitoring and reporting progress by recording the progress achieved in meeting each product's success criteria. Thus, if the time forecast shows that a product is forecast to be delivered late, the product quality log may show that the delay is due to a failure related to quality.

The product quality log is a simple report that follows the life cycle of each product, showing to what extent each of the product's steps have been successfully achieved. These steps are:

- draft complete;
- review complete;
- changes completed;
- approved fit for purpose (FFP).

Specific columns identify the date on which each step has been completed so that progress can be better managed.

Project forecast report: benefits forecast

Most projects have to be completed before their benefits can be delivered. Therefore, there may be limited value in reporting progress in achieving benefits during the life of the project. However, there are occasions when it can be helpful to assess progress in achieving benefits during the life of the project (Figure 10.11), such as the following:

- The forecast benefits change. The baseline forecasts were underestimated or overestimated. For example, the intended customers from a new market are no longer anticipated.
- Some benefits have been delivered during the project. For example, redundant computer equipment has been removed during the project rather than after completion, resulting in lower maintenance charges.
- There is a desire to compare benefits and costs dynamically during the project. The project steering group is responsible for delivering benefits that outweigh costs by an agreed margin. If it is

to take well-informed decisions throughout the project life cycle, it will help to have management information about the project's accruing and forecast benefits, as well as the costs.

Project forecast report: risk register

The risk register (Figure 10.12) will help the project manager when reviewing the project. The "Factor" column alerts the project steering group to risks or issues requiring their intervention.

Timesheet

The forecast at completion and variance can be calculated automatically, but the actual to date and the estimate to complete must be obtained to allow that to happen. Every time a project forecast report is produced, these figures must be included if it is to have any value. The source of such information will be the people to whom the work has been delegated, so a timesheet is the best way to gather the data. In Figure 10.13, the person completing the form is required to enter data in the grey boxes; all other boxes contain information derived from the project plan.

Earned value analysis

Using reports to determine whether or not a set of expectations will be met is a necessary aspect of effective management. It is also helpful to gain some confidence that a project is currently where it was expected to be. Earned value analysis objectively measures a project's accomplishments in respect of its performance against the time, cost and quality targets.

Earned value analysis depends on a detailed and up-to-date plan being available and it relies on being able to calculate the extent to which any product is complete. Therefore, it is a prerequisite that the plan against which progress is being tracked is product-based.

Figure 10.14 tells the project management team little about the current state of the project. The planned cost is a measure of what should have been spent at each point throughout the project's life cycle. For example, the project should have spent $50,000 at period 6, $75,000 at period 8 and its whole budget by the end of period 10.

FIGURE 10.14 **Planned cost compared with actual cost**

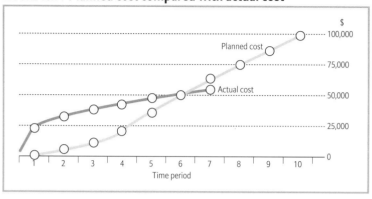

In Figure 10.14 it appears that the actual cost has exceeded the planned cost until period 6, but after that the cumulative actual cost appears to be less than expected. This is not necessarily a time to celebrate, however. This view takes no account of what has actually been delivered at each point, so if the project were suddenly to finish at period 8, although it may be under budget, it may also have produced less than was intended.

Assuming that the project manager has drawn up a product-based plan at the start of the project, it should have been possible to determine the value of each product and its total cost of production. Shown over time, this is called the planned value. At the end of every period, the project manager calculates the value of every product created so far, allowing a proportionate amount for partly completed products. This is the earned value. As progress is tracked, instead of simply comparing the planned cost with the actual cost, the earned value of the products delivered can be compared with the planned value expected (Figure 10.15).

Figure 10.15 shows that progress was better than planned to begin with but fell behind at period 8. However, when the earned value is compared with the actual cost figures used earlier (Figure 10.16) it is higher than the actual cost, which implies that the products that have been delivered have contributed a greater value than the spend to date. Therefore, the project is in a markedly better state than originally illustrated.

FIGURE 10.15 **Earned value compared with planned value**

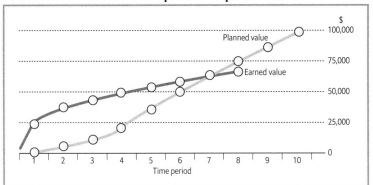

Given the emphasis on the cost of production and the variances that the project manager may wish to identify, the terms "planned value" and "earned value" are often replaced by two better descriptions:

■ budgeted cost of work scheduled (BCWS) – the budgeted cost of work planned in the period being measured;

■ budgeted cost of work performed (BCWP) – the planned cost of work completed in the period being measured.

However, for the technique to work, a third measure is needed:

FIGURE 10.16 **Earned value compared with actual cost**

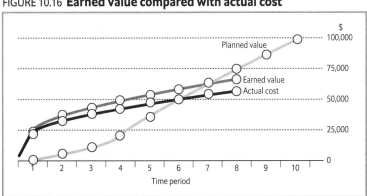

FIGURE 10.17 **Earned value summary**

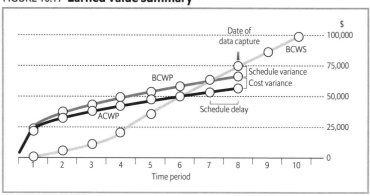

- actual cost of work performed (ACWP) – the cost of work completed to date.

  Now it is possible to calculate:

- cost variation – the budgeted cost of work scheduled minus the actual cost of work planned (how much should have been spent to date based on what has been achieved, minus the amount actually spent);
- schedule variation – the budgeted cost of work performed minus the budgeted cost of work scheduled (how much should have been spent to date based on what has been achieved, minus the amount that was planned to have been spent);
- schedule delay – when the budgeted cost of work scheduled is the same as the budgeted cost of work performed, less the date when the data was captured, measured in days.

Therefore, the example can be extended. Figure 10.17 shows a project that is:

- underspent – the actual cost of work performed is less than the budgeted cost of work performed, so the cost variance is positive;
- behind schedule – the budgeted cost of work scheduled is greater than the budgeted cost of work performed so the schedule variance is negative.

Therefore, having given a value to each product, earned value analysis provides a view of project data that can significantly enhance the management team's understanding of the state of the project.

Quality reviews

Earned value analysis depends on being able to measure the completeness of a product. Without it, performance is measurable only in terms of money spent over time. But regardless of whether earned value analysis is being used as a monitoring and control technique, the successful execution of the plan depends on managing quality as well as time and cost. It follows, therefore, that the project's products' fitness for their purpose should also be actively managed.

While the product quality log tracks the project's progress in meeting milestone targets, it only records the results of a more substantial product review process to which all key deliverables should be subjected. Only in this way can those approving their completion have confidence that they are measurably fit for their purpose.

As a product is being developed, the product description should be used as a definition of what a successful output should look like. In particular, the quality criteria set out the specifier's quality expectations so that the developer can be sure to build them into the product. So, if the quality criteria section asks, "Will the report be limited to no more than 30 pages?", the author can be sure to meet that expectation.

Given that the product description can be complex and that there is usually room for misinterpretation, a quality review is often advisable. This compares the draft product and the product description to determine how far the product can be considered complete.

There are different forms of quality review, each suitable for a particular type of product:

- Testing – where a physical test is necessary, for example a pressure test of a tyre to determine the point at which it would explode.
- Inspection – where a product or service is scrutinised to determine its fitness, for example a visit to premises to evaluate whether they meet health and safety standards.

FIGURE 10.18 **Quality review process**

- Demonstration – where the potential errors are identified by a display, for example a prototype car is demonstrated on a track.

- Formal quality review – where a group of carefully identified reviewers are invited to challenge a product's ability to meet predefined success criteria. This enables errors to be identified and corrected, for example a marketing plan is scrutinised by experts.

- Informal quality review – a less structured version of a formal quality review, where the product is circulated by mail or e-mail so that errors can be identified and corrected.

In many projects, the formal quality review is an effective means of monitoring and reporting the fitness for their purpose of many of its products. The process was first outlined by Michael Fagan in 1976, and he developed it further ten years later. Although originally intended for the software industry, it lends itself perfectly to any form of documentation that has been defined by means of a product description (see Figure 10.18).

Quality review: preparation. This begins during initiation when the product descriptions against which the products will be compared for their fitness for purpose are developed and approved by the project steering group as part of the project plan. The quality plan (a component of the project plan) will contain all product descriptions, together with a list of quality responsibilities identifying who will be responsible for reviewing and approving each product.

Reviewers should be selected with care. They should fulfil these roles:

- chair – to ensure that a clear conclusion is drawn from the review;
- scribe – to record the actions and decisions arising from the review;
- author – to offer insight into the product and its construction;
- reviewers – to identify errors.

The project manager or team leader should also be prepared to attend since the outcome will affect the plan in some way.

To make sure the review is balanced, reviewers should be drawn from a variety of commercial, customer and developer backgrounds. An invitation should be sent to all reviewers informing them of their role. It should include:

- an error list for recording the errors the reviewer identifies;
- a copy of the product description to provide the baseline definition against which the draft product should be compared;
- the draft product to be reviewed.

The scribe should also receive an action form for recording actions and decisions arising from the review. All reviewers should prepare for the meeting by comparing the draft product to the product description, noting errors on their error lists.

A room should be booked and sufficient time allowed to review the product.

Quality review: review. The meeting should start with an introduction of the participants and an explanation of the purpose of the review. Assuming the product is a document, there are several ways to proceed:

- Significant errors are identified as a priority. Thus if the product is critically flawed, a decision to propose rework can be taken before the review has progressed too far.

- Reviewers present and describe their error lists in turn. This lets each reviewer express their particular concerns about the product. The disadvantage is that by the time the last reviewer is reached the errors listed may have been identified and presented by someone else, leaving them feeling as though they have made no contribution.

- Each page of the document is considered in turn. Each reviewer has an equal opportunity to contribute. Furthermore, if the review has to be cut short or overruns, everyone will have reviewed the product to the same place.

- Each quality criterion in the product description is considered in turn, which means that the quality criteria against which to measure the fitness of the product must be sufficiently reliable and that the product descriptions must be of a high standard.

When conducting a review:

- participants should be expected to have prepared thoroughly;
- everyone should aim to work within agreed time limits;
- the authority of the chair should be respected;
- all participants should be tactful and diplomatic;
- the chair should be prepared to reschedule the review if there are too few participants or if they are underqualified;
- the product should be reviewed, not the author;
- the product should always be compared with the product description, not with any personal opinions about what constitutes a "fit" product;
- during the review, errors should be identified, not solutions;
- irrelevant debate should be avoided;
- each reviewer should annotate the product with trivial matters, such as spelling errors.

As the review progresses, the scribe should record the actions and decisions agreed on the action form, being sure to assign each action to an agreed participant. In practice, most of the actions usually fall to the author, who will be expected to produce the necessary amendments. When the review has been completed, the scribe should read back the items on the action form to make sure that they reflect the debate and that those required to take action understand their obligations. They should gather the reviewers' copies of the products annotated with spelling and grammatical errors, together with the errors lists.

The chair is responsible for making sure that the review concludes decisively. The options are:

- approved – the product can be accepted;
- approved subject to amendments – the product can be approved once the actions on the action form are undertaken;
- revise and reschedule (product not ready) – the product is not sufficiently complete or of a suitable standard for review;
- revise and reschedule (product needs significant change) – the product is critically flawed and requires radical redevelopment;
- revise and reschedule (insufficient reviewers) – not enough reviewers attended;
- revise and reschedule (unqualified reviewers) – the reviewers attending were insufficiently qualified;
- revise and reschedule (unprepared reviewers) – the reviewers attending were insufficiently prepared.

Quality review: follow-up. If the review showed that the product was complete subject to corrections, the scribe should give everyone a copy of the action form. The scribe should also give the author the annotated copies of the product.

The author should consider the changes necessary, determine whether they can be accommodated within the time and budget remaining available for this product and inform the project manager of the effect. In turn, the project manager should update the product quality log and after considering the time and cost implications decide whether the author should go ahead and make the changes.

Assuming that the changes can be accommodated according to the plan, the author amends the product using the action form and the annotated copies as a guide. A revised version is then circulated so that reviewers can confirm that the errors they identified have been corrected and that all other actions have been satisfied. Once they have provided proof of their acceptance, the chair can approve the product. This confirms that it meets the planned quality expectations and is fit for its purpose.

Informal quality review. This is a common form of product appraisal which, if managed well, has many of the benefits of the formal quality review but is cheaper to implement. Instead of gathering reviewers together, the product is sent to them via mail or e-mail. The author asks them to identify errors, which he then seeks to rectify in a further version.

While this might appear faster and cheaper than a formal review, it is often less rigorous and may not identify errors in sufficient quantity or quality.

To make sure that the informal quality review is as effective as possible, the author should:

- identify a balanced selection of reviewers to represent commercial, customer and developer viewpoints;
- set a time by which reviewers should return their identified errors;
- provide a budget within which reviewers should work and a cost code to which their time and any costs should be attributed;
- provide a product description against which the reviewers will compare the product, or at the very least, a list of quality criteria to limit the scope of the review (this will stop errors being created by opinions rather than fact).

Both the formal and informal quality reviews seek to lift the fitness of a product to a point at which it is acceptable for use. Creating a product that is fit for its purpose takes time and money, so managers need to be prepared to invest in quality.

Control

Monitoring and reporting will not be effective without control. Once the various reports have been considered, the control cycle moves towards its final position where any corrective actions and decisions are taken to pull the project back onto its intended track. This must be subject to tight governance because the project might easily find itself in a worse position if the wrong decision is made or taken by someone without the appropriate authority.

If organisations are resistant to change and act accordingly with regard to their projects, they will face serious consequences. First, the deliverables arising from their projects will be less able to satisfy the real needs of the users. Second, by pursuing objectives that have become either irrelevant or misplaced, they will spend more than they need to. And third, they will fail to keep pace with the changing world around them and see their more fleet-footed competitors benefit first.

The crucial message is not that change should be accommodated without a care, but that the organisational culture and practices should allow for balanced consideration of the consequences of change for the project.

Deliver incremental change

Many projects grow out of control because they take on too much. There are great benefits in building a programme of much smaller projects, each of which has a greater chance of delivering something quickly which swiftly realises its benefits. In the context of managing change, such projects are less likely to become out of date too rapidly, and stand a greater chance of delivering before the world overtakes them. Alternatively, the project may be of a manageable size, but might still be able to deliver change in increments. This is explored further in Chapter 11.

Establish a baseline

A baseline is an authorised record of a project variable at a specific point in time. It may be set for the project's timescale, budget, scope or benefits, for example. Setting a baseline is like taking a date-stamped photograph of the project. It shows what the project looked like at that point: what it was expected to cost, when it was due to deliver, what it would produce, what value it would confer on the organisation, and so forth. A great benefit of a baseline is to allow the consequence of a change to be assessed so that a decision can be made to accept it or not. Without a baseline, it becomes impossible to know what impact a change may have on any of the project's variables, resulting in either a reluctance to accept any change at all, or the accommodation of changes without knowledge of the consequences.

One of the reasons project managers place such emphasis on obtaining approval of the project plan and business case at the outset is that the project steering group's acceptance of them transforms the documents into the baseline against which success will be measured. Whenever a request to change the project is encountered, for whatever reason and from wherever it may originate, an assessment may be carried out to understand its impact on the project plan and business case. If any of the baseline measures appear to be seriously affected, the project manager may seek the project steering group's approval to have them changed, or "rebaselined".

It follows that each of the variables must be measurable. In this respect, timescale and budget are relatively straightforward to determine: a date on a calendar or a financial value, for example. Subject to the guidance provided in the previous chapter, it is also relatively easy to quantify benefits. The greatest challenge comes when attempting to measure the quality and scope of the deliverables expected from the project.

Of course, there are ways of baselining a project without first defining the scope and quality of its deliverables. It is possible to state a sum of money and request that what is delivered never exceeds that budget. Alternatively, time may be of the essence, in which case the users will receive what has been developed when the clock stops. Neither is unheard of, yet it is worth considering this: once the budget and time have been exhausted, the sole remaining legacy of a project is the deliverable it has produced. For this reason alone, it is worth establishing baselines for the quality and scope of the deliverables first, so that it is easier to negotiate the time and cost required to produce them. This way, quality gets a look-in from the outset, and the impact of change can be measured against it.

FIGURE 10.19 **A table of requirements**

Item	Source	Priority	Description	Owner	Acceptance criteria	Supplier	Complexity	Cost ($)
1	User needs workshop	Essential	20 customer service staff to have been trained in the use of the system	User authority	All trained staff can use the system as intended, unsupervised	Training division	Medium	3,500
2	User needs workshop	Desirable	Client's purchase history retained and available in real time	User authority	Client purchase history is always available, and is accurate	IT division	Low	1,000
3	User authority	Optional	Interface into CRM system to allow nightly synchronisation of customer name and address details	User authority	Customer name and address details are never more than one day out of sync	IT division	Medium	7,000

In Chapter 5, the case was made for creating a set of project success criteria for which time, cost and benefits are all candidates. In addition to these relatively simple measures, users frequently expect that their "requirements" must be met. A requirements specification is a document in which their needs are commonly captured and articulated and for which baselines are recorded. Each requirement must be described as clearly and substantially as possible since it is against such statements that any possible changes will be compared. Changes may take the form of entirely new requirements, those that are no longer needed, or variations of existing ones. When expressing requirements, it may be helpful to capture them in the form shown in Figure 10.19.

The fields identified in the form are as follows:

■ Item. Unique identifying number for the requirement.

■ Source. The person, meeting or deliverable that identified the requirement.

■ Priority

   – Essential: the solution is unacceptable without this requirement satisfied.

   – Desirable: the solution should meet this requirement, but would not be unacceptable without it.

   – Optional: if a solution is possible, it will be accepted, but it is not necessary.

■ Description. Textual description of the requirement.

- ■ Owner. The person to whom ownership of the requirement has been assigned.
- ■ Acceptance criteria. The measures to be used when determining the solution's fitness for purpose.
- ■ Supplier. The person or body who has been assigned the task of developing a solution.
- ■ Complexity. The relative difficulty of developing a solution
  - – Low: the solution (or similar) has been developed before and presents no challenge.
  - – Medium: the solution (or similar) may have been developed before but requires bespoke elements.
  - – High: the solution has not been developed before and will require a bespoke approach.
- ■ Cost. The estimated person-day and/or materials cost of developing the solution.

Having an explicit statement of requirements with relevant baselines allows for the management of the quality and scope of the project's deliverables, especially when a request is made to change either measure. However, since the timescale and budget for the project will, to a large extent, have been based on an understanding of the statement of requirements, any changes to those requirements are likely to have an impact on the project's timescale or budget, or both. It will be in everyone's interests to anticipate what the volume and scale of change are likely to be.

Apply change management practices across all projects

The accommodation of change in a single project may have an effect on other projects in the portfolio. It follows that the project steering group might use similar escalation conditions to raise matters for the portfolio management team's attention, as they may also need to enact contingency measures of their own.

Use a process to manage changes

The process by which both issues and change requests are handled is identical so that the right people are given the best information on which to make the decision they believe to be right. This process makes sure that, if the project's parameters have to change, it is a conscious, intended management control. It is reasonable for a project's timescale to be extended, its budget doubled, or its output to look very different from that originally planned, so long as these changes are agreed under a pre-determined management process and overall the project remains financially justifiable. The control process is illustrated in Figure 10.20.

Change request or issue

Change must be managed, so anyone may raise a change request or an issue on a freely available form (these are often summarised in a change log to give an overview of every change request made and issue raised in order to keep track of progress). This is preferable to allowing changes without control.

FIGURE 10.20 **Control process**

Analysis

Everything known about the issue or change request should be included on the form, which may be circulated widely. The reason for the issue may well be contained in any of the project forecast report's "Reasons" columns. The reasons may be complex, so the project manager should oversee the analysis to make sure the background is clearly explained.

Impact assessment

The effect an actual or potential change may have on the project can be significant and expensive and therefore needs to be evaluated. The project manager must make sure that critical baseline documents are available so that the effect of the change can be assessed accurately. These are the principal baseline documents:

- business case – to assess the effect on benefits;
- user requirements document – to assess the effect on scope;
- solution design document – to assess the effect on the solution's robustness;
- project plan – to assess the effect on timescale, costs and quality;
- risk register – to assess the effect on the riskiness of the project.

If several change requests and issues arise, it may be necessary to have a team of people to assess their effects. This will have a cost implication for the project and is why the control of such changes is linked to the contingency budget. Even if a team is not required, impact assessment can be expensive, especially where the project is complex. The budget needed is not easy to estimate, but if managers record what they have invested, future projects can use the figures as a guideline.

Impact assessment answers these questions:

- What are the time and money implications of this issue or change request?
- How will this issue or change request affect the robustness of the design?
- How will this issue or change request affect the operability of the solution?

To find an appropriately balanced solution, the impact assessment process must involve someone with a commercial focus, a developer to consider the effects on the design and a customer or user to judge how the solution will be affected. The project manager should manage the process and may well promote a particular perspective; however, in the interests of balance, the project manager should take account of other views. Nevertheless, it is not surprising that the effects on time, cost and benefits usually take precedence, because a focus on the commercial point of view is often uppermost in many stakeholders' minds.

Solution proposal

There may well be a number of options and the project manager must make sure they are outlined clearly so that a recommendation can be made. No matter how many solutions there are, all will have an impact on time, cost or quality, and possibly also the benefits of the project, because they are inextricably linked. For instance, if more time is needed, this is likely to affect cost. If the budget must be contained, the product's quality may be impaired. If more functionality or content is required, both the time and cost targets may be compromised. Any solution will usually require a compromise regarding the original expectations. Here is a list of compromises needed to achieve a desired outcome:

- To accommodate a solution while keeping to a fixed deadline:
  - more resources may be necessary;
  - faster resources may be needed;
  - quality and/or quality checks may have to be reduced;
  - the scope of what is delivered may have to be reduced;
  - overtime/weekend work may have to be increased;
  - holidays may have to be cancelled.
- To accommodate a solution while working within a fixed budget:
  - cheaper resources may be required;
  - fewer resources may be employed;
  - quality and/or quality checks may have to be reduced;
  - the scope of what is delivered may have to be reduced;

- – delivery dates may have to be delayed;
- – overtime/weekend work may have to be reduced;
- – holidays may have to be cancelled.

■ To accommodate a solution while meeting the original quality and content expectations:

- – more resources may be necessary;
- – "better" resources may be needed;
- – quality processes, including tests, may have to be improved;
- – customer expectations may have to be better managed;
- – delivery dates may have to be delayed;
- – discounts may have to be offered;
- – some components may have to be deferred until later.

The need to control quality can be mitigated by strengthening the organisation's ability to specify, plan, build and test products by:

■ identifying senior and authorised customers to participate in the project steering group;

■ accommodating requirements through user forums;

■ clarifying and baselining requirements at the start of the project;

■ allowing changes to requirements only through formal change control;

■ keeping customers involved throughout;

■ involving business analysts throughout as advocates for customers;

■ prototyping solutions;

■ setting clear "quality gates" such as the number of faults tolerated at each stage of testing;

■ training those who will take part in testing;

■ managing end-date expectations to avoid compressing the testing;

■ providing incentives for quality, not just timeliness and keeping to budget.

In all cases, further but stark options include:

■ delivering late, despite intentions not to do so;

- delivering over budget, despite intentions not to do so;
- delivering lower quality or reduced scope, despite intentions not to do so;
- if the business case is compromised, cancelling the project.

Decision

If a baseline for time, cost, quality, risks and benefits has been agreed during the initiation stage, the assessment should have produced a clear statement of how the project will be affected by the change request or issue. This is important to determine not only the extent to which those parameters may be affected, but also who should decide whether to accept the proposed solution. It is all too common for critical decisions to be passed down the organisational structure rather than upwards. The project organisation has been specifically designed with degrees of authority given to each level of management that must be respected. Determining who should make a decision to accept or decline a change to the project's parameters is made simpler by using red, amber and green escalation conditions. For instance, if, on assessing the effect of an issue that has taken the project by surprise, it is now forecast to be completed in the project manager's red zone, he must ask the project steering group for a decision. If the forecast completion date falls outside the project steering group's red zone, the decision must pass further upwards to the portfolio management team. If the escalation condition is amber, control remains with the management tier in question, but those above should be alerted.

In all the reports described in this chapter, the red, amber and green escalation conditions are clearly identified so it is instantly possible to determine who is authorised to decide which solution is to be adopted.

Amend plan

Having decided upon a certain course of action, the control cycle has come full circle and either the business case or the project plan, or both, will need updating.

If the solution was approved by the project manager, the updates may include altering the forecast timescales, budgets or quality expectations in keeping with the (now) approved solution.

If the effect of the change request or issue was significant enough to involve the project steering group or portfolio management team, additional changes to the project plan and/or the business case may be required. They will need to approve the new version to make sure it contains the revised parameters created by the impact assessment. These new parameters, possibly involving amended timescales, altered budgets or changed quality expectations, will form the project's revised baseline against which future variances will be measured.

If the degree of change has heightened the anxiety of the most senior authorities in the project, they may decide to make the escalation conditions more sensitive. This will make it more likely that the decision to accept proposed solutions to issues and change requests will be referred upwards either earlier or more often. This gives each level of management dynamic control over the authority of those below.

The importance of effective control

The control process is a sound basis for managing significant change. However, most competent managers delegate, monitor, report and control progress as a matter of course, taking decisions regularly and frequently without recourse to such governance. Even so, overconfidence can be a manager's downfall. Small changes can have a significant and lasting effect on a project. When added together, a number of small, seemingly insignificant variances can quickly add up to a critical slippage that may not only require referring upwards, but also affect the underlying justification of the project.

Effective control mitigates the risk of a project failing one day at a time.

Iterative project delivery

UNDERSTANDABLY, MANY USERS have struggled with the prospect that they may have to wait for months – or even years – for a project to deliver what they asked for. Equally, specialists have been frustrated by the fact that over time, users' needs appear to be continuously changing. This has resulted in progressively longer and longer delays, increasing the likelihood that what the project produces will no longer be relevant, and placing at risk the investment made by the sponsor.

The traditional sequential approach to development, where requirements are gathered and a design created before a solution is eventually developed, tested and implemented, has been the standard for many years, especially in the software industry (where it is commonly referred to as the "waterfall approach"). However, when account is taken of the pace of change, the burden of uncertainty, and our dependence on rapidly evolving digital solutions, it follows that an alternative to the sequential approach may be desirable.

With these challenges in mind, the software industry has spearheaded a development approach which is more and more iterative and incremental in its nature, producing blocks of features and functionality that progressively meet the emerging or prioritised needs of users in a dynamic environment. Figure 11.1 compares the linear sequence commonly associated with waterfall solution development, to the incremental growth and deployment of an iteratively developed product.

The incremental software development approach has become widely known as "agile". It is more helpful to say that agile is not so much a method as a state of mind from which a range of methods have

FIGURE 11.1 **Sequential and incremental development**

emerged, including, but not limited to, Scrum, Extreme Programming (XP), Dynamic Systems Development Method (DSDM) and Feature Driven Development (FDD). This book will not explore or describe each; what is central for leaders and managers to understand is that these are methods to deliver products, whereas change is delivered through projects. This chapter will explore how projects can accommodate agile product and service development methods as an alternative to a more traditional, sequential approach.

Increasing interest in the agile method has led to the need for, and creation of, what is commonly known as the Agile Manifesto*, a set of four values and twelve principles. Given that these arose from within the software industry, they are articulated to underpin iterative, incremental software development.

The Agile values

These assert a preference for:

- individuals and interactions over processes and tools;
- working software over comprehensive documentation;
- customer collaboration over contract negotiation;
- responding to change over following a plan.

---

* https://agilemanifesto.org/

In seeking to promote these values, it is helpful to understand that the items on the left are valued more than the items on the right.

It is as well to consider these values through the eyes of the three perspectives described throughout this book: the commercial sponsors of change, the specialists who build its products, and the users who use or operate them. Users benefit from maintaining a close connection with the specialists, enabling them to define what is needed, quickly experience the products of development, and suggest refinements. The specialists are able to create these products in the knowledge that there will be less likelihood of significant change later in the project, and that what they have produced is valued and appreciated by those who will use and operate it. The commercial interests of those who are funding the work must not be forgotten. Given that they hold the purse strings, their interests will be critical to the work, and often uppermost. This community will be motivated by the benefit of being able to realise a return on their investment with less risk of being undermined by the fast pace of change.

The following principles serve to underpin the agile software development values:

1. Customer satisfaction is ensured through early and continuous delivery of valuable software.

2. Changing requirements are welcomed, even in late development.

3. Working software is delivered frequently (weeks rather than months).

4. There is close, daily co-operation between business people and developers.

5. Projects are built around motivated individuals, who should be trusted.

6. Face-to-face conversation is the best form of communication (co-location).

7. Working software is the primary measure of progress.

8. Sustainable development is able to maintain a constant pace.

9. There is continuous attention to technical excellence and good design.

10. Simplicity – the art of maximising the amount of work not done – is essential.

11. The best architectures, requirements and designs emerge from self-organising teams.

12. The team reflects regularly on how to become more effective, and adjusts accordingly.

As can be seen, these principles have been created with the iterative, incremental development of software in mind. The language suggests that they may not be suited to all projects, especially those with little or no software content. It is certainly possible for some to be translated; for example, in identifying "working software", principle 7 may instead be interpreted to refer to the importance of producing a deliverable, whatever it may be. Others are so closely focused on the software development environment that they take little account of the practicalities of business change; for example, principle 6 assumes that face-to-face communication is always preferable, possible, suitable and necessary.

This is not to say that the features of an agile approach cannot be accommodated within the project management environment, nor that they can only be applied to software deliverables. Indeed, for reasons described in Chapter 2, it is more necessary now than ever before for leaders and managers to know how to deliver change of any sort, incrementally. For example, where a restaurant chain is creating a new menu, a traditional approach may be to design, develop and test every dish before launching the entirely new offering overnight. An alternative, incremental approach may be to engage customers to help develop, test and introduce each dish in turn, so as to build up a portfolio of menu items over time. Both approaches may ultimately take as long and require the same investment to arrive at a similar outcome. However, the incremental, iterative approach has allowed for the dynamic management of changing customer tastes, and the risk that some dishes may not be well received.

Therefore, it is perhaps more accurate to say that there are some projects which can and must be managed to deliver iterative, incremental change, and that there are some which may not be suited to an agile approach. Indeed, the very term "agile" has had unintended consequences. Those who do not understand it, wrongly assume that it confers an ability to produce the same outcome more quickly, or that it can be applied to any project, or that no change in behaviour is needed by those in the user or sponsoring communities for it to be successful. Whichever development approach is to be used – sequential or incremental – is a decision best taken by an educated, informed and capable project steering group, since it is they who are to own and direct the project on behalf of the organisation.

The benefits and risks of an agile development approach

There are some general benefits to be enjoyed by applying an iterative development approach:

- **Increased user engagement**. The close working relationship between users and specialists in an agile environment is a foundation stone on which every other benefit depends. This acknowledges two important principles: first, that project deliverables are being built for users and that the more involved they can be, the more likely they are to operate and adopt what the project creates; and second, that change is a constant pressure on any project and may be managed dynamically and collaboratively.

- **Dynamic change control.** Product changes are managed as they are identified, and are generally of lesser size and consequence as they relate to the product's incremental development. This is not to say that significant changes do not impact the project; the possibility of a change impacting the project's viability remains the same.

- **Increased collaboration.** There is significant and growing demand for agile development approaches from customers and users. This increases the likelihood that they are prepared to engage more collaboratively in the iterative creation of new products and services. Furthermore, the closer working relationship between clients and suppliers, facilitated by agile working, may also lead to the development of new commercial business opportunities and projects.

- **Prioritised requirements.** The combination of significant user participation and dynamic change control allows for – and encourages – the regular and frequent prioritisation of requirements. This ensures that the investment in time and resource is being focused on those needs which are considered to matter most.

- **Greater likelihood of product acceptance.** It is widely recognised that the use of regular and frequent iterative development cycles within an agile approach allows for the incremental creation of the product, ironing out issues and faults, and introducing improvements at every moment throughout the process. This increases the likelihood that the product will be accepted when presented for approval. This is in stark contrast to the more traditional sequential approach where a product's fitness for purpose is ultimately measured against criteria which may have been defined many weeks, months or even years ago.

- **Increased likelihood of use.** The more engaged and involved the users have been in the development of their product, the more likely they are to adopt it for use when the project comes to a close.

- **Opportunity for faster return on investment.** The possibility of more frequent product releases allows for the progressive realisation of commercial benefits. This also provides an opportunity for suppliers to introduce phased payment plans, resulting in a more even and regulated revenue flow.

- **Commercial proposition.** The benefits of iterative development may be offered by suppliers, thereby increasing the opportunities to secure new business.

To counterbalance the benefits, there are, of course, several risks in applying an agile development approach:

- **An absence of a clear and common understanding of the features, benefits, nature and practice of agile.** It is common for any method or approach to be misunderstood, or for independent pockets of understanding to develop which are inconsistent. To address this, agile delivery must be treated as any other method or approach; those who are to be involved in its application must be engaged and educated in order for the desired behaviours to become sufficiently adopted.

- **Agile development comes in many forms, which may become confused.** As noted earlier, agile may be thought of as a mindset from which a number of approaches have emerged. Before assuming that an organisation can adopt the relevant behaviours, it is essential to have settled on a method which is robust, reliable, appropriate for the nature and culture of the organisation and, above all, proven.

- **A commercial return is eclipsed as user needs are pursued.** The commercial value of what may be an attractive feature to a user, may not outweigh the investment needed to develop it. In mitigation, the sponsor and user authority must work in close collaboration to ensure that both user and commercial interests are met.

- **An academic understanding of the agile development approach is mistaken for the expertise needed to manage a project**. This can result in a poor investment and the loss of opportunity to observe and experience the benefits. When using any new method, it is certainly helpful to be advised by someone who understands it. However, it is also vital that those advisors can offer their expertise within the context of a working environment within which significant sums of time, money and energy are being invested. The approach must be applied according to the risk and opportunity it may address, and tailored and tuned according to the needs of the project and the organisation. If it is implemented in its purest form, it may not be seen as relevant to the real needs and experience of those who have to deliver change.

- **Users and customers misunderstand what is meant by agile delivery, resulting in a failure to meet their expectations.** Agile is a word that suggests the ability to move quickly and easily. Customers may consider this to mean that they will get what they were expecting, faster. A specialist might assert that the customer may gradually get what they were expecting by being able to engage and participate in the process of iterative development.

■ **Sales and account management colleagues misunderstand what is meant by agile delivery, resulting in a false expectation being sold.** As above, in those projects where one organisation is supplying its products and services to another, those who promote the benefits of an agile approach to the customer may also misunderstand how it is intended to operate, and sell a promise which cannot be met. Furthermore, the need for a continuous and close working relationship during the sales negotiation phase and during delivery is not widely appreciated. Therefore, the salesforce must be engaged and educated so as to fully understand not only the opportunities which agile development can offer, but also its challenges. Only then may they make clear the commitment expected from clients and users.

■ **There is a belief that agile development is incompatible with fixed price delivery, threatening the organisation's ability to meet customer's demands for both.** In commercial contracts between one organisation and another, it is common to develop agreements where clearly defined deliverables are created for a fixed price. This is perfectly compatible with an agile development approach, so long as certain important caveats are understood:

  – that the customer will participate fully in the product's development, providing the time and resource needed throughout;
  – that any changes to the product's features (as defined in the contract) are subject to management through commercial change control;
  – that before a fixed price is agreed, the features of the product and a plan for its creation (including the number of iterations) are agreed.

Sequential or incremental development?

Many technical considerations may be relevant when deciding which approach to adopt. After the relative pros and cons of each have been debated, the specialist member of the project steering group will be best placed to gather relevant insight and to add their authority to whatever conclusion is reached.

Whether an incremental approach to development is to be applied to software, or to non-software deliverables – or even to a combination of both – the central question for managers of change is this: If an incremental development approach is to be used, what is the consequence for the project's management environment? This book has promoted an approach to change and project management because it has been proven to provide the governance necessary to deliver lasting benefit for any kind of change. As has been noted throughout the book, the quality and quantity of management applied to a project must be tuned and tailored in proportion to its nature, risk, criticality and relative priority.

This rightly assumes that all projects are different. To determine that all projects must develop their deliverables in the same way can create a constraint that may favour some projects but harm others. Some projects, or parts of projects, are simply not suited to an agile approach. For example, the benefits of a bridge may not be realised in increments. Nor is it always possible to deliver a change in people's behaviour in defined or time-specific chunks. Therefore, each project must be assessed according to its own needs to determine which is the most appropriate method.

Here are some considerations when determining whether an incremental development approach is suitable:

- **Whether the business case would commercially benefit from – or not be compromised by – a progressive realisation of benefits.** For example, an incremental approach may allow for benefits to be realised much earlier than otherwise planned; a project to remove leased but unused hardware may be able to yield a return whenever batches of kit are sent back to the leasing company, rather than having to wait until all of the hardware has been located and processed. This is a fundamental consideration; without knowing the consequence of the development approach on the project's underlying commercial justification, the benefits may be put at risk. It is commonly argued that agile development breaks a project into smaller pieces so that each iteration may be delivered one at a time. However, without consideration of the business case, this approach may place the entire endeavour at risk. For example, if a project is required to make an upfront investment in some computer hardware, the incremental delivery approach must be able to deliver significant enough commercial benefit in sufficient enough time to pay back these early costs and maintain the confidence of the investors.

■ **If some or all of the project's deliverables are naturally suited to incremental development**. As noted above, incremental delivery does not suit all types of deliverable. Where it may be decomposed into a collection of usable or operable features or functions, incremental development and delivery may be possible. Software is a good example of this. However, if the project is required to design, develop and implement the architecture on which the software will ultimately operate, this component of the project may have to be developed in a more traditional, sequential manner.

■ **If the project is about to begin.** It is rarely helpful to impose a development method on a project which is already under way. The decision as to which development approach is to be used should be made by the project's own authorities, when it is being initiated.

■ **Whether the environment is subject to change.** The ability to react effectively and efficiently to change must be a feature of any project management environment. If the requirements of the project are considered relatively stable it may be appropriate to apply a traditional development life cycle. However, if the project is seeking to meet the needs or demands of an audience that is naturally dynamic, such as customers, an incremental approach will allow for many small changes to be swiftly addressed.

■ **Whether the user and/or specialist communities are ready, willing and able to deliver change in this way.** Given the importance of close collaboration between users and specialists, very large projects may not be suited to an agile approach. Furthermore, some user communities are not willing, interested or capable enough to collaborate as closely and for as long as may be required. However, smaller endeavours, characterised by individuals or teams that are enthusiastic, knowledgeable and able to engage with each other may be well suited to the approach. A successful collaboration also depends on the capabilities of the specialists; they must be sufficiently familiar with the agile mindset to both practice and promote it to others.

The incremental development cycle

Relevant terms associated with this form of development will be explained as they are encountered in the sections that follow. However, it is helpful to first understand the features of a development iteration, as illustrated in Figure 11.2.

An iteration is usually considered to be a two- or three-week, rigidly time-bound cycle of development work. It commences with a planning phase that determines how the resources available to the iteration are to be assigned to the work. The scope is determined by a senior member of the user community who maintains a prioritised list of what is needed in the product. When work is under way, the product is developed to its next incremental level. This may represent the addition of new features and functions or the refinement of those that already exist. Daily update meetings are held, at which each member of the team shares their progress and plans with the team. The iteration review is where the developed features or functions are demonstrated

FIGURE 11.2 **An iterative cycle**

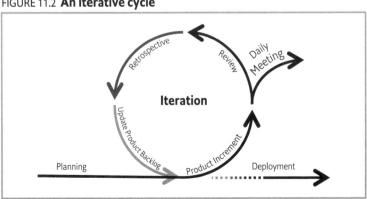

to determine their quality and state of completion. An iteration retrospective allows both the senior member of the user community and the iteration team leader to understand and refine how the team is working. Thereafter, the backlog of work is updated to reflect what has or has not been delivered, and what, if any, further additions and changes have been requested. It is then possible for the increment to be deployed into the operational environment.

What may be seen from this cycle is that it very closely mirrors the sequential development life cycle, but in miniature; a product is planned, developed, tested and deployed, and lessons are learned to allow for improvement. That said, there are also some features that are not contained within the cycle, such as cost-justifying the entire endeavour, determining how many such iterations there must be to deliver the vision, educating communities to operate and use the product, encouraging the adoption of new practices and behaviours, and determining the extent to which the intended benefits have been realised. Effective change and project management must do all of these things. For this reason, it is important to recognise that agile development approaches sit within a broader management framework.

If it has been determined that a project is to deliver some of its products by means of an agile approach, even if only in part, the governance may be tailored, as would be the case for any project. Taking the subject areas in the order presented in this book, here are the key features of the project's management environment that may be tuned to accommodate an incremental, iterative approach to developing and releasing deliverables.

Roles and responsibilities

Allowing for the fact that there are a great many different agile approaches, there are several common or popular roles that deserve to be compared and contrasted with those already described in this book.

Reference has been made to a senior member of the user community who is accountable for the product that the project is to deliver. From an agile perspective, this person is commonly referred to as the product owner. They are accountable for the creation, prioritisation and maintenance of the list of what is to be included in the product, known as the product backlog. This rightly suggests that, in common with the role of the project steering group's user authority, the product owner is also accountable for the product's fitness for purpose at each deployment, and at the eventual close of the project. This requires them to engage closely with both the wider user community and the development team to ensure that focus is maintained on those features and functions which are of greatest priority.

Furthermore, they must have a close and effective working relationship with the sponsor to ensure that the requirements of the users are balanced against the need to deliver a commercially viable outcome. Given the importance of this role, it follows that it should be represented by a single person and that they must be granted the authority to discharge their responsibilities as a key member of the project steering group.

Also noted in an earlier example in this chapter was the manager of the iteration. This individual may be variously called the scrum master, sprint leader or iteration leader, depending on which form of agile development is being practised. They are accountable for the planning,

FIGURE 11.3 **An organisation structure for a project using mixed approaches to development**

monitoring and control of each iteration to produce the features of the product that the product owner has identified.

In this way, their activities may be similar to that of a project manager or team leader. However, when designing the project's organisational structure, it is important not to assume that one is a replacement for the other. It is questionable whether the manager of an iteration may also be the project's manager. Depending on the nature of the project, it may also be required to produce deliverables and outcomes that cannot be created by means of an agile approach, including educated users, customers who behave differently, a new company operating model, replacement hardware or any number of deliverables that are unique to that project. Therefore, it is possible that the iteration manager will report to a project manager as would any leader of a workstream. The example in Figure 11.3 imagines a project with a significant amount of non-IT business change (such as education and behaviour change activity), plus some procurement and systems development activity.

Articulating and promoting the vision

In Chapter 5, it was noted that the vision may be articulated according to a variety of perspectives, these being commercial, specialist and user. As a senior user authority, the product owner is accountable for describing and promoting the output expected by the user community. They may do this by creating the product vision. This is the part of the entire project's vision, which specifically describes the product's future state. This sits alongside the sponsor's business case, which describes the intended commercial outcomes, some of which will be realised through benefits arising from use and operation of the product.

As a means of describing the journey from the present to future state of the product, the product owner may also create a product roadmap, expressing the probable development of the product over time in pursuit of the product vision.

Planning risks and rewards

The business case is as central to a project which uses an agile approach as it is to any other form of development. The fact that the product of the project is to be developed iteratively means that there is a possibility for some benefits to be realised as the project progresses. This progressive realisation of benefits can be reflected in the cost-benefit analysis. While the early arrival of benefits may appear attractive, the costs must also be tracked to ensure that the project remains likely to deliver a commercially viable outcome in the long term. Given the iterative nature of the product's development, it is easy to allow the cost of the project to run away while incremental changes are delivered and new features are added to the backlog.

Every iteration must be considered within the context of the business case as both a contributor to benefit and cost. Just as a change request to a more traditional, sequentially developed product must be considered for its impact on the plan and on the business case, iterative development must be no different. In other words, while the interests of the users and specialists are being satisfied during the iterative development process, the commercial viability of the entire project must not be forgotten. A project of this nature will also have an end, and must deliver clearly measurable benefits as might be expected from any other form of project.

Planning quality

As for any development approach, quality is an important component to plan, monitor, control and deliver. This is eased by having users and specialists participate in close harmony and proximity. Furthermore, while an agile approach allows for the product to be described from the outset for which quality criteria will be necessary, it also determines that it will be delivered in increments and iterations, as features are added and refined progressively. Therefore, while each cycle of iterative development is time-constrained to two or three weeks, it is also determined by the features which it will deliver and the quality criteria it must meet. The product owner is accountable for ensuring that users' quality expectations are specified, planned, built, tested and delivered. To this end, the product vision can be helpful in describing the product not only in terms of its objectives, but also by the measurable standard to which it must aspire. Equally, the product backlog that lists and prioritises the items for inclusion, must also make clear what

FIGURE 11.4 **A product breakdown structure for a project using an agile development approach**

quality expectations each incremental delivery must meet. Therefore, quality criteria may be used to articulate the fitness for purpose of any deliverable, whether it is produced as result of an agile iteration or as the end product of a more traditional sequential life cycle.

Any project which adopts an agile development approach may continue to benefit from quality-centric planning, as described in Chapter 7. Consider the simplified example in Figure 11.4 of a product breakdown structure for a computer system which is to be developed using an agile approach.

Although the agile approach seeks to lessen the focus on creating "comprehensive documentation", some records are helpful as evidence of decisions and choices. Examples contained in the scope of this project are the product vision, the product roadmap, the epics (which is a term used to describe a group of requirements) and user stories (which are more detailed needs described from a user's perspective). Although each epic might be seen as a number of component user stories, they are not represented on the product breakdown structure in hierarchical relationship to each other, but as separate, individual deliverables. This is because, in identifying the user stories, the epic does not become a redundant product; both the described epic and the articulated user stories are deliverables to be created by the project.

Next, it is necessary to consider the order in which the deliverables may be developed, taking into account the iterative nature of the approach, as shown in Figure 11.5.

Before entering the period of iterative development, this project will first create the product vision and roadmap. This eases and facilitates the identification and development of the epics which, as noted above, must be clearly articulated. This allows for the user stories to be identified and described from which the backlog is developed. Note that the backlog is referred to in this example as the "updated product backlog". This recognises that the backlog is an ever-changing deliverable which will exist in many states during the life of the project, reflecting the users' changing needs and priorities.

Thereafter, the iterations are identified as deliverables. Note that an iteration is not a deliverable but a process by which to create one. In this example, the iteration's output is working software. Therefore, the naming convention recognises that each iteration must deliver

FIGURE 11.5 **A product flow diagram for a project using an agile development approach**

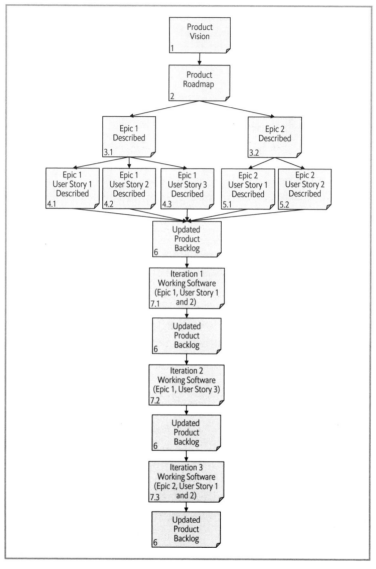

something of substance that meets a defined quality standard. If not already contained in the epic, user story or product backlog, that quality standard may be articulated as a product description, as described in Chapter 7.

Planning time and cost

As also noted in Chapter 7, there is a close relationship between time, cost and quality. If any one of these is to be rigorously enforced, it requires that the others must be flexible. The quality of what can be achieved in a fixed number of weeks must be tailored to fit. Therefore, when planning what an iteration must deliver (as described above), due account must be taken of the number of resources available, and the users' expectation of what might constitute a product of sufficient quality. The process to arrive at a plan (the details of which were described in Chapter 8) remains the same, but with the following small clarifications:

- With time constrained to a limited number of weeks for each iteration, what each cycle produces must be clearly defined. If not, it must be accepted that, if an iteration cannot produce what was expected, a revision of priorities in the backlog must follow.
- The estimation of the resources needed for each iteration is related to the volume of work to be completed within a fixed period.
- The value and cost associated with any delivery will be of particular importance to the sponsor, given that each cycle has the potential to produce not only a deliverable, but also the realisation of commercial benefits.

What becomes apparent is that there are some aspects of change that may not be so easily created by a process of iteration. For example, the communication to, and education of, users or customers who are to receive the new features or functions, may not suit an agile development approach. The adoption of new practices and behaviours is equally important and must somehow be planned into the project. The procurement of materials or technology may also not be suited

FIGURE 11.6 **Agile and non-agile work in a Gantt chart**

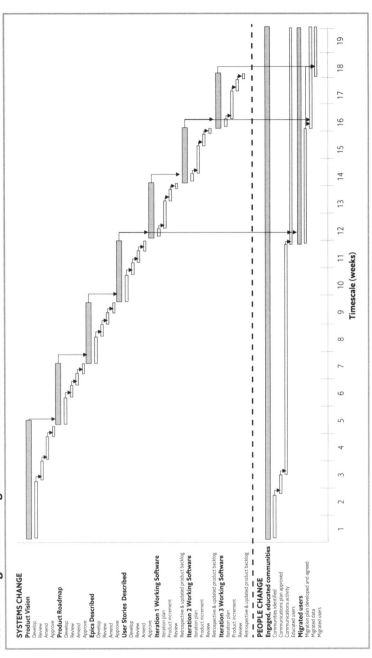

to being delivered in this way. So, it is to be expected that, while some deliverables lend themselves to iterative development, others do not. Therefore, there is a need for a plan that combines agile and traditionally developed products. An example of how agile and non-agile work may sit alongside each other in a plan is illustrated in the Gantt chart representation in Figure 11.6.

The work to deliver a new computer system follows the sequence identified in the product flow diagram in Figure 11.5. The schedule is based on a planning condition that each iterative cycle must be of a two-week duration. Beneath the dotted line, some people-change activity has been added. Engagement and education are considered to be continuous work that run alongside the systems change activity. The migration of users to the new system also appears beneath the line, particularly because of its close dependence on the behavioural-change activity. Some dependencies also exist between the iterative cycles and the migration of users. In this way, agile and non-agile work can be accommodated within a single plan.

As each iterative cycle is intended to complete with the deployment of the latest product increment, it is also possible that there is some people-change activity which must immediately follow. Such post-deployment activity might include the production and promotion of iteration-specific education and communication materials, or the management of questions arising from its introduction. The way in which this may be shaped and planned is illustrated in Figure 11.7.

The planning of an individual iteration must be accommodated within the two- or three-week cycle. This begins with the product owner's selection of items from the product backlog. This must take account of those items' relative priority and the strategic vision for the product's development contained in the product roadmap. Due consideration must also be given to the benefits which the iteration will realise, relative to the cost of development. The iteration may be characterised by certain features which are not only important, but which may also be promoted to the user community in a way that facilitates their understanding and adoption of it. Therefore, it can help to determine a set of quality criteria by which to judge the fitness for purpose of the iteration's output. With this knowledge, the iteration leader prepares a plan for the two- or three-week cycle, taking account

FIGURE 11.7 **Detail within the Gantt chart**

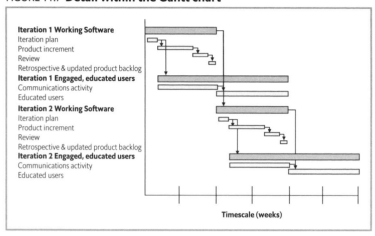

of the need to develop the identified items, review the working output, consider the effectiveness of the team, update the backlog, and deploy the product increment.

Initiating projects

While users and specialists may be motivated to quickly commence the agile development of the project's product, the same five questions first outlined in Chapter 1 apply for this form of project as any other. It remains essential to know that the project is commercially justified and has been prioritised alongside every other endeavour; it will be competing for resources that may be in need elsewhere. A considered organisational structure will allow for the determination of who is to participate in the leadership and management of the project. A project plan must establish the commensurate levels of time, money and quality within which the project must operate. And the remaining governance for change control, risk management and communication must be put in place. Only when initiation is complete should the authority be provided for the commitment of resources to the project.

Project delivery

Given the challenges of managing change in a dynamic environment, the same aspects remain subject to control in an agile development as they do in any other. The control cycle, described in the previous chapter, serves the same purpose. However, some of the mechanics of operation are different.

Project steering group controls

These are no different from those described in Chapter 10 and should be applied according to the demands of the project steering group participants and the riskiness of the project itself.

Project manager controls

In addition to any regular progress management activity which the project manager considers necessary (as described in Chapter 10), there is also the opportunity to manage progress within each iterative cycle; this is one of the great features of agile development. On the assumption that an iteration is of a fixed duration, whoever is charged with the management of the iteration – be that the project manager or iteration leader – there are four aspects that must be controlled and regulated:

- **Effort/cost**. The resources required to deliver what has been included within the scope of the iteration must be sufficient to deliver the product increment. If progress falls behind, there is the option of drawing in further resources in greater number or expertise, or gaining the product owner's authority to reduce the scope or quality of what the iteration is to produce. If this choice is exercised, the product backlog may be updated with any items that cannot be delivered during the present iteration.

- **Change.** Change may be managed at a dynamic level within the iteration, allowing users and specialists to adjust the quality of the emerging product as development proceeds. Change may be managed by the product owner between iterations as the product backlog is continuously reappraised and prioritised. Project-level change may also be managed in the way described in the previous chapter.

■ **Quality**. Users have continual access to the emerging product as it is developed in increments. Furthermore, with a review built into the iteration cycle, there is further opportunity to determine the product's fitness for purpose. In this way, the quality life cycle is contained within an iteration, in addition to any other quality management activity which is necessary or desirable within the project.

■ **People.** Maintaining a motivated and engaged team is no less important in an agile environment. In addition to using their intuition, the iteration leader has the formal opportunity of the daily meeting to observe and maintain enthusiasm for the work, and to address any concerns.

The illustration in Figure 11.2 identifies the daily meeting. This is a time-boxed opportunity for members of the team to advise on what has been completed, what is due to be completed, and what barriers there may be to completion. The emphasis is on the quality and completeness of each individual's respective work. For this very reason, clear product quality criteria (as can be found in a product description) can be of immense value for determining what constitutes a complete piece of work. Quite commonly, this meeting is performed standing up to maintain the emphasis on brevity. It may also be performed in front of a task board. This is a physical, visual representation of those items which are to be started, those which are under way, and those which are complete.

Project closure and beyond

As noted above, many controls are exercised within each iterative cycle. The same is also true of some of the events that take place at the end of a traditional, sequentially organised project.

The retrospective is a planned opportunity for members of the team to consider what lessons may be learned from the recent iterative cycle. In this way, it is comparable to the lessons learned event described in Chapter 13 and is in keeping with the agile manifesto that states that "regularly, the team reflects on how to become more effective, and adjusts accordingly". With the emphasis on a quicker pace, a smaller scope and reduced paperwork, the retrospective for an iteration may be brief and undocumented. However, the same essential questions are asked of those who participated:

- What went well?
- What did not go well?
- What may be done to improve?

A lessons learned review agenda may be used (see Chapter 13) although it may be significantly shortened to no more than 45 minutes in total.

In a more traditional, sequentially planned project, the deployment of the product is commonly expected at the end when it is subjected to progressive levels of testing before being released into the operational environment. This may seem very different from the way in which product increments are deployed from an agile development iteration. However, while the number and frequency of releases are greater, the care and attention given to each release should be no different. This is because each deployment represents a handover from a project team to business-as-usual. Trivial as an individual product increment may seem in the grand scheme, it represents a change to the way in which the organisation works, and carries with it the potential to change people's working practices and behaviour, for good or bad.

Project closure removes the machinery of management that has wrapped around the entire project, regardless of which development approach has been applied. However, at the point at which the project steering group is asked to approve the recommendation to close the project, particular attention should be paid to the state of the product backlog, the product roadmap and the product vision. This will allow for an assessment of what items had been originally anticipated for inclusion, and what was ultimately delivered within the constraints of time and money available. It may be at this time that further increments are discussed or encouraged. This is quite reasonable and legitimate, on condition that the commitment of any further investment is managed within the governance of a project, and within the context of the many other changes which the organisation may be planning.

Finally, benefits realisation, although a feature of incremental change, must be measured in the long term to ensure that the associated change in working patterns and behaviours have taken place and are now being practised as a second nature.

Agile development in practice – a case study

A very large, global organisation had been using a system called TIM to record and report how workers spent their time. At the end of a working week, everyone entered into TIM the number of hours they had spent on different business-as-usual activities and projects. Importantly, the project data were compared with plans to determine whether the work was progressing on track, and served to identify where corrective action may be necessary. Of course, the data held in TIM was useful to a great many managers since it allowed for the creation of reports detailing measures of productivity, resource demand and supply, financial positions and so on.

TIM had been adapted over the years to suit the organisation's specific needs. Many business processes had been developed to fit around TIM's idiosyncrasies. This also affected the culture of the organisation; people could be heard to say that "TIM needs you to do your timesheet" or "TIM won't let you see that report". Many people had become expert in the use and operation of TIM to the extent that their jobs depended on its continued use.

So when the supplier of TIM announced that the system would be retired at the end of the following year, the organisation had a difficult decision to make. Should it stick with TIM and maintain it in-house, accept a new solution from the supplier, or develop something new? It chose the latter.

Having done so, two projects were outlined that were to be delivered one after the other. The first would replace TIM with like-for-like functionality from a new software package, called CLAIRE. After a period of stabilisation, the second project would provide incremental improvements in order for users of CLAIRE to benefit from many of the new system's additional features. It may come as no surprise to discover that the first project followed a traditional, sequential life cycle, and the second was conceived of as a series of agile increments.

The second project was overseen by a project steering group composed of three key stakeholders who represented the perspectives described in Chapter 4.

■ The sponsor was the IT director who had committed the organisation to invest in CLAIRE and benefit from system and process performance improvements, reductions in headcount and, of course, the avoided risk of continuing to depend on an unsupported computer system;

■ The specialist interests were represented by the account manager from the company which developed CLAIRE and was helping to implement and tailor it;

■ A new participant – the product owner – was introduced to represent the users of the new system.

The success of the business case for the second project depended on further risk mitigation, and productivity and procedural improvements leading to resource reductions to which department managers had committed.

With contributions from scores of users, the product owner developed the product vision and roadmap. These helped to determine that some significant new features would be delivered during the course of five, time-bound agile development cycles, covering:

1. Portfolio management – using CLAIRE functionality to help anticipate, plan, monitor and control clusters of projects;

2. Project planning – encouraging project managers to adapt their planning practices to fit the more structured work-flow encompassed in CLAIRE;

3. Project reporting – increasing the quantity, quality and scope of project reports to facilitate better control;

4. Management accounting –specifying and developing new reports and processes to improve the management of budgets and resources;

5. Off-shore resource management – deploying CLAIRE to a group of colleagues who had not been in scope during the initial rollout in the first project.

Much of the above was well suited to the incremental nature of an agile approach. For example, CLAIRE's portfolio management functionality was assessed by the product owner, who determined which of the key features were most attractive for inclusion in the first agile cycle. A team of developers and users was formed and a scrum leader appointed. Daily stand-up meetings were conducted with the team in front of a Kanban board to monitor and maintain progress. The scrum leader worked closely with the product owner to maintain control of scope, quality and team effectiveness.

However, not all of the work was perfectly suited to the use of an agile approach. While the second cycle (project planning) included the development and deployment of some more of CLAIRE's software features, it also required that the organisation's cohort of project managers adopt some behaviours and practices that were, to many of them, quite alien. For example, previously they had not been required to approve a project worker's weekly timesheet. This had been instead left to the worker's line manager who knew very little about each specific project and would sign the timesheet without question. Since each project manager was accountable for the time charged to their project, it seemed perfectly reasonable that they should take on this responsibility. However, there was significant resistance from many who were faced with the prospect not only of having to take on what they considered to be an additional administrative burden, but who were also reluctant to be held accountable for their project's budget.

With this practical challenge in mind, the project plan was composed of a series of agile iterations that delivered new functionality, but with longer periods of accompanying activity designed to engage and educate a project management community on which the business depended.

Summary

Agile – and incremental development – has been referred to as a mindset. What has been described in this chapter may suggest that an organisation needs to undergo a period of change to fully comprehend and practise the management of iterative, incremental product development. Compared to a sequential approach, an agile approach may represent an entirely new way of working. For an organisation to achieve a new mindset suggests, as noted throughout this book and especially in the final chapter, that it is able to discover, articulate and embed new practices and behaviours.

Support and assurance

WORKING ON A PROJECT can be confusing and demanding for people new to change management. Even those familiar with the language, the processes and the responsibilities will need some help.

A common way of providing help is to use a support/assurance function to:

- assist the project manager and project team;
- assure the project steering group that the project management environment is, and continues to be, fit for its intended purpose;
- assist and assure the portfolio management team in their governance of the portfolio.

The support/assurance function can have a variety of names, such as:

- Project office
- Project support office
- Project management office
- Programme office

There is no typical structure, position or remit for a support/assurance function since it provides a tailored set of products and services to a specific audience whose needs are many and various.

FIGURE 12.1 **Support/assurance structure**

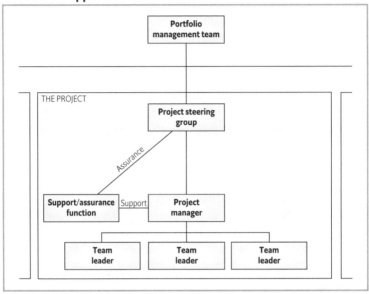

The need for, and benefits of, a support/ assurance function

A support/assurance function is not always essential. Much will depend on the size, criticality and risks of the changes being delivered and the needs and experience of the people working on the project and within the wider organisation.

Project managers may benefit from having some administrative responsibilities removed, freeing them to manage more effectively. The project steering group may benefit from the independent assurance that their project is in safe hands. The portfolio management team may be unable to function effectively without the regular management information they need to make critical decisions.

The variety of people that the support/assurance function is there to serve suggests that its positioning is critical. The structure illustrated in Figure 12.1 will support a project manager and assure the project steering group.

However, to serve a portfolio management team, the support/

FIGURE 12.2 **Support/assurance structure outside the individual project**

assurance function should be outside any individual project, as in Figure 12.2.

A combination of both may be needed if the project manager, project steering group and portfolio management team all need support and assurance, as in Figure 12.3.

Therefore, the help provided by the support/assurance function and the way it is delivered will depend on who is to be served. Given this, the benefits of an effective and efficient support/assurance function can be:

■ better use of scarce skills;

■ development arena for project management expertise;

■ faster and more accurate impact assessment of changes and risks;

■ application of common standards;

■ stronger application of a common management discipline;

■ central and single repository for management information;

FIGURE 12.3 **Support/assurance function for all parties**

- flexible service provision according to need;
- greater confidence in alignment of projects to strategic imperatives.

Introducing and operating a support/assurance function entails costs. In addition to running overheads, the satisfaction of one audience usually comes at a cost to another. For instance, providing management information to the portfolio management team suggests that the project managers will be required to gather the necessary project data but they will see no benefit from doing so. Therefore, the support/assurance function must have a clear and approved remit.

Support and assurance definition report

This document describes what a support/assurance function offers and how it will do so. Its success will be judged by answering these questions:

- Does it identify a steering group of sufficient authority to direct it to a successful outcome?
- Does it identify a support/assurance function manager of sufficient experience to plan, monitor and control it effectively?
- Does the solution address the identified issues and opportunities?
- Have all potential constraints been addressed?
- Is its position in the organisation clear?
- Are customers of the support/assurance function specifically identified?
- Have the products and services it is there to provide been prioritised to make sure the benefits are realised swiftly?

A support and assurance definition report should cover the areas listed in Table 12.1.

TABLE 12.1 Support and assurance definition report

Background	An outline of how the proposal for a support/assurance function has come about so that the environment within which it is to be introduced may be fully understood.
Issues and opportunities	A detailed explanation of the reasons a support/assurance function is considered to be an appropriate solution.
Constraints	What matters will constrain the way in which the support/assurance function operates?
Governance	How will the support/assurance function be structured?
Products and services	What will the support/assurance function provide, to whom and in what order of priority?

Background

As many people will have an opinion about what needs the support/assurance function must satisfy, this section must describe the principal drivers. These will be more fully expressed in a business case, but until then, this section must provide a background of sufficient depth to make sure it is clear why the support/assurance function is being considered.

Issues and opportunities

This section must fully express the challenges and opportunities faced by each customer of the support/assurance function. The section can be divided by customer type (project manager, project steering group, portfolio management team, and so on). Failure to clearly identify the issues and opportunities may result in an expensive support/assurance function that adds little value.

Constraints

Many factors will affect the remit of the support/assurance function. This section should consider the following areas, not all of which will be relevant in every case:

- **Who is to be served?** This statement must be consistent with the needs expressed in the issues and opportunities section.
- **Customer expectation.** How will each of those to be served judge the success of the support/assurance function? Are their expectations contradictory? Have their expectations been prioritised?
- **Shared resource.** Is the support/assurance function to be responsible for providing project resources across a portfolio? For instance, are people with project planning experience to be made available according to project demand?
- **Organisational scope.** Where will the line be drawn between its responsibilities and those of the finance team, the resource demand/supply team, the management information team, the head of project management, and so on?
- **Skills and experience availability.** To what extent are the specialist competencies already available within the organisation? Will they need to be sourced from outside?
- **Internal structure.** What internal organisational structure will be suitable? How senior must it be? What will be the internal reporting structure?

- **Delivery structure.** Will specialist services be delivered by support/assurance function team experts or will all its team members deliver all services?

- **Professional development.** Will participants be drawn from the project management resource pool, or will they seek to join it? What would be the next career step for the support/assurance function manager?

- **Administrative support.** Is the support/assurance function expected to deliver administrative services either wholly or in addition to other offerings?

- **Advisory.** To what extent will it be expected to provide "expert" support and assurance? Would the team members be known for their proficiency as project management professionals?

- **Culture.** Is there a history of attempts made at implementing a support/assurance function? Is the concept new to the organisation? How ready is the organisation to accept the investment it will need to make?

- **Phasing/growth/maturity.** Will it be a permanent or temporary function? If it is not expected to outlive the project(s) it supports, how will it be disbanded?

- **Location.** Will it need to be physically based in a particular location? Can it operate "virtually"? Could the team be split, and if so, how?

- **Technology.** How can technology be used to help deliver its products and services? How much is already automated and centralised? To what extent would technology be needed to allow the products and services to be effectively utilised?

- **Methodical approach.** Will it be expected to develop and/or administer the organisation's approach to project management?

- **Impartiality.** Where will the line be drawn between the responsibility to support and potentially having to audit the project? Will the people working in the support/assurance function be mature enough to manage such challenges? What form of assurance could it offer: project management health checks, internal project audits, externally resourced project audits?

■ **Value for money.** Will the team charge for its services? If so, how? How will the quality of service be assured?

Failure to overcome such constraints could lead to the increased likelihood of serious risks. For example, the support/assurance function may:

■ be seen as an ivory tower, resulting in a loss of respect and reputation;

■ fail to deliver real value and create instead a financial burden for the organisation;

■ not deliver soon enough, resulting in a loss of faith in its ability to support the organisation;

■ not offer its members a development path towards a clear and desirable objective, resulting in their demotivation.

Governance

The definition report must show how the support/assurance function will be structured and governed. It might be relatively simple to create a team or department within the line structure to deliver the necessary products and services, but this suggests a permanency that may not be appropriate. If the team are to support and assure those temporary management environments called projects, it is sensible to develop the support/assurance function along similar lines; it would not become a fixed body and would need to demonstrate its continued relevance throughout its lifetime, just like a project.

In this way, the support/assurance function would be:

■ justified by a business case;

■ owned and directed by a team of sponsors;

■ managed by a project manager;

■ controlled by a plan;

■ required to deliver value in stages, throughout its life, adding more value at each stage;

■ able to close when its purpose has been achieved.

Since the purpose and value of a support/assurance function are often questioned, treating it like a project demonstrates to its customers that it faces the same challenges as a project, will benefit from the application of principles and techniques described in this book, and is shown to be credible by the way it responds to them.

Therefore, if it is to be justified by a business case, its intended benefits must be clearly outlined and quantified by a set of sponsors. Whether or not they are called a project steering group is up to them; it may be more appropriate to call them a support/assurance function steering group, comprising the following:

■ **Sponsor.** A person representing the body that will commercially sponsor the support/assurance function, who might be an existing project sponsor, a department line manager or possibly a member of the portfolio management team.

■ **Developer representative(s).** A person (or people) who can offer an authoritative view on how the support/assurance function is to be constructed, governed and made active. They may have operated one previously or come from a third-party project management specialist.

■ **Customer representative(s).** This person (or persons) would be very important, providing the success criteria by which the support/assurance function would be judged. Depending on the audiences to be served, the customer representative could be a project manager, a project steering group member, a member of the portfolio management team, or a combination of all three.

The project manager, or more appropriately the support/ assurance function manager, will be responsible for development and implementation according to an approved plan drawn up to satisfy the expectations set out in the business case. It must show how the support/ assurance function can be enabled to deliver value to its customers as soon as possible, and how that the value can be maintained or increased over time.

Products and services

Below are some common products and services demanded from a support/assurance function.

To support and/or assure the portfolio management team

- contribute to the development and continued management of the portfolio plan;
- develop and maintain the organisation's methodical approach to project management;
- monitor progress of all projects against the portfolio plan, prepare portfolio forecast reports and alert the portfolio management team to variances;
- assure the integrity of products being delivered by the portfolio particularly regarding:
  - scope, to confirm that duplication or omissions are minimised;
  - value, to provide assurance that projects are delivering to cost with a clear focus on benefits management;
  - competencies, to ensure that the organisation's skills are being applied effectively and efficiently;
  - timescale, to determine that projects remain focused on time targets and that dependencies are being honoured;
  - strategic fit, to assure the portfolio management team that projects have been prioritised to meet the organisation's strategic imperatives;
  - compliance, to demonstrate that standards and procedures are being respected;
- conduct health checks and propose solutions;
- assess and advise on the implications of changes to the portfolio plan;
- provide support in using tools or techniques for managing the portfolio or projects;
- identify and satisfy training needs;

- develop and maintain a register of the organisation's project resources and skills;
- facilitate portfolio co-ordination and communication sessions;
- track and measure the realisation of benefits from projects.

To support and/or assure the project steering group

- help to link projects to the organisation's strategic imperatives;
- advise on initiation procedures;
- advise on identifying and managing benefits in the business case;
- help the sponsor to maintain the business case;
- help to prepare project steering group meetings;
- propose and/or conduct project health checks;
- advise on closure procedures;
- support the sponsor during the benefits realisation stage.

To support the project manager

Planning:

- help the project manager to prepare the project plan;
- facilitate and/or administer planning sessions;
- assist in developing estimates;
- help the project manager prepare changes to plans where escalation conditions have been breached;
- propose recovery actions where escalation conditions have been breached

Control:

- make sure that time recording and forecast reporting procedures are being applied;
- produce the project forecast report for the project manager, alerting him to key variances;
- administer change control procedures;
- assess the effect of change requests and issues;
- facilitate the regular identification of risks;

- maintain and update the business case, particularly regarding costs;
- make sure that all quality controls are applied through maintaining the product quality log;
- attend quality reviews when appropriate to make sure they are adequate;
- assist in closing the project.

Administration:
- co-ordinate all quality control activities;
- check or complete timesheet information on behalf of all project resources;
- minute all project meetings;
- administer the project's configuration management;
- identify training requirements and assist in their resolution;
- gather improvements to the approach to project management.

Consultancy:
- coach project personnel in project management;
- provide project planning support and assistance to all project personnel;
- provide guidance on assorted specialist matters;
- develop and/or support automated tools or techniques;
- provide support to improve the accuracy of estimates.

When the products and services desired are identified, needs should be prioritised so that a pilot phase can provide the most important ones to start with, adding others over time.

Defining, validating and implementing a support/assurance function

The product flow diagram in Figure 12.4 shows how to implement the support/assurance function as a project.

This approach allows for effective project management principles

FIGURE 12.4 **Product flow diagram**

to be applied to developing and implementing the support/assurance function while its operation is subject to continued phased benefit reviews to determine whether or not it is delivering value.

Key products in the approach are as follows:

- **Business case.** To justify why the support/assurance function is necessary and to set targets against which it must be seen to perform.

- **Support/assurance function definition report.** As described above.

- **Communications document.** To describe the audiences, methods of communication and messages needed to promote the support/assurance function so that all essential stakeholders are engaged.

- **Recruited support/assurance function personnel.** To develop and deliver the range of products and services. This may begin with support from specialist third parties but can eventually be delivered internally.

- **Developed tranche one products and services.** The support/assurance function must offer a range of products and services that will be popular with and benefit its customer(s). The first tranche must satisfy an immediate demand and make sure the investment in the support/assurance function can be justified.

- **Operational environment.** This may be a physical space for the support/assurance function to occupy or a virtual web or intranet environment through which it can operate.

- **Common data repository.** Since it is almost inevitable that the support/assurance function will be asked for project management information, the core data must be gathered and held somewhere. This usually begins as a spreadsheet from which some of the reports described in Chapter 10 are produced. However, most organisations quickly outgrow the storage capacity and capabilities of a spreadsheet and need to develop ever-more sophisticated data management tools. This list gives an idea of the data fields needed to produce sensible management information:
  - Project name
  - Project manager
  - Project sponsor
  - Customer representative(s)
  - Developer representative(s)

- Dependent projects
- Milestones/deliverables name
- Time escalation conditions – red, from and to
- Time escalation conditions – amber, from and to
- Time escalation conditions – green, from and to
- Milestone/deliverable quality reviewers
- Approval authority
- Baseline start date
- Baseline end date
- Forecast/actual start date
- Forecast/actual end date
- Start date variance (calculated)
- End date variance (calculated)
- Time within escalation conditions? (calculated)
- Reason for time variance
- Draft completion date
- Quality review "invitation sent" date
- Quality review "baseline review" date
- Quality review "review complete" date
- Quality review outcome
- Quality review number of changes
- Quality review "changes complete" date
- Quality review "approved fit for purpose" date
- Resource name
- Resource escalation conditions – red, from and to
- Resource escalation conditions – amber, from and to
- Resource escalation conditions – green, from and to
- Resource baseline items
- Resource baseline unit value
- Resource baseline total (calculated)
- Resource actual to date items
- Resource actual to date unit value
- Resource actual to date total (calculated)
- Resource estimate to complete items
- Resource estimate to complete unit value
- Resource estimate to complete total (calculated)
- Resource forecast (calculated)

- Resource variance (calculated)
- Resource within escalation conditions? (calculated)
- Reason for resource variance
- Quality measure
- Quality escalation conditions – red, from and to
- Quality escalation conditions – amber, from and to
- Quality escalation conditions – green, from and to
- Quality measure baseline
- Quality measure actual to date
- Quality measure success % (calculated)
- Quality within escalation conditions? (calculated)
- Reason for quality measure variance
- Benefit name
- Benefit escalation conditions – red, from and to
- Benefit escalation conditions – amber, from and to
- Benefit escalation conditions – green, from and to
- Benefit baseline
- Benefit actual to date
- Benefit estimate to complete
- Benefit forecast (calculated)
- Benefit variance ($ and %) (calculated)
- Benefit within escalation conditions? (calculated)
- Reason for benefit variance
- Risk description
- Risk escalation conditions – red, from and to
- Risk escalation conditions – amber, from and to
- Risk escalation conditions – green, from and to
- Risk likelihood
- Risk impact
- Risk factor (calculated)
- Risk mitigation
- Risk contingency amount

■ **Piloted products and services.** This is the first time that the tranche one products and services will have been provided to a real customer of the support/assurance function.

- **Project closure report.** This will close the project and initiate the benefits realisation phase(s).
- **Customer engagement review.** This will determine how far the customers of the support/assurance function are satisfied with the quality and form of its products and services. It must not only determine their happiness with what has been delivered, but should also ascertain their future needs so that the support/assurance function can respond.
- **Reassessed business case.** This will ensure that there remains sufficient enthusiasm, a market and enough funding for the support/assurance function to continue.
- **Developed tranche two products and services.** The second tranche must satisfy the maturing needs of the support/assurance function's customers. Usually, their number and sophistication increase, but the support/assurance function must be prepared to reduce its offerings if the market so demands, or to close if necessary.
- **Operated products and services.** As each benefits realisation phase progresses, more refined products and services may be provided.

A flexible function

A support/assurance function should always be sensitive to the needs of those it serves. Since its value will be judged by its customers, it should not be seen as permanent but rather as a flexible part of an ever-changing environment. Therefore, the support/assurance function should be developed as the product of a managed project so that its value is assessed at every stage.

13

Project closure and beyond

A PROJECT CAN BE CLOSED TOO QUICKLY as people seek to extricate themselves and identify their next role. They believe remaining involved would be worthless because if the work planned has been completed, what can be gained from any further project stages?

When a project is completed in a well-considered way it provides the chance to learn valuable lessons, to make sure the project delivered everything in the way it was intended, to measure the benefits it promised to deliver, and most importantly, embed the essential changes in behaviour that enable those benefits to be enjoyed

To do this, it is helpful to consider completion as:

- Project closure – where the project is closed down with the same management rigour as when it was initiated.

- Benefits realisation – where the emerging benefits promised in the business case are monitored, measured and, where possible, controlled to a point where they finally outweigh the whole-life investment.

A project is complete when the closure stage is deemed successful. Benefits realisation is a post-project period owned and administered by those who commissioned the project, as illustrated by the project life cycle (Figure 13.1). Crucially, it is during this period that much can be done to ensure that true change is achieved, not merely the delivery of something which has the potential to facilitate it. It follows that the leader of the change – in all likelihood, the project's sponsor – must retain a commitment to embed the new behaviours that release the

FIGURE 13.1 **The project life cycle**

benefits. Failing to do so may result in the presence of new systems, processes, products and services, all of which appear impressive but which are not adopted by their respective communities. Without the adoption of change, it cannot be said to exist.

It is helpful to first consider the governance that sits astride closure and beyond.

Project closure

This formal stage enables the management environment to be dismantled only when the project has met the project steering group's success criteria. They keep control of the project until they – and only they – agree it can be disbanded.

Closure asks whether the project has resulted in a product of sufficient quality, within acceptable timescales and budgets, and that should deliver the intended benefits. Therefore, the project steering group must find out from the project manager to what extent the expected time, cost and quality targets have been met.

The project closure report

The project manager answers by drawing up a project closure report (see Table 13.1) which provides quantitative measures for the project steering group to use in making their decision to close the project.

TABLE 13.1 **Project closure report**

Baseline documentation	The documents against which successful completion is being measured.
Background	An outline of the project's history so that any anomalies are fully understood.
Project summary	A detailed review of planned versus actual measurements to determine whether the variances would prevent a decision to close the project.
Matters outstanding	Any matters that remain unsettled.
Post-project governance	What management environment is needed for the post-project period leading towards the final measurement of realised benefits?
Other closure criteria	What additional closure criteria must be satisfied, if any, for the project steering group to make their decision?
Recommendations	What options are there for closing the project?
Proposed action	What outcome does the project manager propose? How will post-project governance be implemented?

The report's success will be judged on the answers to these questions:

- Does it provide sufficient information for the project steering group to close the project with confidence?
- Is the information accurate and up-to-date?
- Is all information internally consistent?
- Does it clearly outline a course of action for the benefits realisation stage?
- Does it fully describe the roles and responsibilities of those who will take part in the benefits realisation stage?
- Does it provide enough information about the governance of the benefits realisation stage for the portfolio management team to approve the post-project management environment?

Baseline documentation

Generally, the documentation will be the business case (success criteria section), project governance report (containing the project plan), the user requirements document and the solution design document. Version numbers should be listed to make sure that success is being measured against the most recently approved versions of the documentation.

Background

The composition of the project steering group should be described to make it clear that those seeking to close the project are those who have directed it so far. The course of the project's progress should be outlined, identifying changes relevant to understanding its state and variances at the point of closure.

Project summary

This section should list the following:

- Project success criteria. These are outlined in the business case. The report must show how far these success criteria have been met (see Table 13.2, for example).
- Budget (see Table 13.3, for example). The project steering group will want to know the reasons for any variances and the details

TABLE 13.2 **Project success criteria**

Baseline project success criteria	Actual project success	Variance	Reason
Does the new computer system process twice as many trades per day as the previous one?	Original system processed 950 trades per day. New system has been shown to process 1,900 trades per day successfully.	**0** **GREEN**	
Does the new office provide each of the 350 staff with at least 36 sq ft of desk space?	Office provides 400 people with at least 36 sq ft of desk space.	**+50 people** **AMBER**	Capacity was allowed for staff who may join office in the future.
Have all new staff been recruited by the end of June?	All new staff were recruited by August, but at no risk to the project.	**−2 months** **AMBER**	Three of the nine intended staff were unable to join by June. However, they were not critical to the success of the project.
Have the new facilities been secured within budget?	See budgetary review below.	*See budgetary review below.*	See budgetary review below.
Have the new office operating procedures been made available to the Tokyo office as a priority?	Tokyo office received new operating procedures before other colleagues.	**0** **GREEN**	

should be noted here. In Table 13.3, even a positive variance of $500 is shown as amber, representing money requested but not used and which must be handed back to the portfolio management team.

■ The project steering group should also know about monies committed but for which the liability has not yet been recorded (usually because the invoice has not been received). This identifies costs to be attributed to the project after closure and for which the cost codes must remain open.

■ Timescales (see Table 13.4, for example). The project steering group must know the reasons for any variances and details should be noted here.

Matters outstanding

This section should list the following:

■ Additional products –any products included beyond those originally anticipated.

■ Excluded products – any products which, although planned, were not delivered (for instance, "documented operating manual").

TABLE 13.3 **Budget**

1	2	3	4	5	6	7
Resource item	Original baseline	Last authorised baseline	Invoiced at completion	Forecast total	Variance with original baseline	Variance with last authorised baseline
Human resources	$32,000	$42,000	$42,000	$42,000	**–$10,000** **RED**	**$0** **GREEN**
Non-human resources	$29,500	$29,500	$25,500	$29,000	**$500** **AMBER**	**$500** **AMBER**
Capital costs	$4,000	$4,000	$4,000	$4,000	**$0** **GREEN**	**$0** **GREEN**
Total	$65,500	$75,500	$71,500	$75,000	**–$9,500** **RED**	**$500** **AMBER**

Notes:
Column 1: resource type, summarised from project plan
Column 2: as approved in project governance report
Column 3: as approved in notification (where relevant), dated dd/mm/yy
Column 4: as identified on finance ledger, dated dd/mm/yy
Column 5: taking account of committed and planned spend, not yet invoiced
Column 6: variance if the amended baseline had not been approved by the project steering group on dd/mm/yy
Column 7: variance, based on approved changes to the project plan following notification (where relevant), dated dd/mm/yy

■ Additional benefits – any benefits added to the business case or augmented since its original approval.

■ Excluded benefits – any benefits removed from the business case or reduced since its original approval.

■ Change requests and issues – the change log will show the status of change requests and issues at the point of closure. Some changes may have been deferred until a later phase or release or may have been declined altogether.

Post-project governance

The benefits realisation stage does not fall within the project's governance. If closing the project means that every aspect of the management environment will be dismantled, there is an increased likelihood of not knowing fully whether the benefits will be achieved.

TABLE 13.4 **Timescales**

1	2	3	4	5	6
Product/ milestone	Original baseline	Last authorised baseline	Actual end date	Variance with original baseline	Variance with last authorised baseline
Initiation	10/04	01/05	01/05	−20 days RED	0 days GREEN
Delivery Stage 1	30/07	28/08	28/08	−29 days RED	0 days GREEN
Delivery Stage 2	28/09	30/10	30/10	−32 days RED	0 days GREEN
Closure	30/10	30/11	30/11	−31 days RED	0 days GREEN

Notes:
Column 1: key deliverables or stages summarised from the project plan
Column 2: as approved in the project governance report
Column 3: as approved in notification (where relevant), dated dd/mm
Column 4: as contained in the most recent project plan, dated dd/mm
Column 5: variance if the amended baseline had not been approved by the project steering group on dd/mm
Column 6: variance, based on approved changes to the project plan following notification (where relevant), dated dd/mm

This section of the project closure report must cover the following:

- The outcome expected of the benefits realisation stage – the report required, its content and the success criteria which, when met, will determine that it is complete.
- The time it will take.
- Who will monitor the stage, identifying those responsible for measuring the benefits and any operational costs that accrue during it.
- The data and/or metrics to be used to measure them; these need to be identified for each project benefit together with the specific means by which its realisation will be measured.
- When and how benefits will be monitored, measured, compared with those planned and (if necessary) steered towards a successful outcome. Pre-scheduled events should be listed to update the business case with actual costs and benefits.

Other closure criteria

There should be few other closure criteria. Examples are:

- Has a suitable post-project governance been proposed?
- Are all participants in the post-project governance comfortable and familiar with their roles and responsibilities?
- Have all project cost codes been prepared for closure?

Recommendations

This section should describe the circumstances under which the project should be closed. This may mean that a straightforward decision is required to close the project as planned. Alternatively, it may be necessary to recommend a postponement of some of the project to a supplementary stage, for example where a part of the project cannot be delivered within the planned time or budget. In more extreme circumstances, it may be recommended that the key deliverables are not to be used in the operational environment, for instance where the product does not meet quality expectations. In any case, the recommendation should not come as a surprise to the project steering group, which should have been kept informed of progress throughout the project.

Without such governance being placed around project closure, benefits realisation can all too easily become unmanaged and unfocused, resulting in a failure to monitor realised benefits adequately and, ultimately, not knowing whether the project was a success.

Proposed action

This describes the steps that must be taken to reach the closure decision and to put in place the governance of the post-project benefits realisation stage described in the post-project governance section.

It is important to state when the benefits reviews will take place so that those involved can note them in their diaries. Additionally, the responsibility for delivering and approving the final benefit realisation report must be made clear so there is no doubt about ownership.

Project closure process

The project closure process (see Figure 13.2) is relatively straightforward, although since closure means different things to different people, it must satisfy their varied needs.

For the project steering group closure means:

- The investment made in the project has come to an end.
- A period is beginning during which the emerging benefits must be seen to outweigh the actual project costs and increasing operational costs.
- The customer representative(s) must make sure that the business-as-usual environment is able to operate the project's product.
- The developer representative(s) must make sure that support is available to customers.

For the project manager closure means:

- Work identified on the project plan is complete, so the plan must be brought up-to-date and filed.
- Post-project actions must be handed over to the post-project governance team, whatever that may be.

FIGURE 13.2 **Project closure process**

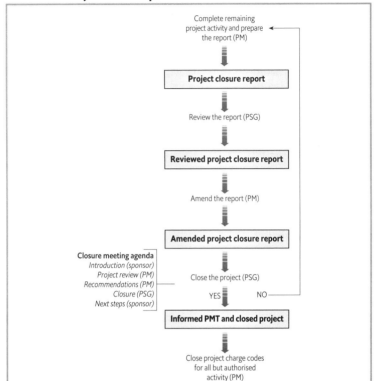

- Project cost codes must be prepared for closure, making sure that only committed and authorised spend is charged to them.

- Project team members must be told of the closure and their line managers instructed to seek new engagements for them.

- The project manager must give feedback to each team member for use during their regular performance appraisals.

- Sufficient budget must remain available to fund a "lessons learned" meeting, which should be scheduled for a time that suits as many project participants as possible.

Lessons learned report

This is the result of a lessons learned review, which gathers and communicates as much information as possible to generate greater future management efficiencies.

The report is often less valuable than the review itself; it is hard to think of many projects where the first step has been to review the lessons learned from the past. In many organisations, individual learning contributes to the improvement of company procedures and standards more than the rectification of systemic faults and anomalies when a project has been completed. However, the report may provide useful information to a new project's first risk identification workshop.

The success of a review of how the project was governed can be judged by whether:

- representatives of all levels of management were involved in the review;
- it was held near enough to the end of the project so that participants in the review remembered things clearly and accurately;
- both positive and negative aspects of project management were given sufficient consideration;
- improvement actions were clearly identified;
- the individuals responsible for carrying out those actions have been identified;
- each action has a timetable for completion.

The report's proposed structure (see Table 13.5) helps to determine how the review is conducted.

Project background

This can be copied from the project closure report.

Objectives

These depend upon how open the organisation is about learning and growing. A common set of objectives is:

TABLE 13.5 **Lessons learned report**

Project background	A brief outline of the project itself for readers who are not participants in either the project or the review.
Objectives	What is the purpose of the review, and what are the measures of success?
Scope	How widely is the management of the project being reviewed? What exclusions are there, if any?
Observations	What observations did the participants identify?
Lessons learned	What lessons can be learned from those observations?
Action plan	What is the plan to implement the lessons?

- to allow all participants to feel that they have had the opportunity to contribute to the growth of the organisation's project management capabilities;
- to identify specific project management improvements that can be implemented in future.

A lessons learned review can be conducted not merely at the end of a project, but also at the end of a project stage. Clearly it can help improve project management if there is a willingness to learn and improve throughout the project rather than just at the end.

Scope

The purpose of the lessons learned review is to consider how well the project was managed. To avoid confusion, it may be necessary explicitly to exclude non-management matters, such as a technical review of the computer system or bridge or building that the project delivered. Inclusions can be described by listing the area of project management to be considered, such as:

- organisation, roles and responsibilities;
- communications and stakeholder management;
- plans, planning and delegation;
- monitoring, reporting and management information;
- project control, including change control;

- quality management;
- risk management;
- benefits management.

Observations

A lessons learned review should promote good practice and help eliminate poor habits. The observations should be straightforward statements without qualification. For example, a positive observation from a debate about monitoring and reporting might be: "The project forecast report was used for the first time and helped to identify variances." A negative observation might be: "Too many preventable issues arose because the monthly risk identification session was too infrequent."

Lessons learned

This section describes the lessons to be learned from the positive and negative observations and is the reason for the report. For example, a lesson to be learned from the positive observation above could be: "All projects should be encouraged to use project forecast reports (and, at the very least, make sure that variances are clearly identified)." A lesson to be learned from the negative observation above could be: "Risk identification sessions should be more frequent for all similarly sized/scoped projects."

Action plan

This shows how the lessons are to be embedded in the organisation's project management culture (see Table 13.6, for example).

Lessons learned review

This usually takes place a week or two after the project has been closed. Those invited to take part should come from all levels of the project's management, including team members, team leaders, the project manager, the project steering group, customers, suppliers, the project steering group and, if the project was of sufficient size, criticality or risk, members of the portfolio management team.

TABLE 13.6 **Action plan**

Number	Lesson	Action(s)	Success criteria	Who?	Due date
1	All projects should be encouraged to use project forecast reports (and, at the very least, make sure that variances are clearly identified)	Introduce project forecast report to Project Ace, Project King and Project Queen.	Projects Ace, King and Queen adopt the project forecast report and use it fully without supervision.	DK	dd/ mm/ yy
2	Risk identification sessions should be more frequent for all similarly sized/scoped projects	Increase frequency of risk identification sessions for Project Jack.	Project Jack conducts two-weekly risk identification sessions.	PT	dd/ mm/ yy

Given the importance of allowing everyone to contribute fully and equally, the review is usually best managed by an external or impartial, seasoned and assured facilitator, possibly found in, or through, the support/assurance function.

The agenda should be as follows:

- introduction;
- ground rules;
- observations;
- break;
- lessons learned;
- action plan.

Introduction

The introduction should be made by a member of the project steering group, ideally the sponsor. This lends authority to the review and provides an opportunity to promote the value of the output to all participants. The introduction must also allow the sponsor to state the objectives of the session. Given that some participants may not have been involved throughout the whole life cycle, some limited project background will be necessary. This will also help set the scope of the review.

Ground rules

An occasion where unhappy memories may have to be revisited can be upsetting for individuals and disruptive. Emotions can cloud the desired outcome, so the facilitator should set out the rules of engagement at the outset. The list below is not exhaustive, but is a starting point for developing a set of rules participants should abide by:

- **Park issues.** If a matter is debated for longer than five minutes without resolution, it is "parked" on a flip chart and revisited outside the session.
- **Work within the agenda.** The agenda approved by the sponsor should be respected. If there is not sufficient opportunity to discuss something, it may be parked.
- **Respect the facilitator.** The facilitator is there to allow the session to progress effectively and efficiently.
- **Prepare in advance.** Participants should be encouraged to think in advance about the observations and lessons they wish to raise.
- **Criticise the governance, not individuals.** If criticisms are to be made, they should be levelled at the project's governance rather than the people who developed or operated it.
- **Speak one at a time.** This will enable observations and solutions to be identified more quickly.
- **Make your point clearly.** Think about what you wish to raise and use language participants will understand.
- **Make your point once.** Time is limited, so avoid labouring a point.
- **Make your point politely.** Do not allow emotions to create unnecessary tension.

Observations

Everyone attending will be keen to offer their views, positive or negative, so some structure is necessary.

The two approaches below depend on breaking the group into smaller teams:

■ **Tailored group topics.** Each group has a specific set of topics they must review, including those identified in scope (see Lessons learned report above). A set of starter questions may be provided to help each group explore the issues relating to their topic. For instance, one group may be assigned risk management and their starter questions might include: Were risk management events conducted sufficiently frequently? How effective was the project in mitigating risks?

■ **Common group topics.** Each group is presented with a list of all topics falling within the scope of the review. The same starter questions may be provided to assist groups. This approach has merit if everybody wants to cover every topic.

The result is a flipchart sheet listing the positive and negative observations arising from each group's discussion, with three or four highlighted as the most significant (see Figure 13.3).

During the session, the facilitator should move around the groups to make sure they are progressing to schedule and that the output is as required. At the end of the session, each group should be given a few minutes to present their highlighted observations.

FIGURE 13.3 **Positive and negative observations**

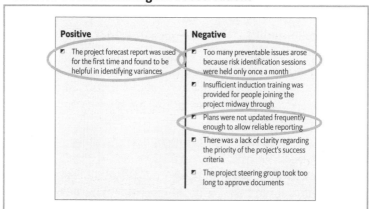

FIGURE 13.4 **Positive and negative observations and lessons learned**

Positive	Negative
✓ The project forecast report was used for the first time and found to be helpful in identifying variances	✓ Too many preventable issues arose because risk identification sessions were held only once a month
✓ *LESSON LEARNED: All projects should be encouraged to use project forecast reports and, at the very least, to ensure that variances are clearly identified.*	✓ *LESSON LEARNED: Risk identification sessions should be more frequent for all similarly sized/scoped projects*
	✓ Plans were not updated frequently enough to allow reliable reporting
	✓ *LESSON LEARNED: Project plans must be updated at a frequency no less than every two weeks*

Break

The observations session can be draining, not least because people often focus on the negative aspects of the project. The break allows participants to recover and prepare for the next session, which is intentionally upbeat and focused on improvements.

Lessons learned

Participants return to their groups to consider the highlighted observations. Their objective must be clearly stated: to identify improvements that can be introduced to the project management approach. For each highlighted observation, they should identify at least one practical way of overcoming the issues and promoting those matters considered positive.

Each group's results can be noted on a sheet of flipchart paper (see Figure 13.4).

During the session, the facilitator should move around each group with an eye to the schedule and the required output. At the end of the session, each group should be given a few minutes to present the lessons it has identified.

Action plans

It is essential to create an action plan for the event to have any value. It is not sufficient to have identified lessons within the review; the changes necessary to the project management governance must be made if the improvements are to make any difference.

The action plan must state what the action entails, how its completion will be measured, who has responsibility for completing it and by when. The responsibility for making sure the actions are carried out should be assigned only to participants in the room.

Once the action plan is agreed, the sponsor who backed the review must publicly take responsibility for seeing it to a successful conclusion. The project manager should not take on this burden; he may well be assigned to another project and his responsibilities will lie elsewhere. The sponsor, however, has continuing accountabilities after the project has ended, including the continuous improvement of the organisation's approach to project management. Contributions to this will come from the actions taken as a result of the lessons learned review.

This is not the sponsor's only remaining responsibility. Having proposed that a package of benefits may be delivered by the project on or after its completion, the organisation may rightly expect each sponsor to remain responsible for, and committed to, the realisation of those benefits.

Benefits realisation

This period follows the closure of the project; it is when the intended benefits are expected to grow. The governance put in place for the project is no longer present and besides, it would be unnecessary and inappropriate for the activities ahead. The objective of the benefits realisation stage is to make sure that the benefits outweigh the investment according to the targets outlined in the business case.

For the change to be considered successful, these questions must be asked:

- Who has responsibilities during this period?
- How will the mounting costs and benefits be monitored, measured and controlled?
- When can the period come to an end?
- How will the organisation reward success or failure?

- Can the benefits be shown to have contributed to planned business objectives?
- Have the desired changes, initially anticipated by the leadership team in the vision, been adopted?

Roles and responsibilities

Since it commissioned the project, the portfolio management team has ultimate responsibility for both a successful conclusion to the stage and the realisation of benefits that sufficiently outweigh the investment. It is also responsible for commissioning projects that contribute to the strategic growth and development of the organisation. Consequently, although the portfolio management team considered the project sufficiently worthwhile to merit investing the organisation's money, the sponsor promoted the project and persuaded others to follow. Therefore, it makes sense for the portfolio management team and the sponsor collaborate to steer any remaining activity needed to assure the realisation of changed behaviour and the benefits that follow.

The sponsor may have a line role to which they must return, but they also have the additional responsibility of monitoring, measuring and controlling the mounting costs and benefits during this period, so many organisations provide help, often from the support/assurance function. Specifically, the sponsor can draw upon the skills of a project specialist who can devote time to the monitoring and measurement of costs and benefits. Where a project/programme support function does not exist, an expert may be identified to take on the monitoring and measuring role. In either case, this frees the sponsor to exercise authority where variances in expected costs or benefits are identified. The sponsor alone is expected to bring the realisation of benefits back on track.

Once a project has been completed, it is not uncommon for its sponsor to work in an entirely different part of the organisation. If that makes it impractical for the sponsor to discharge his continuing responsibilities for benefits realisation, the portfolio management team should identify someone to do so, particularly focusing on someone who has the leadership capabilities to deliver change. Without such an authority in place, the benefits and costs may not grow at their intended rate and the project might yet be deemed a failure.

Monitoring, measurement and control

Tracking benefits and costs during the benefits realisation period should be reasonably straightforward if:

- the monitoring and measurement mechanisms have been expressed clearly enough in the business case; and
- changes to the intended benefits, costs or monitoring and measurement mechanisms have been accommodated in the business case during the project.

Each benefit and cost item must be monitored and measured separately. Table 13.7 gives an example of some benefits identified in a business case in Chapter 6.

TABLE 13.7 **Quantifying benefits ($)**

	Year 0	Year 1	Year 2	Year 3	Year 4
Increased revenues	–	5,000	60,000	60,000	70,000
Increased customer satisfaction	–	5,000	10,000	10,000	10,000
Competitor removal	–	–	20,000	20,000	20,000
Customers from new market	–	–	30,000	30,000	40,000
Cost savings	–	8,000	10,000	11,000	11,000
Headcount savings	–	5,000	5,000	5,000	5,000
Removal of redundant IT kit	–	3,000	5,000	6,000	6,000
Total	–	13,000	70,000	71,000	81,000
Cumulative total	–	13,000	83,000	154,000	235,000

The relevant facts extracted from the business case are as follows:

- Customer satisfaction is measurable before, during and after the project through a survey.
- A 5% improvement in customer satisfaction between year 0 and year 1 is envisaged as a direct result of this project.

- In year 2, it will increase by a further 5%.
- It will remain stable during years 3 and 4.
- The increase in revenue will come from newly satisfied customers spending more on the organisation's products and services.
- The 5% improvement in customer satisfaction will lead to a $5,000 increase in sales in year 1, a further $5,000 in year 2, and then stabilise at $10,000 for the remainder of the whole life of the venture.
- The lower costs will come from headcount savings because fewer customer service staff will be required.
- The 5% improvement in customer satisfaction will lead to a reduction in headcount, creating savings of $5,000 per year, every year for the remainder of the whole life of the venture.

Therefore, during the benefits realisation period, the sponsor is responsible for making sure the benefits accrue according to the benefits realisation plan. In the example in Table 13.7, this means that the plan must allow for the following to be measured or recorded in a consistent way:

- customer satisfaction before the project begins and at least every year thereafter;
- customer revenue before the project begins and at least every year thereafter;
- the number of customer service staff before the project begins and at least every year thereafter;
- the operational costs of the implemented solution.

Benefits realisation is as much about monitoring and controlling the operational costs of implementing the solution to make sure that they do not exceed the planned amount as it is about monitoring the benefits. The margin, the difference between costs and benefits, is ultimately what matters as stated in the business case.

The costs identified in the business case in question are shown in Table 13.8.

If the project was completed at the end of year 0, the subsequent costs must be monitored and controlled, and the way in which they are to be measured must be recorded in the benefits realisation plan.

TABLE 13.8 **Costs over time ($)**

	Year 0	Year 1	Year 2	Year 3	Year 4
Resources	1,300	12,250	16,820	12,600	19,850
Consumables				1,000	
Hardware			28,000		
Software			17,000		
Environmental				11,000	
Accommodation	500	1,200	1,200	1,200	1,200
Expenses	700	2,400	1,600	1,600	3,200
Total	2,500	15,850	64,620	27,400	24,250
Cumulative total	**2,500**	**18,350**	**82,970**	**110,370**	**134,620**

Each measurement of costs or benefits must be planned to take place at a certain time, to cost no more than a specified budget and to satisfy a set of success criteria. For this example, these would be as follows:

- Does the plan enable customer satisfaction, customer revenue and headcount levels to be determined in a way that can be measured year after year in the same way?
- Where possible, have survey dates been selected to coincide with other organisation-wide events to minimise the duplication of effort?
- Can it be shown that the variances in customer satisfaction, revenue and headcount may be attributed to this project?
- Where possible, has the same person been responsible for monitoring throughout the benefits realisation stage?
- Have all elements contributing to operational costs been separately and accurately measured?

By showing how the time, cost and quality expectations of the benefits realisation period are to be managed, the benefits realisation plan bears many of the hallmarks of a regular project plan and should be treated no differently. As the plan is used to determine where variances have occurred, the sponsor is responsible for keeping the costs and benefits in line with the plan. Throughout this stage the sponsor's responsibilities are similar to those of the project manager during the project itself.

Achieving strategic change

The monitoring, measurement and control of costs and benefits during the benefits realisation period described above are sufficient if the benefits have been stated in commercial terms. However, if the project was undertaken to enable the success of a programme or to contribute to the wider strategic needs of the organisation, the portfolio management team will expect that link to be demonstrated.

Particularly where information technology is concerned, it is sometimes more difficult to show the extent to which a contribution has been made to strategic, rather than overtly commercial, success factors. However, there is a way to trace the audit trail from project outcome to strategic imperative. Called the "benefits dependency network", it was developed by John Ward and Joe Peppard of Cranfield University in their book, *Strategic Planning for Information Systems* (3rd edition, John Wiley and Sons, 2002).

Figure 13.5 shows how the software self-installation project

FIGURE 13.5 **The benefits dependency network**

on the left can be shown to contribute to two of the organisation's strategic imperatives on the right. The link between them is formed by the assertion that the project will deliver an "enabler", a feature that facilitates achieving a change in the way the business works. In this case, users are able to pick software from a list to self-install without recourse to experts. This change, if carried out, will benefit the business through faster installation of software and fewer calls to the service desk. These fit the business's investment objectives, which were to improve user and service-desk productivity, both of which are measurable. If the productivity improvements meet the intended targets, progress will be made in achieving the organisation's strategic drivers. Service will improve as users have more time to spend with customers, and productivity will improve as the service-desk team are able to do more with their time.

Additionally, since Table 13.9 was created when the portfolio was being developed, it can and should be used to determine each project's actual contribution to the organisation's strategy. As each project is completed and enters its benefits realisation phase, each statement

TABLE 13.9 **Project contribution to strategy**

Strategic imperative	Project 1	Project 2	Project 3
The company securing $500,000 worth of recurring revenues during the coming year from clients that have always previously paid one-off payments.	Direct	Indirect	Absent
The company delivering three implementations during the coming year of its standard product in seven weeks rather than nine.	Absent	Absent	Absent
The company implementing its own project management method based upon an industry-recognised standard during the coming year.	Indirect	Absent	Absent
Contributing to the company delivering two projects in the coming year using the new project management method.	Absent	Absent	Absent
The company reducing its turnover of staff of more than ten years' experience by 20% during the coming year.	Absent	Direct	Absent

should be changed from the original "Will this project contribute to...?" to "Did this project contribute to...?".

The benefits realisation report

The sponsor should produce regular benefits realisation reports for the portfolio management team. Depending on how long the benefits realisation stage lasts, they may be needed every three months to a year. The concept and content are similar to that of the project forecast report. The project forecast report provides a regular update on progress towards the intended project target; the benefits realisation report takes a snapshot of the mounting post-project costs and benefits, and clearly shows variances so that the stage can be managed and brought to a successful outcome.

The success of a business realisation report can be judged by whether it:

- shows what progress has been made since the preceding report;
- identifies variances in intended operational costs and benefits;
- explains fully how variances arose;
- describes how variances will be addressed;

TABLE 13.10 **Business realisation report**

Summary	A table to summarise the actual and forecast operational spend and benefits realised, identifying variances and escalation conditions.
Variances	An analysis of the key variances.
Corrective actions	A description of what will be done by whom to address the key variances.
Changes to benefits realisation stage governance	A narrative to determine what, if anything, must be done to change the governance of this stage to increase the likelihood of success.
Conclusion	To provide an opportunity for the author to summarise the outcome of the review.
Recommendations	To allow the author to propose how the benefits realisation stage should continue, if at all.

- determines who is responsible for any proposed corrective actions.

  With these criteria in mind, Table 13.10 lists what should be included in a business case.

Summary

A table like Table 13.11 can be included.

This example is based on an assessment of costs and benefits during year 2 of the business case, and illustrates the following points:

- Variances are shown "to date" (the difference between the planned to date and actual to date figures) and as forecast "on completion" (the difference between the baseline and forecast figures). This enables the sponsor to assess the likelihood of the intended margin between costs and benefits being achieved.

- Variances, whether positive or negative, are subject to red, amber and green escalation conditions because the portfolio management team should be alerted to any significant variances. For instance, "removal of redundant kit" has realised its full benefit after year 2, but was not planned to occur until after year 4. The portfolio management team may wish to examine this because it may indicate the kit was removed before it was sensible to do so.

- Since the original business case was developed, two new benefits have been identified, "improved employee morale" and "avoidance of identified risks". These are shown with a zero baseline because they were not anticipated. This makes sure the portfolio management team is alerted to their recent inclusion.

Variances

The benefits realisation report must contain all the information needed to answer any questions it raises. Variances should be described fully, not merely by referring to the numbers in the table.

TABLE 13.11 **Actual benefits and costs**

	Baseline	Planned to date	Actual to date	Estimate to complete	Forecast	Variance to date	Variance on completion
Benefits							
1 Increased customer satisfaction	35,000	15,000	15,000	20,000	35,000	0	0
2 Competitor removal	60,000	20,000	20,000	40,000	60,000	0	0
3 Customers from new market	100,000	30,000	35,000	70,000	105,000	5,000	5,000
4 Headcount savings	20,000	10,000	9,000	11,000	20,000	-1,000	0
5 Removal of redundant kit	20,000	8,000	20,000	0	20,000	12,000	0
6 Improved employee morale	0	0	1,000	4,000	5,000	1,000	5,000
7 Avoidance of identified risks	0	0	1,000	10,000	11,000	1,000	11,000
BENEFITS TOTALS	235,000	83,000	101,000	155,000	256,000	18,000	21,000
Costs							
1 Consultancy	2,500	2,500	2,500	0	2,500	0	0
2 Human resources	61,520	29,070	35,000	32,000	67,000	5,930	5,480
3 Consumables	1,000	0	0	1,000	1,000	0	0
4 Hardware	28,000	28,000	29,000	0	29,000	1,000	1,000
5 Software	17,000	17,000	17,000	0	17,000	0	0
6 Environmental	11,000	0	500	11,000	11,500	500	500
7 Accommodation	4,800	2,400	2,500	2,300	4,800	100	0
8 Expenses	8,800	3,000	3,000	5,800	8,800	0	0
COSTS TOTALS	134,620	81,970	89,500	52,100	141,600	7,530	6,980
NET	100,380	1,030	11,500	102,900	114,400	10,470	14,020

Corrective actions

Corrective action must be proposed for every variance, and an intention to do nothing should be also documented. A simple table can be used (Table 13.12).

Changes to governance

The benefits realisation stage may take several years to be completed, so it is not unusual for those involved in it to move to new positions or for changes to the wider organisation to affect the emerging costs and benefits. The sponsor should use this section to record the changes.

TABLE 13.12 **Corrective actions**

	Actions	Success criteria	Responsibility	Due date
1				
2				
3				
4				
5				

Conclusion

The author should summarise the report, clearly stating the extent to which the realisation of benefits is on track.

Recommendations

This section allows the author to propose a course of action to the portfolio management team. This may suggest that the realisation stage is complete and that no further reviews will be necessary, or alternatively that subsequent reviews must be carried out. Whatever the recommendation, it must be made sufficiently clear so that the portfolio management team know how they are expected to respond.

Project success from effective project management

On the assumption that:

- the vision was clearly articulated and effectively promoted;
- the original business case was robust and reliable;
- it was maintained during the life of the project;
- there was effective management of time, costs, quality, risks and change;
- the "lessons learned" report identified improvement actions that have been accommodated into the methodical approach;
- there has been a determination to maximise the benefits and minimise the operational expenses during the benefits realisation stage;
- there is every chance that the final benefits realisation report will show that the realised benefits outweighed the actual project and operational costs by the amount anticipated in the business case. If, happily, this is the case, it can be said that effective project management has led, intentionally, to a successful outcome.

However, a well managed project does not always lead to a successful change. For example, a new toll road that has been delivered to time, cost and quality expectations may only result in a successful outcome if drivers decide to use it. There are a great many challenges to address when seeking to embed new behaviours or values. As noted in Chapter 10, education can provide users with the skills, knowledge and confidence needed to use or operate whatever it may be that the project is about to deliver. Equally, there is much which may be done after project closure to increase the likelihood that the anticipated changes will be understood, enacted and adopted.

Overcoming obstacles to change

Personal barriers to change

Notwithstanding the institutional barriers to change that were considered in Chapter 2, every individual faced with change will react to it in some way, based on their unique character. If all of the methods suggested throughout this book thus far have been applied, it is to be hoped that many people will embrace the change as a personal opportunity. However, it is unrealistic to expect that everyone will be persuaded of these benefits. The prospect of imminent change may cause many concerns to surface.

If there has been a failure to describe the vision sufficiently well, it is possible that the problem or opportunity facing the organisation has not been adequately comprehended by individual members of the workforce. For example, the absence of a "burning platform" as described in Chapter 2 may have resulted in an individual's sense of complacency. Until or unless they become aware of the issue or opportunity faced by the organisation, it may be difficult or impossible for them to understand the likely impact on their own fortunes. It follows that the vision – and the motivating reason for needing to change – must be promoted as soon as possible, so that individuals have the greatest opportunity to understand it, and to familiarise themselves with the personal consequences it may bring.

Some people are naturally cautious of those who have management roles. Sometimes the management team may have given them good cause to be that way; the practice of rewarding leaders in spite of poor institutional performance does very little to foster trust. Thus, individuals may harbour a natural suspicion of those in authority. Under such circumstances, it may be possible for them to imagine outcomes that are inaccurate. Indeed, it is not unusual for individuals to catastrophise a situation, inflating the consequences of change into something much worse than it might otherwise be. For example, an announcement that a business is preparing to open a new office abroad may cause a suspicion to emerge that an existing office will have to close in consequence, even if management asserts that nothing could be further from the truth.

Once communicated, the proposed solution may itself come under the personal scrutiny of various members of the workforce. It may be that an alternative solution is considered preferable; for example, instead of investing abroad, some may feel that an investment could be made in the existing office. No matter how well assessed the option selected by the management team may be, some of the workforce may well challenge it on the basis that it cannot be made to work. Using the same example, critics of the plan to increase reliance on workers abroad may feel that they will not be able to meet the same standards of quality or productivity reached by the existing workforce.

Going further still, the proposed or emerging change may have some features that render it repellent to members of the workforce, either because of their individual dislike or disgust of what the change represents, or because the workforce operates more broadly in a community that is set against certain working practices. For example, in the UK, since introducing automatic doors on railway trains, there has been increasing pressure to remove the human guards whose job it is to ensure that passengers are on board and that trains can leave the station safely. Strikes have ensued because the workforce, backed by a powerful union, has declared the removal of guards to be an unsafe practice, placing passengers at risk. Whether or not the strikes have been about the safety of passengers or the security of jobs is a matter on which the management team and the workforce appear to have been unable to agree.

For many centuries, the prospect of the introduction of new technology has resulted in strong and sustained emotional reactions. When individuals are able to imagine what change may mean for them personally, it is possible to react in extreme ways, not least because the imagined or real threat of losing power and control over one's future can be terrifying. When many individuals are faced with the same existential threat, it is not uncommon for them to organise themselves into pressure groups, as noted previously in Chapter 2. For example, when individual workers took to destroying newly developed textile machines in the early nineteenth century, the Luddite movement was born, lasting five years and resulting in the use of legal and military force to bring it under control. More modern examples may yet include the arrival of autonomous vehicles, the increasing use of robotics, and the growing opportunities presented by artificial intelligence. All such changes may face a similar, emotional reaction from people who feel that their livelihoods and futures are threatened.

Humans are social beings. Places of work are where many people come to be a part of a community. This can represent more to them than merely a group of colleagues with whom they work. Friendships blossom and connections are formed. The prospect of a change that may impact their social environment can disrupt an individual's ability to perform. It is often the case that people leave their places of work because it no longer provides the sense of social well-being or community for which they yearn; for many, a workplace may be an individual's central or only social environment. While appearing irrational to others, something as simple as being required to move from one desk to another might cause an individual to feel resentful, angry or anxious. Similarly, the personal cost of change must always be considered as a factor when estimating the effort needed to embed new values or behaviours. If the consequence of a change to an individual's working pattern is that they are required to commute or be away from home for longer, they may understandably resist it. In turn, this can lead to the disruption of what may have been conceived of by managers as a relatively simple or straightforward change.

A management team's reaction may be to promote the rewards of the change, especially by expressing its benefits to the institution. However, when faced with something that may impact them personally, an individual may quickly disregard the request to be a "good corporate citizen" and focus instead on whether they are being rewarded well enough for what they are being asked to do. For example, the recent introduction of some new working practices caused the responsibilities of a group of project managers to increase significantly. Many began to question whether they were sufficiently well rewarded to adopt the new behaviours which were being asked of them. One by one, members of this important workforce decided that the personal burden of increased and additional reporting responsibilities was too great. A very large number left, and with them, so did much of the expertise on which the organisation depended. For others, the burden of work was not so much the issue as the fear of being unable to cope with new pressures, especially since so many people had already left. For those workers who felt trapped in their roles, unable to leave the organisation for fear of greater losses, the imposition of new responsibilities was too much of a burden.

Stages of coping with change

In truth, periods of intense change at work can lead to anxiety, sickness and, in extreme cases, suicide.

Research* suggests that restructuring, redeployment and more demanding production targets can result in impossible levels of stress for some workers. Change, managed poorly, can have catastrophic outcomes for individuals.

People's personal reactions described in many of the examples above serve to illustrate the five typical stages of coping with change, first described by strategic change expert Colin Carnall.†

Somewhat similar to the five stages of grief developed by Swiss-American psychiatrist and creator of a stage-model of human grief Elisabeth Kubler-Ross, it begins with denial, a belief that the proposed change will never happen. This may be characterised by an assertion that the change can never be made to work, or that previous attempts to change have already been unsuccessful. Faced with the stark consequences of change, an individual may become highly resistant, especially if their personal well-being is placed at risk. For example, in the face of a new worker's time-recording system, many individuals refused to complete their weekly timesheets, choosing instead to revert to the old system with which they were familiar. During this period, a person's focus may be diverted from their normal work pattern and performance may begin to slip. It is possible that self-esteem may briefly grow as the individual gains confidence in a belief that when change fails to materialise, they will be proven correct.

As new systems, working practices or behaviours become more visible, there follows a defence of the status quo, where an individual may assert that the change must be resisted. In the example described above, when the older time-recording system was removed and workers had no alternative but to use the new system, many refused to report or record their time at the end of the week. Although management's reaction may be to introduce penalties for such behaviour, caution

---

* Waters, Sarah et al. (2016). When Work Kills. Journal of Public Mental Health. Retrieved from https://www.emerald.com/insight/content/doi/10.1108/JPMH-06-2016-0026/full/html
† Carnall, Colin. (2018) *Managing Change*. Oxford, UK: Routledge.

FIGURE 13.6 **Coping stages**

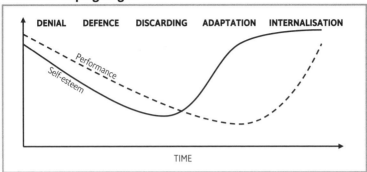

Source: derived from Colin Carnall, *Managing Change*, 2018, Routledge, London

should be exercised for some time to allow individuals to come to terms with the change.

A turning point is achieved when an individual recognises that reversion to the methods, practices and behaviours of the past is no longer possible; they are discarded. Although their self-esteem may begin to grow, performance may yet remain poor as their transition commences. Discarding may be a period fraught with risk for the individual as they experiment with new feelings associated with their acceptance of the change. This is a point where management may feel able to declare victory, but to do so would be premature. Indeed, it may be necessary to invest in educational resources in readiness for the coming stage.

Adaptation is a time not only for the individual to transform into the state imagined in the vision, but also for the institution itself to recognise and accept that mutual change may be required. Modifications may be necessary to the deliverables created by the project; for example, a more engaged and adapting workforce may identify faults or improvement opportunities that the organisation would wish to accommodate. It follows that many of the educational interventions described in Chapter 10 may need to be applied, reapplied or refined. These may also be helpful in addressing frustrations that arise among the workforce as the solution, which has been promoted for so long and so hard by the leaders of change, is revealed to be imperfect or fallible.

Internalisation is characterised by the treatment of new working practices, relationships, systems, structures and behaviours as the "new normal". The reality of the proposed change is that it is here to stay, and has been adopted as second nature. In other words, the new state of business-as-usual is in place.

Not everyone experiences these stages in the sequence described. Some individuals or communities may become stuck in a particular stage. Others may move forwards and backwards as the different features of complex change are encountered. During this time, it is important that managers and leaders accept this reaction as both likely and normal. Although a transactional leader's or manager's reaction may be to introduce penalties for a failure to comply, a transformational leader will recognise that this process may be lengthy. One of the most important investments that may be made is in time. An effective change leader will recognise that, even if the project has been executed efficiently, iteratively or even speedily, the time it takes for people to adapt may be significant. While there are many techniques which may encourage behaviour change, a community affected by change takes time to comprehend it, adapt to it and, occasionally, heal.

Knowing that each individual will face a unique and personal journey towards a new way of working or behaving, it follows that change leaders face quite a challenge. They must succeed in understanding each individual, or groups of individuals, sufficiently well as to know how they may be best motivated to change. There are a range of tools and techniques which may provoke an increased desire to participate in change, or if not, to tolerate it.

Leadership and management interventions to encourage adoption in the post-project period

Some mention has already been made above of motivational techniques that can support an organisation during a period of change. Educational interventions, many of which can be introduced during the life cycle of the project, were described in Chapter 10. What follows are further methods to encourage the adoption of new practices, especially helpful during this post-project period when the workforce is coming to terms with the prospect of behaving in a new way.

Celebrating success

People should be notified of success whenever a notable win has been achieved; this will partly compensate for the many times when issues or problems have hindered progress. It may have been possible to do so during the life cycle of the project, especially if it has delivered periodic releases of new functions or features. It is particularly helpful to mark the moment of movement into the post-project period of benefits realisation. Commonly, this is an opportunity for project team members to enjoy a party. However, while they are moving out of a period of turbulence, the communities of users and operators are about to enter one. Therefore, it may be helpful to mark the end of a project, and the beginning of the realisation period, as a moment that both communities are able to celebrate together. For example, in publicly celebrating the completion of the project, a change leader may also address those who are to inherit its deliverables, offering gratitude in advance for a period during which they may experience disruption and anxiety. A leader may even go so far as to extend any celebratory activity to include those who will be affected by the change.

Post-live support

Leaders may offer reassurance after any "go live" activity to ensure there is continued emotional and practical support for those who may be now working in a very different cultural or operational environment. Continued practical support in the use or operation of a new product or service may be provided very simply. However, all projects are unique. For example, projects which seek to deliver operational cost-reductions through redundancy exercises may have to provide significant and complex support to those who are about to encounter a period of intense emotional disturbance. In addition to the provision of outplacement advisors, counselling support may be an extremely welcome and necessary service.

Tailored performance indicators and role profiles

People must clearly understand what is expected of them. If a project is to bring about a change to a role, this must be reflected in the relevant role profiles or job descriptions. To encourage them to act differently, workers must also be sufficiently motivated to focus on their new responsibilities instead of their old ones. Key performance indicators (KPIs) are a means by which to describe the characteristics of changed behaviour. Although these may be included in the role profile, they are more commonly set at the beginning of a year so as to provide a tailored target for varied members of the workforce. Used thoughtfully, leaders may design them to articulate the behaviours expected during and after a period of change.

Performance measurement

With targets set, the mechanisms for determining the extent to which people have been meeting their new responsibilities and performance targets must be in place. If a programme of periodic or annual performance assessments is already in place, there may be scope to ensure they are timed to coincide with points in the change cycle when a measurement is necessary. If performance reviews are not already in place, a change programme may be considered as an excuse to introduce them. In any case, role profiles and targets are of no value if a worker's performance is not assessed against them.

Tailored rewards

Meeting the demands of a performance measure does not always have to result in a reward; it may simply signify that the worker in question is delivering what is required of them. However, it can be appropriate to offer rewards when responsibilities and targets have been met, especially when these may have changed as a result of an uncomfortable or demanding period of transformation. Better still, the offer of a reward can itself transform the way an individual behaves, serving as an incentive to change. Of course, incentive schemes must be carefully tuned to ensure they encourage the correct behaviour. For example, it may be helpful to introduce a commission scheme to reward salespeople who generate revenue from a newly targeted retail sector.

However, if the incentive to sell to corporate clients remains more attractive, it should come as no surprise if the sales force continues to focus on them instead of the intended retail customers. Unless the existing commission scheme for corporate sales is also adjusted accordingly, the incentive to generate retail sales may be insufficient to change existing sales practices. There may also be moral or ethical questions raised about rewards. Some UK doctors in general practice have been offered cash incentives to resist referring certain patients to hospitals. While this may produce the desired outcome of a reduction in demand for over-subscribed hospitals, the possible consequence on patient well-being has been questioned.

Tailored penalties

Penalties may also be a necessary or helpful motivational tool for some people. As above, while penalty schemes can be made to work well, they are also fraught with risk. Given that money or privileges may be withheld for failing to adopt a specified practice, workers are likely to apply the rule in a way that minimises their exposure to the penalty. This too can have unintended consequences. For example, a bus company was frustrated that its drivers were failing to complete their routes on time. The drivers were encouraged to do so with the introduction of a penalty scheme; a percentage of their bonus would be withheld if they completed their route outside of an agreed limit. While this had the desired effect of greatly improving punctuality, it was achieved at the expense of customers; if a driver feared they would not reach the depot on time, they would simply not stop for waiting passengers.

Knowledge transfer

With the prospect of the emergence of a new steady state, the leaders of change may seek to progressively diminish their role in favour of migrating responsibilities to the organisation's business-as-usual managers. This is a process that can serve to empower both through the receiving-team's acquisition of new knowledge or skills, but also through public demonstration that the change governance is being progressively removed. This transference of ownership is an important sign, and should not be merely symbolic. It should be accompanied by the handover of relevant project and change management materials,

FIGURE 13.7 **A roadmap to deliver change**

Example: A roadmap for a capability transformation programme

OUR VISION

- Focused, motivated and informed change owners who are accountable for justifying and delivering benefits
- An informed, educated and engaged community of change managers
- Projects which are prioritised and aligned to the organisation's strategic imperatives
- Project Managers who are accountable for delivering projects to a successful conclusion
- A common method by which projects are managed

Uptake, Engagement and Performance Measurement

Reward and Recognition

Managed Issues

Celebrated Change

Educational handbook

Behaviour-based education

Leadership sponsored launch

Trained PMs

Updated key performance indicators

Updated role profiles

Short Term Win: assessment using Minimum Standard allows viability of all projects to be known and addressed

Project management minimum standard

Shared insight of future state

PM engagement events

Performance baseline

RISK: Senior management commits to nothing more than instructional training for PMs

QUESTION: How do we prepare the PM community to embrace continued change?

RISK: We fail to manage PM resistance now, which undermines our ability to change behaviours later the library of frequently-asked-questions (and answers), all educational and training collateral, and promotional materials. For example, where a new computer system has been installed, knowledge transfer will be an important moment when IT operations and its own help desk take responsibility for the continued support of the system, and that the learning and development function accepts that its delivery of a continued programme of systems training signifies its shared accountability for maintaining the workforce's competence.

Effective issue and problem management

The delivery of anything new often brings with it faults, issues and problems. The users and operators of whatever the project has delivered will be well placed to identify where things aren't working properly. Leaders must show that any issues are addressed so they don't become a reason for people to resist the change. This may involve the implementation of problem management systems and processes, facilities to capture and respond to frequently-asked-questions, and a help desk to provide practical and emotional reassurance.

Quite apart from the advantages of using a project to create a deliverable of some significance, interventions to facilitate effective behavioural change have been described in Chapter 2, Chapter 10

FIGURE 13.8 Interventions to deliver change

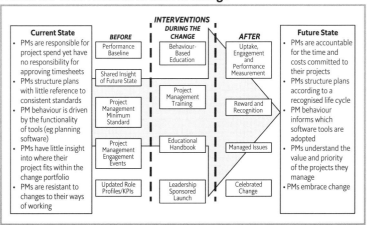

and this chapter. Drawing these together into an example, Figure 13.7 describes the key features of an organisation's vision, and identifies those interventions considered necessary to realise it.

There is a combination of techniques to engage and educate stakeholders, and to embed new practices and behaviours.

Figure 13.8 imagines the user journey which may be undertaken by a single community to be affected by this change. In this example, a future state is foreseen where project managers demonstrate markedly different behaviours. Interventions have been planned to contribute to their transformation.

Therefore, the mechanics of management and the art of leadership must be brought together during closure and beyond to increase the likelihood that change – in all its guises – takes place as intended.

Embedding effective project management

A METHODICAL APPROACH for using projects to deliver lasting business change may represent a change in itself for many people in an organisation. To succeed, any approach to designing, implementing and embedding a new way of working must take account of the fact that it must be a culture-changing exercise. If project management behaviours are not modified at both the individual and organisational levels, the desired transformation will not take place.

As in many projects, realising the benefits of introducing a new approach will take time. During this time, the leaders of the change must manage carefully the expectations of the many stakeholders who will be affected by the outcome. For some, it may be a difficult experience; their workload may increase, or they may be required to work in a way that is not instinctive. Others will relish the opportunity to embrace practices that they see as enhancing their professional lives. Those who seek to design, implement and embed the new approach will need to deliver an outcome that neither panders to, nor exiles, either of these two extremes. A managed approach is essential, so using a project to embed project management in an organisation is an effective way of accomplishing it. For the rest of this chapter, this project will be referred to as the project management improvement initiative.

Establishing a case for change

It is important to demonstrate the link between projects and business change objectives – one delivers the other – so there must be a clear indication from the outset that an investment in project management

TABLE 14.1 **Capability maturity model**

	Level 1: Initial	Level 2: Repeatable
Project alignment to business imperatives	No alignment of projects to business strategy. There is no clear expression of a portfolio of projects, or a change agenda.	Mandatory and strategic projects are identifiable. Most attract senior sponsorship.
Benefits management	Projects are initiated without any cost/benefit analysis being undertaken. The benefits delivered are never measured.	The scope of mandatory and strategic projects is defined, enabling cost/benefit analysis to be regularly undertaken.
Methodical approach to project management	There is no articulated, methodical approach to project management. Project work is mostly indistinguishable from business-as-usual.	Only core processes and deliverables are documented and applied to mandatory and strategic projects. Knowledge of a Methodical approach is shared among a limited few. Support tools are used sporadically.
Stakeholder management and project organisations	Projects are managed using the business-as-usual structure. The terms "project manager" and "project sponsor" are occasionally used.	In the organisation there are individuals who are known for their ability to manage or sponsor projects. Other stakeholders are identified but rarely engaged. Project steering groups are formed for mandatory or strategic projects.

Level 3: Defined	Level 4: Managed	Level 5: Optimised
A defined portfolio of projects exists for which each has a clear sponsor. Each project's intended contribution to the organisation's advancement is described.	Decisions about which projects to promote and pursue are based on business and project performance metrics.	The planned or actual contribution made by each project to the organisation's strategic advancement is regularly reappraised and used to improve future change agendas.
An approach to benefits management exists. Scope is defined for all projects. A cost/benefit analysis is completed for all projects.	The benefits management approach is applied to all projects. Benefit-related data are gathered throughout the life cycle and used to facilitate stop/start decisions.	The actual benefits delivered by each project are measured and used to determine choices for forthcoming projects. Sponsor rewards are linked to the delivery of benefits.
All processes and deliverables are documented. Some integration with business-as-usual systems and procedures exists. Project data are being gathered centrally. Immature support/ assurance function in place. Support tools used consistently.	Processes and deliverables are being applied in common across all projects. Project and business-as-usual systems and procedures fully integrated. Decisions based on reliable information. A mature support/ assurance function employs sophisticated tools and techniques.	Projects, and the methodical approach, regularly examined to identify and implement improvements. Recognised project management standards set by accredited bodies could be met.
The project roles are understood. Project practitioners are a recognised group. A portfolio management team manages the portfolio. Project steering groups exist for most projects. An approach to stakeholder identification exists.	The competencies of project managers and members of the project steering group are known, allowing the selection of a tailored project management team to be more precise. The project management team operates to a commonly understood process. Stakeholders are actively managed.	The organisation's change agenda is delivered by tailored project, portfolio and programme structures which accommodate relevant stakeholders.

	Level 1: Initial	Level 2: Repeatable
Quality management (planning, monitoring, reporting and control)	Project success criteria are misunderstood and undefined. Project delivery focuses only on achieving time and/or budgetary targets. Quality control and assurance activities are rare.	Project success criteria are defined for mandatory and strategic projects. Some common project deliverables have been identified and described. Assurance and control activity is applied to key projects and deliverables.
Resource and cost management (planning, monitoring, reporting and control)	Resources and costs are managed through existing business-as-usual channels. Project resource and cost plans do not exist, or can only be constructed under instruction. Budget targets are frequently missed.	Techniques exist for estimating resources and costs. Standard reports are available for key projects. Resource tracking and cost management are applied to mandatory and strategic projects.
Time management (planning, monitoring, reporting and control)	Project time schedules do not exist, or can only be constructed under instruction. Delivery dates are frequently missed.	Techniques exist for estimating timescales. Standard reports are available for projects. Time management techniques applied to mandatory and strategic projects.
Risk management	There is no approach to risk management. Projects are regularly surprised by unforeseen events. The organisation invests in troubleshooters to fix problems.	Some organisational risk management is applied to select priority projects. An approach to risk management is used for mandatory and strategic projects.

Level 3: Defined	Level 4: Managed	Level 5: Optimised
An approach to quality management is well documented. Most projects are subjected to some form of independent quality assurance. Most deliverables are subjected to quality definition and control.	All projects apply the quality management approach, allowing quality expectations to be specified, planned, built, tested and accepted. Evidence exists of all completed deliverables. The support/assurance function provides support and assurance services. Libraries of common project deliverables exist.	Project and deliverable success/quality criteria are regularly reappraised in light of changes. Projects regularly commission quality assurance activities (eg, health checks). Recognised quality standards set by accredited bodies could be met.
Resource selection and cost estimation approach is applied by most projects. Reporting is standardised. Demand and supply management is understood as a concept and practised to some degree.	Resource control and cost management is integrated with organisation's other systems and procedures. Management information is available in a variety of tailored formats. Demand and supply management works effectively.	Lessons are learned from underestimates and overestimates. Demand forecasts are regularly used to facilitate resource movement across the organisation. Management information is used extensively to facilitate control.
Timescale estimation approach is applied by most projects. Reporting is standardised. Links between time, cost and quality are understood but not fully managed.	Timescale management is integrated with organisation's other systems and procedures. Management information is available in a variety of tailored formats. Time, cost and quality are managed through an integrated plan.	Lessons are learned from underestimates and overestimates. Management information is used extensively to facilitate control. Time, cost and quality expectations are commonly traded to meet strategic or commercial targets.
A risk management approach exists and is applied to most projects. Metrics are used to identify contingency amounts. Risk mitigation is allocated to those with suitable authority.	Project, portfolio and programme risk management is aligned to organisation-wide risk management. An approach to contingency management is commonly applied.	Well-articulated contingency amounts are a common feature of project, portfolio and programme plans, and are traceable to identified risk mitigation activities. Lessons are learned from exposure to risk so that future change initiatives accommodate suitable mitigations.

	Level 1: Initial	Level 2: Repeatable
Change management	Little or no management of project scope takes place, resulting in fluctuating expectations of time, cost, quality and benefits.	Baselines for time, cost, quality and benefits are set for mandatory and strategic projects. Some change control is applied to such projects.
People management	Project management expertise largely unrecognised. High turnover of project-related staff. Project expertise remains undeveloped.	Key staff engaged in multiple projects. Exposure to more complex or risky projects is the only development route.

will directly contribute to the organisation's ability to meet its agenda for change.

It is sensible to remind managers of their personal and organisational objectives so that they grasp the relevance of the proposed changes. Some examples of business objectives which effective project management can contribute to are:

■ achieving demanding financial targets;

■ overcoming competitive challenges;

■ being able to respond swiftly to change;

■ being recognised for excellence in product and service delivery;

■ offering opportunities for staff development;

■ learning without customers having to identify improvement opportunities.

The case for a project management improvement initiative can be made more compelling by comparing the organisation's existing project

Level 3: Defined	Level 4: Managed	Level 5: Optimised
A change control process exists and is applied to most projects. Metrics are used to manage the demand on contingency budgets.	Project change control is aligned to portfolio change management. Approved authorities are in place at all levels of the organisation to agree or decline changes, subject to clearly stated escalation conditions.	The organisation plans its contingency budgets based on the amounts required by previous projects.
Multiple development paths defined to facilitate project management career progression. The support/assurance function facilitates recruitment of project practitioners.	Individual performance aligned to career development. Demand and supply management of specific skill types is widely practised.	The performance of project practitioners is measured and managed, ensuring that the organisation develops the competencies it needs. Project management career path integrated with industry standards. Tailored recruitment campaigns facilitated by active skills management.

management capabilities against an index. This puts aspirations into context and shows how challenging it may be to achieve the desired level of expertise. A capability maturity model provides simple measures of an organisation's state of development. There are five levels:

- Initial – where a chaotic, unstructured approach is self-evident. Success depends on a combination of chance and the personal energy of those driving change.
- Repeatable – where there is evidence of prior success being repeated.
- Defined – where a methodical approach to project management is evident and documented.
- Managed – where the approach is integrated with wider business management and measurement of performance is possible.
- Optimised – where feedback from practice and innovation is incorporated into the organisation's documented and cultural

approach to project management so that it becomes self-improving and self-sustaining.

Table 14.1 presents a capability maturity model for project management, covering the topics contained in this book.

The analysis can be illustrated. Table 14.2 shows an organisation's position on a simple scale of project management maturity. Despite some limited peaks, this organisation's maturity is no more advanced than the lowest measuring item, and is therefore level 1.

There are several models of maturity for project management. Among the more structured is the Project Management Institute's Organisational Project Management Maturity Model (commonly called OPM3). It seeks to provide a way for organisations to understand project management and to measure their maturity against a comprehensive, broad-based set of best practices. It also helps organisations wishing to increase their project management maturity to plan for improvement.

Although many potential sponsors may be persuaded by the prospect of a comparison with an industry norm, many will wish to judge their organisation's improvements against its own past performance. This

TABLE 14.2 **Project management maturity**

	Level 1: Initial	Level 2: Repeatable	Level 3: Defined	Level 4: Managed	Level 5: Optimised
Business alignment					
Benefits management					
Systematised approach					
Stakeholder management					
Quality management					
Resource and cost management					
Time management					
Risk management					
Change management					
People management					

TABLE 14.3 **Questionnaire**

No.	Current state	Disagree	Agree

Project alignment

No.	Current state	Disagree — Agree
PA1	Our company strategy does not exist in documented form	1 2 3 4 5 6 7 8 9
PA2	Our company strategy contains contradictions and/or gaps	1 2 3 4 5 6 7 8 9
PA3	Most projects proceed, regardless of their relative contribution to our strategic objectives	1 2 3 4 5 6 7 8 9
PA4	The priority of business or change opportunities depends on the seniority of the sponsor	1 2 3 4 5 6 7 8 9
PA5	We do not have a commonly understood expression of our projects' contribution to our company strategy	1 2 3 4 5 6 7 8 9
PA6	We do not use our company strategy to validate our selection of projects	1 2 3 4 5 6 7 8 9

Benefits management

No.	Current state	Disagree — Agree
BM1	All projects proceed, whether or not there is an articulated justification	1 2 3 4 5 6 7 8 9
BM2	Project success is measured only in terms of meeting time, cost and quality expectations	1 2 3 4 5 6 7 8 9
BM3	At the end of a project, we cannot quantify what benefits were delivered	1 2 3 4 5 6 7 8 9
BM4	We have never established whether a project delivered us the desired outcome	1 2 3 4 5 6 7 8 9
BM5	Once a project has begun, we do not revisit its justification	1 2 3 4 5 6 7 8 9
BM6	We have lacked the information and/or authority to stop projects when necessary	1 2 3 4 5 6 7 8 9
BM7	We reward revenue generation	1 2 3 4 5 6 7 8 9
BM8	We do not offer rewards to those involved in delivering successful projects	1 2 3 4 5 6 7 8 9

No.	Current state	Disagree	Agree

Systemised approach

No.	Current state	Disagree ··· Agree
SA1	Project work is largely indistinguishable from business as usual activity, and is delivered by people who work mostly in the business as usual environment	☐☐☐☐☐☐☐☐☐ 1 2 3 4 5 6 7 8 9
SA2	We have limited or no access to an impartial assurance service	☐☐☐☐☐☐☐☐☐ 1 2 3 4 5 6 7 8 9
SA3	We are failing to either gather or apply lessons that we should have learned from previous projects	☐☐☐☐☐☐☐☐☐ 1 2 3 4 5 6 7 8 9
SA4	We invest in project management tools that deliver little value	☐☐☐☐☐☐☐☐☐ 1 2 3 4 5 6 7 8 9

Project organisations

No.	Current state	Disagree ··· Agree
PO1	There are multiple, independent sponsors who provide direction to single projects	☐☐☐☐☐☐☐☐☐ 1 2 3 4 5 6 7 8 9
PO2	When changes are made to our business's organisation structure, it affects the organisation of our projects	☐☐☐☐☐☐☐☐☐ 1 2 3 4 5 6 7 8 9
PO3	The organisation's ability to implement change depends on the complex co-ordination of multiple departments, many of which cannot or will not work with each other	☐☐☐☐☐☐☐☐☐ 1 2 3 4 5 6 7 8 9
PO4	Participants often move in and out of management positions within individual projects	☐☐☐☐☐☐☐☐☐ 1 2 3 4 5 6 7 8 9
PO5	When those involved in a project are unable to make a decision, they turn to the line management structure	☐☐☐☐☐☐☐☐☐ 1 2 3 4 5 6 7 8 9
PO6	Responsibility for delivering project success lies with the project manager	☐☐☐☐☐☐☐☐☐ 1 2 3 4 5 6 7 8 9
PO7	We expect the project manager to make every decision necessary to deliver the project successfully	☐☐☐☐☐☐☐☐☐ 1 2 3 4 5 6 7 8 9
PO8	The clients of our projects have little or no authority in the way in which the project is managed	☐☐☐☐☐☐☐☐☐ 1 2 3 4 5 6 7 8 9
PO9	The suppliers engaged in our projects have little or no authority in the way in which a project is managed	☐☐☐☐☐☐☐☐☐ 1 2 3 4 5 6 7 8 9
PO10	People are unclear about their respective responsibilities and boundaries of authority	☐☐☐☐☐☐☐☐☐ 1 2 3 4 5 6 7 8 9

Planning and control

No.	Current state	Disagree ··· Agree
PC1	Project success criteria are rarely stated	☐☐☐☐☐☐☐☐☐ 1 2 3 4 5 6 7 8 9

No.	Current state	Disagree		Agree
PC2	Project plans consist mainly of a timeline or bar chart	□□□□□□□□□ 1 2 3 4 5 6 7 8 9		
PC3	There is no detailed, clearly articulated list of the specific deliverables that each project will deliver	□□□□□□□□□ 1 2 3 4 5 6 7 8 9		
PC4	While our projects have phases and stages, we rarely halt the project in order to consider its continued viability	□□□□□□□□□ 1 2 3 4 5 6 7 8 9		
PC5	We have frequent senior management project meetings	□□□□□□□□□ 1 2 3 4 5 6 7 8 9		
PC6	We have little confidence in project time and cost estimates	□□□□□□□□□ 1 2 3 4 5 6 7 8 9		
PC7	Key resources become unavailable at short notice	□□□□□□□□□ 1 2 3 4 5 6 7 8 9		
PC8	Time, cost and quality expectations are frequently at odds	□□□□□□□□□ 1 2 3 4 5 6 7 8 9		
PC9	Projects are funded month by month	□□□□□□□□□ 1 2 3 4 5 6 7 8 9		
PC10	Project plans are updated irregularly if at all	□□□□□□□□□ 1 2 3 4 5 6 7 8 9		
PC11	Although we could probably find out how much a project has cost to date, it would be a major exercise for someone to do so	□□□□□□□□□ 1 2 3 4 5 6 7 8 9		
PC12	We are skilled in monitoring spend to date, but rarely do we re-evaluate our earlier estimates	□□□□□□□□□ 1 2 3 4 5 6 7 8 9		
PC13	We report all variances of any amount to senior managers	□□□□□□□□□ 1 2 3 4 5 6 7 8 9		
PC14	By the time a problem is identified, it is too late for any corrective action to have any effect	□□□□□□□□□ 1 2 3 4 5 6 7 8 9		
PC15	At best, we have an informal peer review system in place, but mostly, we don't put any of our project deliverables through a review process	□□□□□□□□□ 1 2 3 4 5 6 7 8 9		

Risk management

No.	Current state	Disagree		Agree
RM1	We pride ourselves on our ability to manage issues and problems	□□□□□□□□□ 1 2 3 4 5 6 7 8 9		
RM2	We alert our senior managers to most risks or issues that we have identified	□□□□□□□□□ 1 2 3 4 5 6 7 8 9		

No.	Current state	Disagree Agree
RM3	Risks or issues are rarely discussed outside the project environment	1 2 3 4 5 6 7 8 9

Change management

No.	Current state	Disagree Agree
CM1	Projects routinely miss time, cost and quality targets	1 2 3 4 5 6 7 8 9
CM2	Expectations fluctuate so much that we are rarely able to state the scope of our projects with any certainty	1 2 3 4 5 6 7 8 9
CM3	The impact of changes is difficult to determine resulting in our being led into an acceptance of them all	1 2 3 4 5 6 7 8 9
CM4	A change is implemented if the person who requested it is persuasive enough	1 2 3 4 5 6 7 8 9
CM5	The project manager has to decide whether or not a change is accepted	1 2 3 4 5 6 7 8 9

People management

No.	Current state	Disagree Agree
PM1	It is important for us to resource our project management teams with people who understand the technical nature of the project	1 2 3 4 5 6 7 8 9
PM2	We have a high turnover of project-related personnel	1 2 3 4 5 6 7 8 9
PM3	We have one or two key project practitioners who are in constant demand	1 2 3 4 5 6 7 8 9
PM4	The career path for any project practitioner is to engage in more, or more complex, projects	1 2 3 4 5 6 7 8 9
PM5	We have little idea how to obtain the necessary project competencies we will need in the coming years	1 2 3 4 5 6 7 8 9

TABLE 14.4

No.	Current state	Consolidated responses Disagree Agree	Future state
Project alignment			
PA1	Our company strategy does not exist in documented form	□□□□□□□■□ 1 2 3 4 5 6 7 8 9	Our company strategy exists in documented form
PA2	Our company strategy contains contradictions and/or gaps	□□□□□□□■□ 1 2 3 4 5 6 7 8 9	Our company strategy is internally consistent
PA3	Most projects proceed, regardless of their relative contribution to our strategic objectives	□□□□□□□□■ 1 2 3 4 5 6 7 8 9	All new and existing initiatives are regularly prioritised against strategic objectives
PA4	The priority of business or change opportunities depends on the seniority of the sponsor	□□□□□□□□■ 1 2 3 4 5 6 7 8 9	Successful project prioritisation comes as a result of each initiative's alignment to commercial or strategic objectives
PA5	We do not have a commonly understood expression of our projects' contribution to our company strategy	□□□□□□□□■ 1 2 3 4 5 6 7 8 9	Projects are derived from and measured against our company strategy
PA6	We do not use our company strategy to validate our selection of projects	□□□□□□□□■ 1 2 3 4 5 6 7 8 9	We measure the extent to which each project contributes to our strategy
Benefits management			
BM1	All projects proceed, whether or not there is an articulated justification	□□□□□□■□□ 1 2 3 4 5 6 7 8 9	Only projects justified by a business case are sponsored

No.	Current state	Consolidated responses Disagree Agree	Future state
BM2	Project success is measured only in terms of meeting time, cost and quality expectations	☐☐☐☐☐☐☐■☐ 1 2 3 4 5 6 7 8 9	Project success is measured in terms of the benefits delivered to our clients and to ourselves
BM3	At the end of a project, we cannot quantify what benefits were delivered	☐☐☐☐☐☐☐■☐ 1 2 3 4 5 6 7 8 9	Retrospectively we can calculate project profitability
BM4	We have never established whether a project delivered us the desired outcome	☐☐☐☐☐☐☐■☐ 1 2 3 4 5 6 7 8 9	We evaluate completed projects to determine the benefits they delivered to us commercially, and to our strategic vision
BM5	Once a project has begun, we do not revisit its justification	☐☐☐☐☐☐☐☐■ 1 2 3 4 5 6 7 8 9	The project's justification is revisited and revalidated throughout the project's lifetime
BM6	We have lacked the information and/ or authority to stop projects when necessary	☐☐☐☐☐☐■☐☐ 1 2 3 4 5 6 7 8 9	We would be prepared and able to stop a project if it looked as though it could fail us
BM7	We reward revenue generation	☐☐☐☐☐☐☐☐■ 1 2 3 4 5 6 7 8 9	We reward profit margin delivery
BM8	We do not offer rewards to those involved in delivering successful projects	☐☐☐☐☐☐☐☐■ 1 2 3 4 5 6 7 8 9	We reward those involved in the project to deliver a defined, articulated commercial or strategic benefit

No.	Current state	Consolidated responses Disagree Agree	Future state
Systemised approach			
SA1	Project work is largely indistinguishable from business-as-usual activity, and is delivered by people who work mostly in the business-as-usual environment	□□□□□■□□□ 1 2 3 4 5 6 7 8 9	Projects are conducted according to a clear and commonly understood approach
SA2	We have limited or no access to an impartial assurance service	□□□□□□□■□ 1 2 3 4 5 6 7 8 9	We have access to a range of independent, impartial sources of assurance to mitigate project risk and confirm the effectiveness of our management
SA3	We are failing to either gather or apply lessons that we should have learned from previous projects	□□□□□■□□□ 1 2 3 4 5 6 7 8 9	We have a means by which improvements can be both captured and applied
SA4	We invest in project management tools that deliver little value	□□■□□□□□□ 1 2 3 4 5 6 7 8 9	The organisation benefits from a range of integrated tools that support the management of projects
Stakeholder management and project organisations			
PO1	There are multiple, independent sponsors who provide direction to single projects	□□□□□■□□□ 1 2 3 4 5 6 7 8 9	The portfolio is managed by a single, unified body which empowers tailored groups to own and direct individual projects

No.	Current state	Consolidated responses Disagree Agree	Future state
PO2	When changes are made to our business's organisation structure, it affects the organisation of our projects	□□□□□□■□□ 1 2 3 4 5 6 7 8 9	Delivery of our operational imperatives is independent of our organisational structure
PO3	The organisation's ability to implement change depends on the complex co-ordination of multiple departments, many of which cannot or will not work with each other	□□□□□□□□■ 1 2 3 4 5 6 7 8 9	Projects are managed and delivered by a tailored group of people, independent of the line structure, who accommodate the demands of all parties
PO4	Participants often move in and out of management positions within individual projects	□□□□□□□■□ 1 2 3 4 5 6 7 8 9	There are distinct, tailored groups of people who deliver individual projects
PO5	When those involved in a project are unable to make a decision, they turn to the line management structure	□□□□■□□□□ 1 2 3 4 5 6 7 8 9	Our project organisations contain the authority within themselves to make the decisions necessary to the project's continued progress
PO6	Responsibility for delivering project success lies with the project manager	□□□□■□□□□ 1 2 3 4 5 6 7 8 9	Authority and responsibility for delivering project success lies with the project steering group

No.	Current state	Consolidated responses Disagree Agree	Future state
PO7	We expect the project manager to make every decision necessary to deliver the project successfully	☐☐☐☐☐☐■☐☐ 1 2 3 4 5 6 7 8 9	We make a clear separation between project "ownership" and its "daily management"
PO8	The clients of our projects have little or no authority in the way in which the project is managed	☐☐☐☐☐☐☐■☐ 1 2 3 4 5 6 7 8 9	The clients of our projects form part of the management team of the project
PO9	The suppliers engaged in our projects have little or no authority in the way in which a project is managed	☐☐☐☐☐■☐☐☐ 1 2 3 4 5 6 7 8 9	The key suppliers of major components of our projects form part of the management team of the project
PO10	People are unclear about their respective responsibilities and boundaries of authority	☐☐☐☐☐☐■☐☐ 1 2 3 4 5 6 7 8 9	All individuals to whom project roles have been assigned have been acquainted with their responsibilities and are comfortable with them

Planning and control

No.	Current state	Consolidated responses Disagree Agree	Future state
PC1	Project success criteria are rarely stated	☐☐☐■☐☐☐☐☐ 1 2 3 4 5 6 7 8 9	Project success criteria are listed and prioritised by those who will take receipt of the project's deliverables
PC2	Project plans consist mainly of a timeline or bar chart	☐☐☐☐☐☐☐■☐ 1 2 3 4 5 6 7 8 9	All plans detail time, cost and quality components

No.	Current state	Consolidated responses Disagree Agree	Future state
PC3	There is no detailed, clearly articulated list of the specific deliverables that each project will deliver	□□■□□□□□□ 1 2 3 4 5 6 7 8 9	Our plans clearly identify deliverables, not just activities
PC4	While our projects have phases and stages, we rarely halt the project in order to consider its continued viability	□□□□□□□■□ 1 2 3 4 5 6 7 8 9	We divide projects into non-overlapping stages
PC5	We have frequent senior management project meetings	□□□□□□□□■ 1 2 3 4 5 6 7 8 9	Senior management project meetings are pre-planned, event-driven sessions at which key decisions are made
PC6	We have little confidence in project time and cost estimates	□□□□□□□□■ 1 2 3 4 5 6 7 8 9	Time and cost estimates are demonstrably based on clearly described deliverables
PC7	Key resources become unavailable at short notice	□□□□□□□□■ 1 2 3 4 5 6 7 8 9	Demand forecasts are regularly used to facilitate resource movement across the organisation
PC8	Time, cost and quality expectations are frequently at odds	□□□□□□□□■ 1 2 3 4 5 6 7 8 9	Time, cost and quality expectations are commonly traded to meet strategic or commercial targets
PC9	Projects are funded month by month	□□□□□□■□□ 1 2 3 4 5 6 7 8 9	Funds are identified and set aside when each project is approved

No.	Current state	Consolidated responses Disagree Agree	Future state
PC10	Project plans are updated irregularly if at all	□□□□■□□□□ 1 2 3 4 5 6 7 8 9	All projects have an up-to-date plan
PC11	Although we could probably find out how much a project has cost to date, it would be a major exercise for someone to do so	□□□□□□□■□ 1 2 3 4 5 6 7 8 9	We know how much any project has cost us to date
PC12	We are skilled in monitoring spend to date, but rarely do we re-evaluate our earlier estimates	□□□□□□■□□ 1 2 3 4 5 6 7 8 9	We regularly re-estimate and report forecast costs
PC13	We report all variances of any amount to senior managers	□□□□□□□□■ 1 2 3 4 5 6 7 8 9	We manage significant variations through escalation conditions so that senior manager deal only with matters for which others are unauthorised or unqualified
PC14	By the time a problem is identified, it is too late for any corrective action to have any effect	□□□□□□□□■ 1 2 3 4 5 6 7 8 9	Project progress reports and meetings are timed to allow sufficient opportunity to anticipate and fix problems
PC15	At best, we have an informal peer review system in place, but mostly, we don't put any of our project deliverables through a review process	□□□□■□□□□ 1 2 3 4 5 6 7 8 9	We review and approve deliverables according to their defined success criteria

No.	Current state	Consolidated responses Disagree Agree	Future state
Risk management			
RM1	We pride ourselves on our ability to manage issues and problems	☐☐☐☐☐☐☐☐■ 1 2 3 4 5 6 7 8 9	We pride ourselves on our ability to prevent issues and problems through effective risk management
RM2	We alert our senior managers to most risks or issues that we have identified	☐☐☐☐☐☐☐☐■ 1 2 3 4 5 6 7 8 9	We alert senior managers only to those risks or issues for which their attention is deserved
RM3	Risks or issues are rarely discussed outside the project environment	☐☐☐☐☐☐☐☐■ 1 2 3 4 5 6 7 8 9	There is an escalation route for risks and issues that may affect the wider organisation
Change management			
CM1	Projects routinely miss time, cost and quality targets	☐☐☐☐☐☐☐☐■ 1 2 3 4 5 6 7 8 9	Expectations and estimates are regularly reappraised and approved to allow appropriate contingencies to be identified to mitigate risks and accommodate change
CM2	Expectations fluctuate so much that we are rarely able to state the scope of our projects with any certainty	☐☐☐☐☐☐☐☐■ 1 2 3 4 5 6 7 8 9	Every project has a set of baselined statements of time, cost, quality and benefits expectations

No.	Current state	Consolidated responses Disagree — Agree	Future state
CM3	The impact of changes is difficult to determine resulting in our being led into an acceptance of them all	□□□□□□■□□ 1 2 3 4 5 6 7 8 9	All proposed changes are subject to consideration via an acknowledged process
CM4	A change is implemented if the person who requested it is persuasive enough	□□□□□□□■□ 1 2 3 4 5 6 7 8 9	Changes are assessed by a balanced combination of people before a recommendation is made
CM5	The project manager has to decide whether or not a change is accepted	□□□□□■□□□ 1 2 3 4 5 6 7 8 9	Approval to accommodate a change is granted only by authorised members of the management team

People management

No.	Current state	Consolidated responses Disagree — Agree	Future state
PM1	It is important for us to resource our project management teams with people who understand the technical nature of the project	□□□□□■□□□ 1 2 3 4 5 6 7 8 9	We have a balance of users, technicians and commercial skills in our project management teams
PM2	We have a high turnover of project-related personnel	□□□□□□□■□ 1 2 3 4 5 6 7 8 9	Our project practitioners develop through continued participation in, and contribution to, our portfolio of projects
PM3	We have one or two key project practitioners who are in constant demand	□□□□□□□■□ 1 2 3 4 5 6 7 8 9	We have access to a community of experienced project practitioners

No.	Current state	Consolidated responses Disagree Agree	Future state
PM4	The career path for any project practitioner is to engage in more, or more complex, projects	☐☐☐☐■☐☐☐☐ 1 2 3 4 5 6 7 8 9	There is a clearly defined development path for all project practitioners
PM5	We have little idea how to obtain the necessary project competencies we will need in the coming years	☐☐☐☐☐☐☐■☐ 1 2 3 4 5 6 7 8 9	We have recruitment campaigns that satisfy our considered project competency demands

helps them see progress in project management being measured in more relevant, and possibly commercial, terms.

The questionnaire in Table 14.3 helps to identify and consolidate the perceptions of different groups of people. It allows them to show how far they disagree or agree with each statement. The results of this survey paint a picture of the concerns of different levels of management at a point in time, providing an indication of where the organisation's priorities lie and a further mandate for change. Further surveys can be conducted during the life of the project management improvement initiative to determine how far improvements are being realised.

Depending on who is invited to take part, the analysis may identify some clear but probably contradictory priorities. For instance, potential sponsors may strongly agree that "projects routinely miss time, cost and quality targets". Project managers may strongly agree that "expectations fluctuate so much that we are rarely able to state the scope of our projects with any certainty". The solution lies in a carefully planned and unified approach to making improvements.

Table 14.4 is an extension to Table 14.3. It assumes that the "consolidated responses" have been gathered, giving some guidance about priorities. Adding some corresponding "future states" allows the overview to be expressed more elaborately.

Given the direction provided by these statements, the vision need not be complex. It may be enough to express it like this:

■ The "future state" cultural change will be achieved by dd/mm/yy through the implementation of self-sustaining measures.

Obtaining a mandate for change

Expressing clearly the opportunities for change is not enough. A sponsor, or sponsors, will be needed to drive, fund and direct the project management improvement initiative. The more senior they are in the organisation, the better. This is not to say, however, that anyone is suitable. Nor is it enough that there is a groundswell of enthusiasm for change. Without sponsorship, the initiative will either fail to start successfully or falter soon after. If the project management improvement initiative is to be managed according to the principles of effective project management, they must be applied in selecting a suitable project steering group to own and direct it.

The sponsor should be a recognised promoter of change, ideally someone who has previously sponsored significant change initiatives for the organisation. He should not be involved exclusively in business-as-usual, no matter how competent he is in managing business operations. He should be senior enough to command the respect of his peers since the role will involve selling and promoting concepts that may be alien or unpalatable to others. Significantly, he should have access to funds and be prepared to commit them over what may be a long period. Ideally, the sponsor will be the person who identified the need for change and who has driven the project management improvement initiative this far.

The developer representative must be an expert in managing projects and understand intimately the "methodical approach", as he must assure the organisation that it will be a robust and reliable solution to its challenges. Sometimes a project management consultant will be hired for this role. It is possible that a second person may be required in an organisation that already has a significant number or complexity of existing systems and processes into which the project management approach is to be accommodated. This person might come from the finance department because of its central role in so many management processes.

The customer representative must make sure that the delivered solution meets the needs of the organisation. It is sensible to choose two people who represent communities that will be affected differently by the project's outcome – the sponsors and the project managers. Consequently, one candidate could be a highly regarded project manager and the other could come from the pool of project sponsors, possibly allowing the sponsor to adopt this as an additional role. Whatever the solution, if it is to work and last, it must satisfy these two people.

Much will depend on selecting an appropriate project manager, not just to make sure that the project management improvement initiative is well planned, monitored and controlled, but also that it is a beacon for best practice. If the initiative is poorly managed, there will be little chance of the benefits it seeks to promote becoming entrenched elsewhere. If the organisation does not have a candidate with the necessary qualifications, the person could be recruited from a project management consultancy. The commitment to a suitable individual should not be underestimated; a project management improvement initiative for a medium-sized organisation may take two years or more to complete.

With a powerful, guiding coalition in place (if only informally at this stage), and an identified project manager waiting to be instructed, the fledgling project management improvement initiative is ready to use the evidence it has gathered to justify its case for change.

Justifying the investment

Most organisations should look for commercial benefits from a project management improvement initiative. Too often, the change is instigated by junior managers who argue that a consistent approach to project management will inherently deliver rewards, but that argument does not adequately support what might be a considerable investment. Working in a common way will, at best, help to avoid repeating work, but that will not persuade the senior management team to adopt the initiative. Instead, having sold the concept to the wider senior management team, those promoting the project management improvement initiative should build a substantial business case to show the range of benefits it can generate.

Typically, these benefits fall into three categories which together make a more persuasive case for the investment. Table 14.5 lists some examples and how they could be quantified.

TABLE 14.5 **Benefits of a project management improvement initiative**

Item	Planning assumption	Value
Increased revenue and margin		
Business opportunities will be increased through existing clients' exposure to the organisation's project management excellence.	Clients buy more products and services from our organisation rather than building them in-house.	n additional projects per year of, say, nn days' effort, which returns a revenue of $nn per year.
Clients recognise the value that the organisation's approach to project management creates.	Existing clients (who are not currently paying for project management) pay for project management.	n projects per year of, say, nn days' elapsed duration where a project manager is allocated full time. Value $nn per year.
Clients recognise that all the organisation's project managers can successfully deliver projects because the approach to project management (supported by training and career development) will ensure better availability of project management practitioners with management skills.	The organisation's sales opportunities are not limited by the availability of project managers.	n additional projects are delivered during the year, the profit from which would be, say, $nn.
The organisation's project management expertise is recognised and so it is used in preference to third-party contractors.	Clients use the organisation's project management.	Revenue for one project manager for one project (full-time for nn days at $nn per day). Value $nn.
Developing a business case for each project will result in improved prioritisation of projects.	All projects will be prioritised according to their value to the business and some projects will be rejected.	One project per year is selected over another on the basis of its greater margin, increasing profit by, say, $nn.

Item	Planning assumption	Value
Senior managers will be more able to direct the progress of the organisation towards its strategic goals via the management of a portfolio of business cases.	All business cases are linked to the organisation's strategic aims.	Strategic success increases the organisation's profitability by nn%, say $nn per year.
Reduction in costs		
As a result of effective planning and reporting, clients recognise their own responsibilities where slippage occurs.	Clients pay the full value of invoices charged to their project.	The discount given to clients via credits in the past year due to disputes was $nn, and the chargeable time not billed was $nn. A nn% improvement would represent $nn annual saving.
Definition of products and quality criteria will reduce rework.	More products are delivered to specification, resulting in less rework.	nn% reduction in the cost of rework, and so a saving of, say, $nn per year based on nn person days per month.
Senior managers and project managers will become more efficient at executing projects.	Reduction in the cost of executing project.	A nn% percent reduction in the cost of all projects, say $nn.
Project managers become more focused on project matters and less distracted by line management pressures.	Project managers spend less time resolving line management issues.	n project managers each save nn days per month. This time could be charged elsewhere, giving revenue of $nn.
Mitigation of risk		
With better planning and risk management, the organisation can competitively bid for fixed-price contracts with a reduced risk of financial loss on the contract.	Fixed-price projects are completed with less variance from cost budget.	Assume $nn of fixed-price work during the previous financial year, including a variance of nn%. The project management improvement initiative reduces variance from nn% to nn%, creating an annual saving of $nn.
Better risk management will reduce the cost to the organisation of the management of issues.	Risks are mitigated before becoming issues.	A nn% reduction in the cost of all projects, say $nn.

Item	Planning assumption	Value
The effort to identify and manage risks is reduced by learning from previous projects.	An established risks register is available to all project managers.	Saving of nn days per month for nn project managers. This time is charged elsewhere at $nn per day giving revenue of $nn

The list in Table 14.5 is not exhaustive, and although it suggests how the benefits of a project management improvement initiative can be demonstrated, it is highly likely that the figures quoted will be disputed in the same way that forecasts usually are. After discussion, the proposed revenue increases, cost savings and mitigation of risks may well be lower, but ideally they should outweigh the proposed costs of the initiative, which may be substantial. In any case, if the organisation is not open to using a disciplined project management approach, a business case is unlikely to persuade it otherwise. In that case, it may be necessary to wait until events (such as a failure to deliver a project) force the issue.

Delivering the change

Figure 14.1 was used in Chapter 1 to show the components of effective project management. Here it is embellished to suggest a priority order.

Any organisation that wishes to manage change effectively needs to know that it is ready, willing and able to select the right projects. Phase 1 encapsulates those component parts of an approach that facilitates the justification, prioritisation, resourcing and sponsorship of change. This is the foundation on which effective change and project management is based. The mechanics of project management may be wonderfully efficient but if they are delivering the wrong outcomes, they are valueless. It is for this reason that investing in managing projects in the right way is only sensible when the foundations are in place. Thus, phase 2 sees the creation and promotion of the methodical approach to project management. Commonly, this takes the form of a documentation which includes processes, templates and role descriptions. However, many organisations which are new

FIGURE 14.1 **The prioritised components of effective project management**

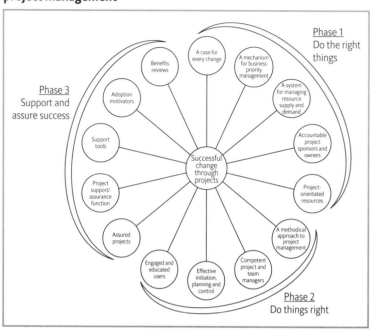

to the management of change may find this hard to digest. It can be helpful to condense the methodical approach into what is commonly called a minimum standard, an example of which is illustrated in Figure 14.2.

This describes what standard of management is expected and is one of the methods first described in Chapter 10 to facilitate change through education. Of course, a degree of basic competence is also necessary among those who are to practise project management. This may be first demonstrated in the effective initiation of projects when the governance is put in place to allow effective onward management.

Education should be provided for sponsors and other senior stakeholders as a priority so that they can persuade others to adopt the approach. Training project managers too early wastes both a precious opportunity and resources. Trainees will return from their courses enthusiastic and capable, only to be thrust into an environment not yet

FIGURE 14.2 **A project management minimum standard**

1. On the Portfolio Management Team's authority, each Project is directed by a Project Sponsor who is accountable for developing and promoting the Project's Business Case, and ensuring that the benefits are realised.
2. The Project Sponsor chairs a Project Steering Group composed of accountable decision-makers who are the project's commercial, user and specialist authorities, and who remain in place for the life of the Business Case.
3. Every project has a clearly identified, single Project Manager to plan, monitor and control the activity of all resources.
4. No project commences without approval from the Project Steering Group of its Project Governance Report which includes:
   a) a clear, populated, documented and communicated project organisation structure, roles and responsibilities;
   b) a Business Case which clearly outlines the available budget compared to the intended, quantified benefits;
   c) a set of base-lined requirements, and a suitable solution;
   d) a base-lined Project Plan which:
      i. clearly identifies deliverables, and when they are planned for testing, delivery and approval;
      ii. shows the cost of delivery;
      iii. describes how the project is to be kept on track.
5. All key deliverables are tested for quality before being considered complete.
6. The Business Case and Project Plan are kept up-to-date at all times.
7. Risks are continuously identified and described, and mitigations planned, monitored and controlled (with the Risk Register showing present status).
8. All projects regularly forecast their status at the point of intended completion, accurately identifying the variance of the project versus the base-lined plan, and ensuring that corrective action is identified, delegated, escalated (where necessary) and managed to completion.
9. All projects work to a base-lined Specification against which changes are managed in a manner which allows for the consequences of any change to be understood, before a decision is authorised (by the Project Steering Group if necessary).
10. An amount of contingency (suited to the degree of project risk and change) is protected by the Project Steering Group, and only utilised on condition of a recorded, costed, value/risk focussed Change Request.

ready for them. Consequently, the position of training and education in the sequence should be considered, using these criteria:

- **Can potential trainees be prioritised according to their seniority?** A first round of senior management briefings will be essential if the drive for change is to come from the top of the organisation. The use of the word "briefing" as opposed to "training" is important as it takes account of the sensitivities of executives who may believe that, for them, training is unnecessary. Trainees should be selected from a carefully considered, prioritised range of participants.

- **Can potential trainees be prioritised by the importance of the projects in which they are engaged?** Some projects may benefit if their participants are trained in project management, but others may be at such a critical point that the introduction of a new approach to project management may do more harm than good. Trainees should be selected from a prioritised range of projects.

■ **Can potential trainees be prioritised according to their development needs?** There will be some for whom an introduction to project management will be an invaluable boost to their confidence and competence. For others, the training will be frustrating and exacerbate existing issues. Involving people of all backgrounds and expertise in projects does not mean that they must all be trained in the principles and techniques of project management. It is better to focus on those for whom the management of projects is an essential skill. In the early stages at least, this may rule out the need to train and educate those who are not involved in the project's management. Trainees should be selected according to their development needs.

A training needs analysis is an important product of the first phase since it allows these points to be accommodated in a thoughtful and planned approach to education. Training is also a way of describing the methodical approach to project management so that a new, commonly understood language can be introduced into the organisation. The training needs analysis becomes both a means of describing how the educational needs of the organisation will be satisfied and the basis of a plan for communication. It can be shown in a simple matrix (Figure 14.3).

FIGURE 14.3 **Training needs analysis**

	Sponsors' project management briefing	Practitioner's project management	Condensed project management overview	Operational project management techniques
Portfolio management team	✓			
Project steering groups	✓			
Project managers		✓		
Project team leaders		✓		
Project team members			✓	
Operational managers			✓	
Operational team members				✓

Groups of participants are shown on the vertical axis and the proposed training events are listed on the horizontal axis. The ticks indicate the events thought appropriate for each audience. The events seek to satisfy markedly different objectives:

- Sponsors' project management briefing – to familiarise the sponsors of change with their obligations so they can communicate clearly with each other and consistently direct the organisation's pool of project managers.
- Practitioners' project management – to provide practitioners with the skills and knowledge to practise the principles and techniques of project management in the organisation.
- Condensed project management overview – to provide non-participants with sufficient knowledge to understand the principles of project management and the organisation's approach to its application.
- Operational project management techniques – to provide non-participants with sufficient skills to practise the techniques of project management in operational areas of the organisation. Such training may be suitable for communities of users who are to find themselves involved in projects but who have not had the benefit of any tailored education in the subject.

These four events allow all potential delegates from project and operational backgrounds to obtain sufficient knowledge and/or skills to participate constructively in a project-focused environment.

The final phase allows for those projects that are now under way to be supported and assured. As noted earlier, assurance may be adopted as a practical series of healthchecks that reveal where any support or corrective action is needed. This may come from, or be co-ordinated by, a support/assurance function, as described in Chapter 12. Tools such as those often used to support the development of plans and progress reports may be considered desirable in a much earlier phase. However, it is only at this point in the process that an organisation has come to terms with its approach and its needs. Therefore, it is recommended that the introduction of tools be delayed for as long as possible until there is already a level of project management maturity sufficient enough to understand what requirements the organisation may have, what tools can address them, and how new tools may be implemented.

As described in the previous chapter, it is helpful to motivate adoption of the approach. Failing to do so can easily result in so much great progress being retarded or terminated. As with any project, the pressure to embed the desired changes must be continuous and unforgiving if, as might be hoped, benefits reviews are to reveal what everyone can agree has been a successful project, and a successful change. Therefore, throughout this entire change it is essential that the organisation delivers some successful projects. Without some early wins to promote the approach, few will see the benefit of the investment. It follows that in selecting projects to which the approach is to be applied, timing must be considered carefully. This will make sure there are milestones throughout the project management improvement initiative that show the value it is delivering.

As project benefits reviews continue, phase 3 not only marks the end of the project management improvement initiative, but also suggests that a significant level of maturity has been reached. Desirable as it may be to conduct benefits reviews in phase 1, it is unlikely that the essential principles underpinning the approach to change and project management will be understood sufficiently and widely enough to allow that to happen. Only because an investment to develop, build and embed an approach to project management has been made in the two previous phases is it culturally acceptable, and possible, to measure realised benefits.

Enjoying the benefits

Introducing a new approach or method to an organisation is, above all, a change to its management culture. In his book *Leading Change*, John Kotter wrote:

> In the final analysis, change sticks when it becomes "the way we do things around here", when it seeps into the bloodstream of the corporate body. Until new behaviours are rooted in social norms and shared values, they are subject to degradation as soon as the pressure for change is removed.

The pressure to optimise competence in project management must be not only continuous and unrelenting but also entire across all parties. It takes an organisation to deliver change; no single individual or group can do it alone. Those who seek to promote and embed the benefits of effective change and project management must be committed to what may be a lengthy and challenging process.

However, the benefits are there to be enjoyed, promising commercial and competitive advantage. Effectively managed projects have the potential to transform individuals and institutions for the better.

Glossary

Cross-references are in **bold**.

Action form	A pro forma used by a **scribe** on which are written the decisions taken and the necessary actions identified during a **quality review**.
Activity network	A technique used to determine a **project**'s **duration** and **critical path** from the activities (or **deliverables**) and their dependencies.
Actual cost of work performed (ACWP)	In **earned value analysis**, what has been spent on the **project** to date.
Actual to date (ATD)	The amount of **budget** or time which has been spent to date.
Agile	A term used to describe any form of **iterative** or **incremental** product (especially software) development approach.
Agile manifesto	A set of 4 values and 12 principles which serve to guide the **iterative** or **incremental** **development** of software.
Analogy estimating technique	A way to estimate the time and cost needed to develop a **deliverable** by comparing it with another deliverable which has similar features and characteristics.

Approved subject to amendments (ASTA)	A **quality review** outcome which allows for the **deliverable** to be approved on the condition that all recorded amendments have been completed and agreed by those who identified them.
Assessment date	The date upon which a project **health check** was last conducted.
Assumption	A condition used for forecasting purposes which has not been proven. An assumption may therefore be considered a risk.
Backlog	See **product backlog.**
Balanced score card (BSC)	A means by which to measure a company's performance taking into account not only financial outcomes but also matters such as customer relationships, business processes and employee skills and engagement that contribute to those outcomes. It was developed by Robert S. Kaplan and David Norton.
Baseline	An approved date or financial value against which all changes (intended or otherwise) may be compared to determine **variance**.
Benefits	The positive outcome sought from a **project** that outweighs the investment made in it.
Benefits dependency network	A technique for tracing the audit trail from **project outcome** to strategic imperative. It was developed and described by John Ward and Joe Peppard of Cranfield University.
Benefits realisation	The **project** phase or process where planned benefits are brought to fruition.
Benefits realisation plan	The section of a **business case** which describes how the organisation intends to measure and deliver the planned benefits.

Benefits realisation report	A document used after **project closure** to determine to what extent the intended benefits have been realised and what further action may be needed to bring them to fruition.
Benefits review/benefits realisation review	A session to determine to what extent the intended benefits have been realised and what further action may be needed to bring them to fruition.
Bottom-up estimating	Used for evaluating the time and cost needed to complete activities or **deliverables** at a low level of detail. (See also **top-down estimating**.)
Budget	The amount of time or money set aside for the completion of a specified **deliverable**.
Budgeted cost of work performed (BCWP)	In **earned value analysis**, the budgeted cost of work which has been completed in the period being measured.
Budgeted cost of work scheduled (BCWS)	In **earned value analysis**, the budgeted cost of work which was planned in the time being measured.
Business-as-usual (BAU)	A term used to describe the regular, non-**project** work of an organisation.
Business case	A document which describes the financial justification for a **project**.
Business plan	A document which describes how an organisation intends to deliver its proposed **business-as-usual** and change agenda.
Capability maturity model (CMM)	A mechanism for describing the varying levels of an organisation's **project management** effectiveness.
Change control	A process for managing the consequences of intended or unplanned variations in a **project**.

Change log	A document used to record and summarise the **change requests** which have been submitted during the life of a **project**.
Change request (CR)	A document which describes an application for a change to be made in a **project**.
Common data repository	A database or other storage mechanism which holds facts and figures about an organisation's **projects** so that management reports about them may be created.
Communications plan	A document which describes how specified **stakeholders** are to receive the messages which are essential to maintain their engagement in a **project**.
Configuration control	A discipline which allows for the management of a **project**'s **deliverables**.
Consensual communication	A communications approach that seeks to involve **stakeholder** communities by actively lobbying for their views.
Consultative leadership	A leadership strategy which seeks to secure success through negotiation.
Contingency	A planned **budget** of time or money set aside to fund the mitigation of identified **risks** or anticipated change.
Continuous renewal	A form of evolutionary change which is characterised by frequent, incremental shifts in the status quo (see also **evolutionary change**).
Control	The taking of corrective action when something has varied from its plan.
Control cycle	The considered process of delegating work, monitoring and reporting progress, and exercising **control**, which leads to the effective maintenance of a plan.

Coping stages	Five phases through which an individual may pass when faced with the prospect of, and passage through, change. First described by Colin Carnall.
Corporate dashboard	A form of report which provides a level and format of management information appropriate for senior managers in charge of a **portfolio** of **projects**.
Cost/benefit analysis	A form of numeric comparison between the costs and benefits of a **project**, planned or actual, to determine its financial viability.
Cost variation	In **earned value analysis**, the **budgeted cost of work performed** minus the **actual cost of work performed** (that is, how much should have been spent to date based on what has been achieved, minus the amount actually spent to date).
Critical path	The sequence of dependent activities with the longest overall **duration** which therefore determines the shortest time possible to complete the **project**.
Customer	A **project**'s **stakeholder(s)** with an interest in the suitability of the **deliverable** to meet their needs as a user of it.
Daily meeting	A time-boxed opportunity for members of an **agile** development team to advise on what has been completed, what is due to be completed, and what barriers there may be to completion (see also **scrum meeting** and **stand-up meeting**).
Delegation	The assigning of work to members of a **project** team.
Delegatee	A person or group assigned work by a manager in the **project**.

Delegator	A person who assigns work to a member of a **project** team.
Deliverable	The output of a process which is both definable and measurable in qualitative terms. Other terms used are milestone or product.
Delphi estimating technique	Used for developing a consensus about an estimate through meetings, questionnaires and surveys.
Democratic leadership	A leadership style which is characterised by encouraging inclusivity.
Developer	A **project stakeholder**(s) responsible for developing and implementing a **deliverable** which conforms to agreed standards and meets the needs of those who will use it.
Directive leadership	A leadership style which is characterised by being instructional.
Discounted cash flow	An approach to forecasting cash flow which takes into account the future value of money.
Discount factor	The amount by which the net difference between future costs and benefits must be multiplied in order to discount it by a specified amount.
Duration	The time between the start and end dates of an activity. In an **activity network**, it is the number of days between the **earliest start time** and the **earliest finish time**, or the **latest start time** and the **latest finish time**.
Dynamic Systems Development Method (DSDM)	An **agile** software delivery approach.
Earliest finish time (EFT)	In an **activity network**, the earliest point at which an activity can finish.

Earliest start time (EST)	In an **activity network**, the earliest point at which an activity can start.
Earned value analysis (EVA)	A technique which objectively measures a **project**'s performance against time, cost and quality targets.
Effort	The time it would take someone to complete an activity if they were able to work at 100% productivity all the time, unfettered by any other work or distraction. Effort is sometimes called "work".
Epic	A sizeable component of work with a defined objective, commonly applied in **agile** development.
Error list	A pro forma used in preparation for a **quality review** on which are written the faults in a **product** identified by the reviewers of it.
Escalation conditions	The terms defining when a forecast breach of targets must be made known to one's superiors, commonly when a **project manager** must inform the **project steering group** that a project is forecast to deliver off target by more than a certain amount.
Escalation management	A management discipline which allows for the creation of certain conditions, the breaching of which enables superiors to take control of a **project** from their subordinates.
Estimate to complete (ETC)	An estimate of the **effort** or cost to complete an activity, **product** or **project** beyond what has already been spent.
Estimating sheet	A pro forma used to record the data that is most relevant to the creation of a **Gantt chart** and **resource plan**.

Evolutionary change	A form of change that is characterised by frequent, i**ncremental** shifts in the status quo (see also **continuous renewal).**
External audit	Similar to an **internal audit**, but conducted by an external party to specific terms of reference in order to identify and attend to any areas of concern within a defined timetable.
Extreme programming	An **agile** software delivery approach.
Feature Driven Development (FDD)	An **agile** software delivery approach.
Financial dependency network	A numeric tool which identifies the financial relationships between **projects**.
Fit for purpose	A term used to describe the suitability of a **product** or service to meet the intended needs of its users; in other words, whether it is fit for their purposes.
Float	In an **activity network**, the difference between the **earliest start time** and the **latest start time**, or the **earliest finish time** and the **latest finish time**. This is the amount by which an activity may slip before it affects any successors. An activity with zero float is said to be on the **critical path**.
Forecast	An estimate or calculation of what is likely to happen in the future. The term is used in many ways in **projects**. For example, in project reports the "forecast start date", "forecast end date" or "forecast benefits" describe what is currently considered to be the planned "start date", "end date" or "benefits", given what is known at the time.

Forecast at completion (FAC)	In project reporting, the total **effort** or cost expected to have been invested by the time a task, **product** or **project** has been completed.
Gantt chart	A diagrammatic tool used to illustrate some of the component parts of a plan, principally the time scale. It was originally developed by Henry L. Gantt in 1910.
Head of project management	The manager of a department or **resource pool** within which the prime resources are **project managers**.
Health check	A means by which a **project** is reviewed (perhaps by invitation) by those involved in the project, often using buddies. The output will be a report identifying opportunities for improvement and areas of strength that could be promoted to others who work on projects. Those working on the project will be responsible for carrying out the actions arising from the health check and there may or may not be a requirement for an external party to check that they are carried out as agreed.
Highlights	Positive events (such as the starting or completion of activities on time and on **budget**) often reported in the **project forecast report** in a section of the same name. (See also **lowlights**.)
Hierarchical communication	A form of communication characterised by messages being disseminated from the top of the organisation, through its various levels.
Iteration	A cycle of product development, commonly used in **agile** developments, resulting in a new **product increment.**

Iterative development	An approach to the development of a service or **product** which results in a series of progressive deployments.
Iteration manager/ leader	The person who manages the incremental development of a **product** or service according to an **iterative development** approach.
Iteration retrospective	The step within an **iteration** within which performance is considered to determine what improvements may be made.
Iteration review	The step within an **iteration** within which the new development **product** increment is considered for its fitness for purpose.
Internal audit	A formal **project** review that takes place perhaps as a result of some evidence of a failing. It should be conducted by someone who is impartial and has the competence to identify opportunities for improvement and propose solutions. It will be the project management team's responsibility to implement these, with progress usually being tracked by the person who conducted the review.
Internal rate of return (IRR)	The discount factor that results when a **net present value** of zero is achieved in a **discounted cash flow**. This financial measure is commonly used to compare one project with another.
Issue	A term used in **project management** to refer to a problem or challenge which has arisen and therefore cannot be prevented, although its effects may still be mitigated to some degree.

Issue management	Identifying, recording, evaluating and controlling the adverse consequences of an **issue**.
Latest finish time (LFT)	In an **activity network**, the latest point at which an activity may be completed before it will start having an impact on other activities.
Latest start time (LST)	In an **activity network**, the latest point at which an activity can commence before it will start having an impact on other activities.
Lessons learned report	A report produced as a result of a **lessons learned review** after the closure of a project describing the management lessons which may be used to improve the execution of future projects.
Lessons learned review	A session to determine the extent to which a recently completed **project** was well managed. The product of this review is a **lessons learned report**.
Lowlights	Negative events (such as the failure to start or complete activities on time or on budget) often reported in the **project forecast report** in a section of the same name. (See also **highlights**.)
Management by objectives (MBO)	An incentive scheme used by many organisations to reward employees for meeting or exceeding specified objectives.
Margin	In the context of a **project**, the difference at a point in time between the actual or forecast financially quantified benefits arising and the actual or forecast total project investment plus operational costs.

Matrix management	The planning and controlling of human resources who are involved simultaneously in **business-as-usual** and **projects**.
Methodical approach	The underlying method and discipline which articulates an organisation's approach to **project management**.
Milestone	See **deliverable**.
Minimum standard	A series of criteria which determine the minimum acceptable level of a product's or service's fitness for purpose (see also **project management minimum standard**).
Monitoring	Comparing actual progress with planned progress.
Net present value	A measurement in present values of the excess or shortfall of future cash flows.
Overspend	Describes where a planned budget has been, or is forecast to be, exceeded.
Person-day	A measurement of **effort**.
Plan	A forecast of future events (see also **project plan**).
Portfolio	A list of **projects** characterised by a common **budget** or department.
Portfolio management team (PMT)	The team charged with commissioning and delivering a value-adding mix of **projects** within a **budget**, aligned with their organisation's strategic and commercial imperatives.
Product	See **deliverable**.
Product backlog	The prioritised list of items for inclusion in the **iterative development** of a product or service.

Product-based planning	A planning technique which provides for the definition of deliverables as a precursor to estimating the timescale and costs of the activities needed to develop and deliver them.
Product breakdown structure	In **product-based planning**, a technique by which a large or complex product is broken down into smaller component parts so that the **project**'s scope may be more readily clarified.
Product description	In **product-based planning**, a technique whereby a product is defined in detail so that it may be more readily estimated, planned, developed, reviewed and approved.
Product flow diagram	In **product-based planning**, a technique whereby a **project** is expressed as a sequence of dependent products, providing the foundations for a **time schedule**.
Product increment	The summation of **product backlog** items included in an **iteration**, plus those items retained from previous developments.
Product owner	A project's user authority where an **iterative development** approach is being used; accountable for the product's entire developmental and operational life cycle.
Product outline	A table summarising the most important characteristics of a list of products.
Productivity	A measure of the efficiency of a resource to deliver a specified product within a defined **budget** and timescale.

Programme	A management vehicle for co-ordinating and implementing an organisation's strategy, specifically by linking together an often complex combination of **business-as-usual** activity and new **projects**, both of which are focused on the delivery of a defined business objective.
Programme office	A body responsible for providing support and/or assurance to those engaged in the management of a programme. (See also **support/assurance function**.)
Project	A temporary management environment, created to deliver a specified output according to a defined business justification.
Project closure	The final **stage** of a **project**. It is only when a project is deemed to have met the success criteria of the **project steering group** that a project can be closed and its management environment dismantled.
Project closure meeting	The last formal meeting of a **project** at which the **project steering group** considers the **project closure report** as a foundation for its decision to close the project.
Project closure report	A document describing the condition of a **project** at the point at which closure is requested, thereby enabling the **project steering group** to make an informed decision.
Project delivery	A **stage** during which the approved **project plan** is used as a guide to deliver the project's products to time, cost and quality expectations.
Project evaluation and review technique (PERT)	A technique that helps identify the **critical path**, **duration** and **floats** of dependent **project** activities.

Project forecast report (PFR)	A report produced by a **project manager** to communicate the present and intended status of a **project** to the **project steering group**, so that corrective actions may be identified to address **variances**.
Project governance report (PGR)	A management document, developed by a **project manager** during the **project initiation** stage, to describe how the targets expressed in the **business case** may be met. It contains a description of the roles, responsibilities and reporting lines of those involved in the project management team, together with the project plan.
Project initiation	A **stage** during which the necessary preparations are made to justify and plan the **project**, and to put in place the management environment which will serve as its foundation.
Project initiation meeting	The first formal meeting of a **project steering group** at which it considers the **business case**, the **project governance report**, the **user requirements document** and the **solution design document** in order to formally take ownership of a **project** from the **portfolio management team**. If the project steering group is comfortable with the project governance report, it will also consider instructing the **project manager** to commence the delivery stage.
Project life cycle	The series of **stages** which allows a **portfolio management team** and a **project steering group** to control the progress of a **project**.

Project management	The principles and techniques used for the identification, initiation, delivery, closure and benefits realisation of a **project**.
Project management minimum standard	A series of criteria which determine the minimum acceptable level of an organisation's approach to **project management** (see also **minimum standard**).
Project management office	A body responsible for providing support and/or assurance to those engaged in the management of a **project**. It may be called the project office or project support office (see also **support/assurance function**).
Project manager (PM)	The person responsible for planning, monitoring and controlling a **project**, to meet expectations of timeliness, cost and quality.
Project office	See **project management office**.
Project outline	A document recording the answers to the most important management questions before a **project** has been commissioned. It is used to seek sufficient investment to fund the **project initiation** stage.
Project plan	A management document produced by the **project manager** as part of the **project governance report**. It is used to show how expectations for time, cost and quality will be met.
Project register	A log of **projects** and some associated detail, used by the **portfolio management team** to assist in the planning, monitoring and control of the **portfolio**.

Project sponsor	The most senior individual involved in a **project** (and **project steering group**), chiefly responsible for leading the project to a successful outcome, specifically ensuring that the intended benefits are delivered and that they sufficiently outweigh the total investment.
Project start date	The date acknowledged and approved by the **portfolio management team** as that at which the **project initiation** stage should or did commence.
Project steering group (PSG)	A **project**'s most senior management authority, composed of experts from customer, developer and commercial backgrounds. The PSG serves as the point from which all original instructions derive, and to which any matters outside the authority of its subordinates can be referred.
Project support office	See **project management office**.
Quality	The features and characteristics of a **product** which affect its ability to meet the defined needs of those who will use it.
Quality control	The process of identifying failures to meet quality expectations and taking the necessary action to correct them.
Quality criteria	Closed questions or quantifiable statements used to describe the extent to which a feature or characteristic of a **product** will meet the defined needs of those who will use it. For example: "Does this glossary explain every term used in this book?" Also called quality measures. (See also **success criteria**.)

Quality log	A table used to record the progress of a **product** through its development life cycle so that a failure of quality at any point may be identified and dealt with.
Quality measure	See **quality criteria**.
Quality method	The various means by which **quality control** may be exercised.
Quality plan	A management document forming part of the **project plan** that describes how the **project** will deliver a **product** which meets the expectations of those who will use it.
Quality review	A **quality method** commonly used to determine by formal or informal means the extent to which a **product** may be considered fit for its intended purpose.
Red, amber, green (RAG)	The colours commonly used to provide a graphical representation of **escalation conditions**. Green indicates that a target is forecast to be met. Amber indicates that it is not, but that the authority to take corrective action remains with the person currently in charge. Red indicates that the escalation conditions have been breached and that the matter must be immediately passed to a higher level.
Resource	An asset used in the development and delivery of a **project**'s output – people, capital, machinery, and so on.
Resource levelling	The process by which the over- and under-utilisation of project resources is minimised. Resource levelling is a function of many **project management** software support tools.

Resource plan	A management document forming part of the **project plan** which describes what resources the **project** will require, when, and how they will be deployed.
Resource pool	A group of people falling within a single management structure, usually with a common skills profile. They might otherwise be called a department or a team from which people may be selected to participate in **projects**.
Resource pool manager	The head of a **resource pool**, responsible for making the most effective use of the people in the manager's charge.
Revise and reschedule (RAR)	An outcome from a **quality review** indicating that the **product** is not ready or needs significant change. Alternatively, this outcome may be because there were not enough reviewers or they were unprepared or unqualified.
Revolutionary change	A form of change characterised by its immediate, abrupt or radical introduction.
Risk	An exposure to the adverse consequences of future events.
Risk evaluation	The process of determining whether or not a **risk** is worthy of the investment needed to mitigate it.
Risk factor	The result of multiplying together the likelihood and impact of a **risk**. This is helpful in determining which level of management may authorise the necessary mitigation(s).
Risk identification	The process of uncovering **risks** to a **project** so that they may be evaluated and assigned for mitigation.

Risk impact	A numeric measure denoting the effect that a **risk** may be thought to have on a **project** or the wider organisation.
Risk likelihood	A numeric measure denoting the probability that a **risk** may become an **issue**.
Risk management	The control of exposure to the adverse consequences of future events.
Risk matrix	A graphical way of showing the relative likelihood and impact of identified **risks** and **issues**.
Risk mitigation	The process by which a **risk**'s impact, likelihood, or both, are made less severe or less painful.
Risk owner	The person or body empowered to authorise the mitigation of a **risk**.
Risk qualification	The process of determining the likelihood and impact of a **risk** so that its **risk factor** may be known.
Risk register	A document used to record identified **risks** and **issues**, together with other information necessary for their management, such as their impact, likelihood, factor and mitigation.
Schedule delay	In **earned value analysis**, when the **budgeted cost of work scheduled** is the same as the **budgeted cost of work performed** minus the date when the data was captured, measured in days.
Schedule variation	In **earned value analysis**, the **budgeted cost of work performed** minus the **budgeted cost of work scheduled** (how much should have been expended to date based upon what has been achieved minus the amount that was planned to have been spent to date).

Scribe	The person assigned responsibility for recording the actions and decisions arising from a **quality review**.
Scrum	An **agile** software delivery approach.
Scrum master	A term commonly used within the **scrum** approach to **iterative** software development, referring to a recognised authority in scrum.
Scrum meeting	A term commonly used within the **scrum** approach to **iterative** software development, referring to time-boxed opportunity for members of the team to advise on what has been completed, what is due to be completed, and what barriers there may be to completion (see also **daily meeting).**
Sequential development	A method of service or **product** development characterised by a linear life cycle (see also **waterfall development**).
Single version of the truth (SVOT)	A term used to emphasise the importance of a clear, current and commonly held interpretation of a **project** plan.
Solution design document (SDD)	A document used to describe how the needs of the users or **customers** of the **project** are to be met.
Sponsor	See **project sponsor**.
Sprint	A term commonly used within the **scrum** approach to **iterative** software development, referring to an **iteration** of software development.
Sprint leader	A term commonly used within the **scrum** approach to **iterative** software development, referring to the person who manages the **incremental development** of software.

Stage	A period within a **project** that has a clearly identified start date, end date, budget and **deliverable**(s), which can be used to facilitate estimating and provide the **project steering group** with points at which the viability of the project may be reaffirmed.
Stage meeting	A meeting of a **project steering group** which takes place just before the beginning of a **stage** (and just before the end of the closure stage) to allow the project steering group to formally confirm (or not) the completion of the previous stage, approve the **plan** for the next stage and reaffirm the project's viability.
Stakeholder	A person or group with an interest in the **project**, whether through their involvement with the change or because they will be affected by its outcome.
Stakeholder map	A graphical technique used to identify a **project**'s **stakeholders**.
Stakeholder matrix	A graphical technique used to prioritise a **project**'s **stakeholders** so that resources may be used efficiently to manage their respective interests.
Standard product/ project estimating technique	Used to identify a cost for a common **product** or **project**, based on knowledge of its size and complexity.
Stand-up meeting	A term commonly used within the **scrum** approach to **iterative** software development, referring to a time-boxed opportunity for members of the team to advise on what has been completed, what is due to be completed, and what barriers there may be to completion (see also **daily meeting** and **scrum meeting**).

Success criteria	Closed questions or quantifiable statements used to describe the extent to which a feature or characteristic of a **project** will meet the defined needs of those who will use it. Success criteria are used to express how the completion of a project will be measured, whereas **quality criteria** are commonly applied to an individual **product**.
Support/assurance definition report	A document used to describe what **products** and services a **support/assurance function** may offer, and how it will do so.
Support/assurance function (SAF)	A body of support and/or assurance to those engaged in the management of a **project** or **programme**. (See also **programme office**; **project management office**.)
Team leader	An individual charged with meeting a **project manager**'s expectations of time, cost and quality through the effective planning, monitoring and control of a team within a **project**.
Time schedule	A representation (often graphical) of a **project**'s timescale.
Timesheets	Forms used to capture the effort invested by members of the **project** team on the development of **products** assigned to them, together with the actual and estimated start and end dates, so that the **project plan** may be updated with progress.
Top-down estimating	Used at the commencement of a **project** to obtain a high-level forecast of its entire timescale, cost and **deliverables**. This may be corroborated with the **bottom-up estimate** created at the commencement of each **stage**.

Training needs analysis (TNA)	A document used to identify the training needs of those involved in **project** work and how, for each individual, they should be met.
Transactional leadership	A style of leadership characterised by the use of penalties and rewards to encourage compliance.
Transformational leadership	A style of leadership characterised by the use of inspiration to encourage compliance.
Underspend	A term used to describe where not all of a planned **budget** has been spent, or is forecast to be spent.
User journey	The set of experiences of a user when interacting with a **product** or service.
User story	A detailed component of work within an **epic**, commonly applied in **agile** development.
User requirements document (URD)	A document used to describe the needs of the **customers** that the **project**'s output must satisfy.
Variance	The difference between the **baseline** and the **forecast at completion**, be it a date or a monetary value.
Waterfall development	A method of systems development characterised by a linear life cycle.
Work	See **effort**.
Work distribution estimating technique	Used to attribute proportionate values to **project stages** or resource types, based on knowledge of those values for previous projects.

Index